The Rishonim

The

Based on research by
Rabbi Shmuel Teich

Edited by
Rabbi Hersh Goldwurm

Historical introduction by
Rabbi Hersh Goldwurm

הסטוריה

The ArtScroll History Series®

Rabbis Nosson Scherman / Meir Zlotowitz
General Editors

Rishonim

Biographical Sketches of the Prominent
Early Rabbinic Sages and Leaders
from the Tenth–Fifteenth Centuries

Published by

Mesorah Publications, ltd

FIRST EDITION
First Impression ... August, 1982

Published and Distributed by
MESORAH PUBLICATIONS, Ltd.
Brooklyn, New York 11223

Distributed in Israel by
MESORAH MAFITZIM / J. GROSSMAN
Rechov Bayit Vegan 90/5
Jerusalem, Israel

Distributed in Europe by
J. LEHMANN HEBREW BOOKSELLERS
20 Cambridge Terrace
Gateshead, Tyne and Wear
England NE8 1RP

ARTSCROLL HISTORY SERIES®
"THE RISHONIM"
© *Copyright 1982 by MESORAH PUBLICATIONS, Ltd.*
1969 Coney Island Avenue / Brooklyn, N.Y. 11223 / (212) 339-1700

ISBN
0-89906-452-3 (hard cover)
0-89906-453-1 (paperback)

סדר במסדרת
חברת ארטסקרול בע״מ

Typography by Compuscribe at ArtScroll Studios, Ltd.
1969 Coney Island Avenue / Brooklyn, N.Y. 11223 / (212) 339-1700

Printed in the United States of America by Moriah Offset

Publication of this volume

has been made possible by a grant

from an outstanding patron of Torah.

Himself a talmid chacham of note,

he generously fosters the cause

of intensive Torah study

by young and old.

For himself, he prefers anonymity;

but his life is a crescendo

of accomplishment.

~§ Table of Contents

◈§ Publisher's Preface

Mesorah Publications Ltd. proudly presents *"The Rishonim,"* a book that offers biographical information and perspectives on the life and times of the great Torah sages who flourished from the end of the Geonic period until just before the codification of the *Shulchan Aruch.* The *Rishonim,* who thrived from the tenth to the fifteenth centuries, led the Jewish people during the turbulent and often persecution-filled years when our people established settlements and great Torah academies in the Mediterranean countries and Western Europe. They shaped the methodology and application of Scriptural, Talmudic, and Halachic learning, and all succeeding generations followed in their footsteps.

By giving brief biographies of the greatest individuals of the period, tracing the rebbe-talmid relationships, showing their chronological development, and sketching the growth and dispersions of the various Jewish communities, this work will enrich the learning and perspectives of students of Torah. As the introduction makes clear, such research was never uppermost in he mind of Torah scholars, nor should it be. However, it is helpful and enlightening in many ways, as a reading of this book will quickly demonstrate. To help the reader gain a broad picture of the era, the book includes many maps, charts, and indices, among them an index matching authors with their most important *sefarim.*

Heretofore, works of this nature in English have been written by scholars of secular inclination. To them, R' Yehudah HaLevi was a poet and Rambam was a philosopher-physician. To the people of the Torah, however, such figures — as well as the 300 others in this book — are distinguished mainly because of their contribution to Torah scholarship or their leadership of Israel in its constant struggle to maintain its identity as the "Nation of Torah."

Of particular interest and importance, this book contains a sweeping introduction providing a historical perspective on the spread of Jewish settlement and the development of new communities during the centuries covered in this book. A similar volume is now in preparation on the *Acharonim,* the leading sages from the fifteenth century onward.

This book is based on research generously provided by Rabbi Shmuel Teich, a distinguished *talmid chacham* and author.

It was edited and prepared for publication by Rabbi Hersh Goldwurm who also wrote the introduction. Although his stature as a *talmid chacham* and commentator is well known from his authorship of many tractates in the ArtScroll Mishnah Series and the Book of Daniel, Rabbi Goldwurm is also a historian of note.

We are grateful to Rabbi Avie Gold whose considerable talents have been expended lavishly to make this book complete, accurate, and accessible to the reader as a research tool. We are also grateful to the entire Mesorah staff: Mr. Stephen Blitz, Yosef Timinsky, Mrs. Shirley Kiffel, Mrs. Faigie Weinbaum, Mrs. Judi Dick, Lea Freier, Chanee Freier, Edel Streicher, and Esther Glatzer.

Rabbi Sheah Brander has coped magnificently with the graphic aspects of this work, such as maps, charts, and clarity of presentation. Long known as a master of his craft, Reb Sheah earns new accolades with this volume.

We are also especially grateful to the anonymous patron who has sponsored this book. His goal in life is to make possible new generations of sages who will do in our era what the *Rishonim* did in theirs. We are privileged to have been found worthy of his regard.

Rabbi Nosson Scherman / Rabbi Meir Zlotowitz

Rosh Chodesh Menachem Av, 5742 / July 1982
Brooklyn, New York

Historical Introduction

The Migrations of Torah

Benefactors

In his approbation to *Shem HaGedolim* (the classic work on rabbinic bibliography by Rabbi Yosef Chaim David Azulai) Malbim says eloquently that just as it would be unnatural for one who has enjoyed the lavish hospitality of an anonymous host not to be curious about the identity of his benefactor, so it is insensitive of the Talmudic scholar or layman not to be greatly interested in learning at least something about the lives and attainments of the greats of generations gone by. Rambam in his commentary to the Mishnah in *Avos* (1:17) divides all types of speech into categories and describes as 'desirable' the kind of speech that lauds the sages and recounts their virtues.

Historically, the Torah community did not assign high priority to research into the lives of even its **greatest** mentors. As the flippant, but true, folk idiom expresses it, "We are **more** concerned with what Rashi says than with the color of his eyes or the style of his clothes." It is undeniable that rigorous analysis of every nuance and implication of the words of Rashi, Rambam, Ramban and so on far outweighs the comparatively trivial study of their lifestyles. That Rashi was a wine merchant and that Rambam was a physician is of infinitely lesser import to the Nation of Torah than (in the expression of Meiri) that Rashi was גְּדוֹלֵי הָרַבָּנִים, *the Greatest of the Teachers,* and that Rambam was גְּדוֹלֵי הַמְּחַבְּרִים, *the Greatest of Codifiers.* Quite naturally, therefore, much of the "human interest" type of material to which modern society assigns so much importance is secondary in the eyes of the Torah scholar. Nothing is more important than the role of a sage as a link in the chain of Torah tradition; by comparison, anything else is virtually meaningless. For this reason, little was ever recorded about the personal lives of the great majority of our Torah luminaries. Consequently, as the biographies in this book will show, we have only scant knowledge about some of the authors whose works are monumental in the development and shaping of Torah knowledge.

The purpose of this book and the volumes that will follow it is to briefly recapitulate the major facts about the most important Torah figures of past centuries. Aside from fulfilling what Malbim considers the natural obligation to know about our benefactors, the information contained in this volume will lend depth and perspective to the learning process as well. The student will often benefit from knowing the chain of teacher-student tradition. For example: From whom did someone learn? Was he aware of the writings and teachings of those with whom he differs? What were the philosophical differences between scholars of various schools? What historical event brought about the cross-leavening of various national traditions?

Geographical Separations

In order to give the reader a sense of historical development we have listed the sages according to the approximate time and chronological order in which they lived and taught. For the same reason we have grouped them according to the various geographical locations where they flourished. To the modern mind, it often seems insignificant whether a prominent rabbi or rosh yeshivah is in *Eretz Yisrael* or America; modern communication has shrunk the world and made virtual colleagues even of people living thousands of miles apart. But in the middle ages communications between the various communities was almost nonexistent and a major development in one region had scant, if any, influence in another. The influence of Rashi and the French Tosafists, which shaped the Talmudic methodology of Germany and Northern France, did not penetrate to the Iberian Peninsula until a much later date when the specific Sephardic style of Jewishness and Talmudic scholarship had already attained its full development. Similarly, Rambam was almost unknown and certainly misunderstood (as we shall see below) in Germany and France during the Tosafist period.

In this book, we have divided the biographies into four geographic areas: 1. The Sephardic Region, including Spain, North Africa, and *Eretz Yisrael*; 2. France-Germany; 3. Provence; 4. Italy.

We have grouped the scholars of the Oriental and North African communities with those of Spain because of the great similarities in their approaches. Indeed the greatest personality of North African Jewry and the one who has laid his stamp upon it — R' Moshe ben Maimon — was a refugee from Spain, who received his early education in that country.

The Moorish conquest and rule of most of the Iberian Peninsula and the Moslem imposition of the Arab language and culture upon it served to open Spain to the influence of its neighbors on the shores of the southern Mediterranean. The open channels of communication to the entire Moslem world of that day acted as a homogenizing factor giving a certain sense of unity to the Jewish communities in this region. Migration to and from the diverse and far flung corners of the Arab Caliphate strengthened this tendency. Even that most remote corner of this world — Yemen — whose Jewry retains to this day a style distinct from those communities commonly (but perhaps erroneously) called Sephardic or Spanish did not escape being profoundly influenced by the personality and writings of Rambam.

Since northern France and Germany were united in learning and culture, with much cross-fertilization between them, we have grouped them together as one community. Provence, the southern part of France, was midway between Spain and France in more ways than geographically. As we shall see below, in many ways it was both a blend of Spain and France and mirrored the sharp differences between the two lands. The last of the regions was Italy, which developed an identifiable Jewish community of its own.

The Geonic Era

The sages of the generation after the completion of the Talmud (500 C.E.) are known as Rabbanan Savurai. They encouraged the continued growth of the Amoraic academies at Sura and Pumbedisa in Babylonia (Iraq), expounded the Talmudic interpretations transmitted to them by their predecessors, and edited the text of the Talmud. The functioning of the two ancient academies was interrupted for a short time because of government pressure, and their reopening in 589 marked the beginning of the Geonic Era, which continued to flourish for almost 450 years, climaxing with R' Hai Gaon, who died in 1038.

The Geonim directed the academies of Sura and Pumbedisa, continuing the educational activity of the Amoraim and Rabbanan Savurai. Students attending the academies were supported by a fund maintained by gifts sent in from all points of the Diaspora. Each academy had a fund, usually under the charge of the Gaon of that yeshivah, who distributed it according to his discretion. Also, the Geonim were vitally concerned with practical halachic application, interpreting Talmudic principles to decide questions of Jewish law and procedure.

The two academies were invested with judicial authority, and the presiding Gaon acted as supreme judge. Often he would present his academy with questions that were sent in from all parts of the Diaspora. These were discussed and the answers recorded by the secretary according to the directions of the Gaon. A large number of the Geonic responsa originated in this way. Many other responsa were written by the Geonim themselves after consultation with the academy. The Geonim had legislative powers as well; they issued *takanos* [enactments] for the purpose of safeguarding the spirit of Jewish life. For example, they decreed that debts of a deceased and the *kesubah* [i.e., the widow's settlement] might be collected from the *movable* property of the estate, where no real property was available. The Geonic enactments were issued jointly by both academies.

The Geonim were usually elected by the distinguished scholars of the academy, but on occasion would be appointed by the *Reish Galusa* [exilarch]. Although they were entirely independent of the head of the Babylonian Jewry, and were even empowered to examine documents and decisions originating in his *beis din* [court], the Geonim, together with prominent members of both yeshivos, paid a yearly visit to the home of the *Reish Gelusa* to render him homage, because he was descended from King David.

Not only were the Geonim empowered to deal with all religious affairs of the Jews of Babylonia — their word was law among Jews throughout the Diaspora as well. These turned to the Geonim of Babylonia for clear Talmudic interpretation and application, and virtually no important action could be taken without their approval, for the legacy of Torah authority had fallen to them. The two academies were the centers of world Jewry.

In the course of the tenth century, however, even before the Babylonian schools ceased to exist with the death of R' Hai Gaon, other centers of learning arose, from which were promulgated teachings and decisions that superseded those of the Geonim. The gifts which the Jews of Spain, North Africa, Egypt, and *Eretz Yisrael* had regularly contributed to the support of the Babylonian schools were decreased and eventually discontinued, since the Jews of those communities now had the priority of supporting the scholars and yeshivos of their own lands.

In order to help provide perspective on the countries where the various sages lived, we offer a country by country review of the history of each land and its Jewish community.

I. The Sephardic Lands

The settlement of Jews in the Iberian Peninsula is very ancient. According to the tradition preserved by Spanish Jewry (see *Don Yitzchak Abarbanel*, commentary to end of *Kinos* and to *Ovadiah* 1:20), the earliest

Spain

Jewish settlers were brought to that country by Nebuchadnezzar following his destruction of the First Temple, and fifty thousand Jewish captives were brought there by the Romans when they destroyed

Jerusalem and the Second Temple. However, next to nothing is known about these early Jewish settlements.

With the disintegration of the Roman empire, Spain was invaded and conquered by successive waves of migratory Germanic peoples from the north, first by the Vandals (409 C.E.) and soon afterward by the Visigoths (412 C.E.). Historians have supposed that before their conversion from Arian Christianity to Catholicism, the Visigoths were tolerant in their treatment of the Jews, but this impression is probably based more on the dearth of historical material pertaining to this period than on evidence of the good will of the Arian Christians. Indeed, an extant letter written in the year 418 by a bishop of Majorca tells of the forced conversion to Christianity of the Jews on the neighboring island of Minorca. A significant number of the Minorcan Jews were martyred and the survivors submitted to baptism.

In the year 589 the Visigoth king Recared adopted Catholicism and presently decreed restrictions on Jewish freedoms. King Sisebut (612-21) tried to enforce Recared's anti-Jewish laws and added to them. In the following year he issued an edict giving the Jews a choice between baptism and expulsion. It seems however, that the government was unable to enforce this decree. Sisebut's successors did not distinguish themselves for toleration of dissident faiths, with the possible exception of Swintila

(621-31). King Ervig (680-7) renewed the oppression of his Jewish subjects; he influenced the Church Council to countenance forced baptism. Further persecution was introduced at the Church Concil of 694, where Jews were accused of plotting to seize power in the country and massacre the Christians.

In the year 711, the Arabs and the Moors crossed the straits of Gibraltar from Morocco and in only three years conquered the entire Iberian Peninsula, which became the kingdom of Andalusia (Vandalusia). The Jews, many of whom had been forced to accept baptism publicly, while secretly observing Judaism, welcomed the Arab conquerors with open arms and aided them in the conquest. Being a ruling minority, the Arabs needed the services of loyal citizens to help them rule the country. Thus many Jews entered the service of the government and a climate favorable to the growth of a vigorous Jewish life was created. Jews from other countries in the East flocked to Andalusia.

In the beginning, the provinces in the Iberian Peninsula were ruled by governors responsible to the Umayyad Caliphate in Damascus. Factional strife between the original conquerors, who had been mainly Berber (Moorish) tribesmen from North Africa, and the Arabs appointed to various positions of power, as well as internal struggles among the diverse Arab clans, weakened their hold over the country. In 750 the Abbasid family overthrew the Damascene Umayyad caliph in a bloody coup. A scion of the Umayyad dynasty, Abd-er-Rahman escaped and was invited by some noblemen in Spain to lead an insurrection against the central caliphate in Damascus. In 756 the Caliph's forces were defeated and Abd-er-Rahman I established an independent caliphate in Andalusia, with Cordova as its seat of government.

The rule of the Cordovan caliphs was benevolent and liberal in comparison with other regimes of the period. Jews were allowed to hold high positions and great influence at the caliph's court. Chisdai ibn Shaprut, a scion of the noted Ibn Ezra family, was the right hand of Abd-er-Rahman III (912-61) and a patron of Jewish scholarship. His position gave him the opportunity to intervene favorably for his less fortunate brethren in the Byzantine empire. In that period Spain was perhaps the most enlightened country in the world, and the study of science and philosophy flourished there. This did not fail to leave its imprint upon Spanish Jewry, which was attracted to these studies. The preoccupation of the Arabs with poetry and their language's richness of expression spurred the Jews to demonstrate that the Holy tongue was just as adaptable and versatile as its sister language, and that it could reach the same heights of beauty. Naturally this gave an impetus to the study of the language itself. The climate that nurtured the great *paytanim* [liturgical poets] R' Yehudah HaLevi and **R'** **Shlomo** ibn Gabirol also contributed to the development of the **early** masters of Hebrew grammar — R' Yehudah ibn Chayug and R' Yonah ibn

Janach. Thus, the period that gave Spanish Jewry its greatest poets also gave birth to the development of Hebrew grammar.

The flowering of Jewish culture was equaled by a heightened level of Talmudic study. The Talmud (*Yevamos* 115b; see *Teshuvos HaRosh* 51:2) reports that a Babylonian exilarch had visited Spain while the *Gemara* was being formulated in Babylon, and the tradition of Spanish Jewry testifies that he transmitted Talmudic learning to them (R' Shmuel HaNaggid cited in *Sefer Halttim* p. 267). Furthermore the entire Talmud had at an early date been committed to writing by a Babylonian savant and sent to Spain (ibid). The same tradition attests to the punctilious observance of the Torah by Spanish Jewry from its earliest history. Before Talmudic scholarship had reached its peak, Spanish scholars maintained a steady correspondence with the Babylonian Geonim and all questions of law were referred to them. *Seder R' Amram Gaon* — the famous treatise on the liturgy and its laws by the Gaon R' Amram bar Sheshna (758-76 C.E.) — was composed in response to a query by Spanish scholars.

Shortly before the decline of the Babylonian Geonate, Providence arranged for an occurrence (990 C.E.)[1] that would have far reaching consequences

The Four Captives
for the entire Diaspora and free its Jews from their dependence upon the Babylonian academies and their scholars. Four great Torah scholars from southern Italy[2] embarked on a sea voyage to raise money for the Torah academies of their country. The four sages were R' Moshe ben Chanoch, R' Chushiel, R' Shmaryah ben Elchanan, and a fourth whose identity and fate are unknown. En route they were captured by Ibn Rumahis, a Moorish-Spanish pirate in the service of the Spanish caliph, who decided to offer them for ransom to four different Jewish communities along the Mediterranean coast. The rabbis wisely kept their identities secret for fear that Ibn Rumahis would extort huge sums in return for their freedom. The pirate carried out his plan with an outcome that was of historic benefit to Jewish life.

R' Moshe (together with his young son Chanoch) was ransomed by the Jews of Cordova, under the leadership of Chisdai ibn Shaprut. The community soon recognized the erudition and eminence of the captive and appointed him their spiritual leader. R' Moshe promptly established an

---

1. This is the date given in most editions of the *Sefer HaKabbalah,* however, historians have pointed out that this must be an error. R' Y. HaLevi (*Doros HaRishonim,* v. 67, p. 298-9) proposes that the correct version is 960 C.E., one year before the death of Caliph Abd-er-Rahman III (al nasser), whose navy captured these four Sages.

2. Southern Italy, specifically the communities of Trani and Otranto, were famous for their piety and learning, as related by Rabbeinu Tam according to the tradition of his forefathers (*Sefer HaYashar, Teshuvos* 46, ed. Jer. p. 90). Other sources attest to Italy's preeminence in Torah scholarship at this early date. Concerning the narrative detailed above, see R' Avraham ibn Daud *Sefer HaKabbalah* and *Doros HaRishonim,* v. 6, pp. 283-305.

academy, and was succeeded by his son R' Chanoch. Between them, they raised a new generation of scholars who would not have to look to Babylon for guidance on every question. R' Shmuel HaNaggid, Talmud scholar par excellence, poet, and statesman, was one of his disciples. Other yeshivos were later established in other Spanish cities. The study of Torah received a further impetus with the arrival (1088) of R' Isaac al-Fasi from Morocco.

Another of the captives, R' Chushiel, was brought to the shores of Tunisia, where he accomplished in the city of Kairouan what R' Moshe did in Cordova. His son, the famous Talmud commentator R' Chananel, and his illustrious disciple R' Nissim (Gaon) ben Yaakov continued his work of making North Africa a major Torah center that became independent of Babylon in matters of Talmudic scholarship.

The third sage, R' Shmaryah ben Elchanan, was ransomed in Egypt. He established an academy in Cairo, where he was succeeded by his son, R' Elchanan. As a result, Cairo, too, became a thriving Jewish community and an important center of Torah knowledge.

The Abbasid Caliphate maintained its power in Cordova from the time of its accession in 750 until early in the eleventh century, but it foundered and

Moslem Power Wanes

fell for the same reason as the Umayyad, its predecessor — Berber discontent. The armies that had conquered Spain originally had been composed mainly of Berber tribesmen, but after the conquest, the Berbers were thrust to the background, while the power and spoils were grabbed by the Arab aristocracy. Their discontent festered until it found the Abbasid Caliphate weak enough to be toppled. In 1012 the Berbers revolted, conquered Cordova and massacred half of its inhabitants. The Spanish caliphate of Andalusia disintegrated and was replaced by twenty-three small city-states. The ruler of Granada, King Habbus, elevated R' Shmuel HaNaggid to the post of vizier and that state flourished and expanded under his able leadership. He was succeeded in his post by his son R' Yehosef, but in 1066 the rebellious Arabs and Berbers of Granada united, killed R' Yehosef, and massacred 4000 of the city's Jews. The remaining Jews were forced to emigrate.

Soon after these events, the Almoravids (al-Murabatin), a Berber dynasty seized power in Morocco, and presently all of Andalusia fell under their sway (approx. 1086). Their Emir Yousuf, although not strictly religious himself, was persuaded to offer the Jews of his realm the choice between conversion to Islam and exile, but an enormous bribe convinced him to be more liberal. As long as this dynasty ruled, the Jewish community in its realm prospered. The rule of the Almoravids was superseded in 1149 by that of the Almohads (al-Muwahidin, "the unitarians"), another Moorish dynasty, which was fanatically dedicated to the propagation of Islam in its most orthodox form. Jews were given the option to choose between conversion and emigration. Many Jews fled. Others outwardly accepted the Moslem religion while secretly adhering to their faith. This sorry state continued for close to a century, when the power of the Almohads waned. Rambam's family was among those that fled Cordova in this period. R' Maimon, Rambam's father, composed his *Iggeres HaNechamah* to console his suffering brethren and to urge them not to lose faith. In later years, Rambam wrote the *Iggeres HaShmad* to clarify the obligations of a Jew when faced with such choices as were presented to the unfortunate Jews in this part of the world. Many of the Jews in Andalusia fled to the neighboring Christian kingdoms of Spain and southern France. The following (13th) century saw the gradual reconquest of Andalusia (Moslem Spain) by the Christian kingdoms in the north, until only the province of Granada remained under Moslem rule. A Jewish community continued to flourish there for the next 250 years until Granada, too, fell to the conquering armies of Ferdinand and Isabella (1492).

Christian Spain

The rule of the Moslems over the Iberian Peninsula was never really complete; almost simultaneously with the Moslem conquest, the Christian reconquest began. The province of Asturias in the northwestern corner of the peninsula was the nucleus around which was founded the ancient kingdom of Leon. Gradually the entire northern coast fell under Christian control as the kingdoms of Old Castille and Navarre (northeast) came into being. Not much is known about the early history of the Jewish communities in these provinces and it may be assumed that the Jewish population was sparse. In the province of Catalonia, at the southeastern tip of the Pyrenees, the important capital Barcelona boasted an old Jewish settlement. We can assume that the Jews in these countries were influenced by their brethren under Moslem rule.

In the eleventh century, when Andalusia ceased to exist as a political unit, the Christian reconquest began in earnest, only to be stopped temporarily by the Almohads. The religious persecution under the Almohad regime caused many Jews to emigrate to the Christian kingdoms. With the waning of Almohad power early in the thirteenth century, the process of reconquest was set in motion inexorably. As the Christians conquered kingdom after kingdom they acquired sizable Jewish populations. Soon the Christian rulers recognized the use they could make of the educated and cultured Jews, and many were elevated to positions of great influence. In spite of the Church's inherent tradition of intolerance, the Jews of Spain generally fared much better than their brethren in central Europe. As long as the reconquest was in progress, the Christian kings needed the good will of the Jews, who in many instances fought in their armies against the Moslems. Spanish Jewry was spared the pain of the Crusades, which ravaged the rest of the European Jewish communities.

In the thirteenth century, when the reconquest was practically complete, and the kingdoms on the Peninsula (Leon-Castille, Navarre, Aragon-Catalonia-Valencia) had taken form, a turning point was reached. Although Jews remained in many positions of power, here and there restrictions were enacted. In Aragon, James I forced the Jews, represented by Ramban, to hold a public dispute (July 20, 1263 in Barcelona) with the convert Pablo Christiani, and required them to listen regularly in their synagogues to sermons aimed at converting them. Ramban's was but one of many such disputations, and a rich polemic literature is the legacy of that fateful period.

Because of the machinations of Jewish courtiers, the Jewish population in Castille became involved in the civil war between Pedro and Henry II, both sons of Ferdinand XI and pretenders to the throne. The Jews were loyal to Pedro and thousands met their death during the war. When Henry was victorious (1369) the political fortunes of the Jews began a steady decline. A fanatical but eloquent priest, Ferrand Martinez, fanned the latent anti-Jewish feeling of the mob and incited them to massacre. In 1390 King John I died, leaving the throne to his eleven-year old son. The ensuing period of upheaval and anarchy was utilized by Martinez to realize his goals. On June 6, 1391, the mob invaded the Jewish ghetto of Seville and killed 4000 of its 7000 inhabitants. The majority of the survivors were forcibly baptized. The flames of murder and violence soon spread throughout the kingdom and beyond its borders into Aragon, Catalonia, Majorca and even beyond Spain's northern border, to Provence. Tens of thousands met a horrible death and even more were forcibly converted. Hundreds of Jewish communities were eradicated. The Jewish communities of Castille and Aragon were ruined. Many Jews emigrated en masse, among them some of the greatest scholars, including Rivash and R' Shimon Duran.

These tragic events were the prologue and direct cause of the subsequent expulsion a scant century later. Some of the converts betrayed their former brethren and turned into rabid Jew haters. Paul of Burgos (Shlomo HaLevi), formerly a very learned and respected member of his community, rose to the position of archbishop and was part of the clique that ruled for the infant king. At the request of the fanatical preacher Vincent Ferrer, Paul drew up anti-Jewish legislation in 1412 reducing the Jews to poverty. He was the author of numerous anti-Jewish polemics, but he was only the most prominent of an odious genre. At their instigation, Benedict XIII, the Spanish antipope, ordered the Jews to take part in a public disputation at Tortosa which lasted for one and a half years (Feb. 7, 1413 — Nov. 12, 1414); R' Yosef Albo was one of the participants. At the conclusion of the disputation the antipope issued a decree severely restricting the liberties of the Jews, including a provision prohibiting study of the Talmud. On the other side of the coin, the newly converted neo-Christians who secretly clung to their Jewish faith were to be an even greater source of trouble. The populace resented these converts' great wealth and influence and hated them with a passion. The professed Jews were accused of secretly abetting their "Christian" brethren.

In 1469 Isabella, heiress to the throne of Castille, was married to Ferdinand, crown prince of Aragon. When she acceded to her regency in 1474 and Ferdinand became king of Aragon in 1479, they jointly ruled over practically all of the territory included in modern Spain (except for Moorish Granada and Navarre). In 1478, Pope Sixtus IV, at the instigation of influential Spanish clergymen, issued a bill authorizing the Inquisition to be reinstituted in Spain. The Inquisition was an old institution in the Church. Originally it had been directed against renegade Christians, but in Spain its purpose was to eradicate Judaizing tendencies among Christians and, especially among Marranos, as the secret Jews were called. Its inquisitors were appointed by the government, which financed the venture and was to reap the profits realized from the confiscation of the rich Jews' belongings. The Inquisition became the law of the land in September of 1480, and on February 6, 1481, the first auto-da-fe [i.e., public burning of "guilty" heretics] caught six victims in its fiery clutches. The excesses of this tribunal caused the Pope (in 1482) to protest and to declare publicly his suspicion that the queen's zeal in this matter was a consequence not of religious fervor, but of cupidity and ambition. However the tempo of the auto-da-fes did not cease, and under the leadership of Thomas de Torquemada, reached new heights of cruelty. It persisted for 300 years and was exported by the Spaniards and Portugese to their possessions in the Americas and Asia.

The religious fanatics surrounding the queen were not satisfied with their successes; they wished to rid Spain of all of its Jews, converted and unconverted. The Jews were accused again and again of luring the converts back to Judaism. On November 5, 1491, Ferdinand conquered the kingdom of Granada, the last enclave of Moorish Spain. This event no doubt freed the king from his dependency on the financial contribution of the Jews to finance his military exploits, and prepared him for the final step — the expulsion of the Jews. On March 30, 1492, the edict was signed. The Jews were to leave by the end of July (the last group left on *Tishah B'Av*) taking along only what they could carry with them. Strenuous efforts and offers of huge payments to the crown by Don Yitzchak Abarbanel could not sway the royal couple. A glorious chapter in Jewish history had reached its conclusion.

The Jews in neighboring Navarre were soon to share the fate of their brethren in Aragon-Castille. This province had a substantial Jewish population dating back to the days when the first king of Navarre had invited the Jews to settle in his domain, where they enjoyed considerable liberty and prosperity until the latter half of the thirteenth century. In the middle of the thirteenth century, when a son-in-law of Louis XI ascended the throne, the country came under French domination. In 1274 after the demise of the king, a civil war, in which the Jews participated, broke out. The French king Philip IV (who in 1306 banished the Jews from his domain) intervened, levied a heavy tax on the Jews and restricted them in other ways. Their situation deteriorated further under the rule of the succeeding French kings. In 1321, the *Pastoreaux* (lit., shepherds) craze spread from France to Spain. The *Pastoreaux* was a fanatical Christian sect that originated in thirteenth century France. In 1320, they massacred many Jewish settlements in southern France, and in the next year the movement crept southward. Navarre, and the Jews of Tudela were attacked. In 1328 it spread throughout the country and the Jewish community was decimated, more than 6000 losing their lives. When Navarre regained its independence in 1329, the new king, Philip III, restricted the rebellious and fanatical priests, but at the same time heavily taxed the already impoverished Jews who left en masse, leaving the kingdom virtually depleted of its Jews. When Spain proclaimed its edict of expulsion, a number of Jewish families were admitted to Navarre, but soon (1498) they were banished from there as well.

The lot of the Portuguese Jewish community had been slightly better than that of its much larger sister communities in the Spanish kingdoms. The

Portugal position of the Jews was favorable and prosperous almost until the bitter end. The rulers of Portugal shielded them from the excesses of the clergy, and the wave of anti-Jewish violence that swept Spain in 1391 did not extend to Portugal. Successive members of the learned Ibn Yachya family held influential positions at the court. Alfonso V (1438-81), whose minister of finances was Don Yitzchak Abarbanel, protected the Jews against mounting anti-Jewish feeling fanned by the clergy. His successor, John II (1481-95), offered temporary asylum and a promise of transportation abroad to 100,000 Spanish refugees in exchange for a hefty payment, but he did not keep his promise. When he did provide ships, they were too few and often not seaworthy, and no measures were instituted to protect the helpless refugees. The unscrupulous ship captains and their crews committed all kinds of violence and mayhem upon the unprotected Jews. Those who were not fortunate enough to leave in time were declared slaves, their children were taken from them, and they were sent to the island of St. Thomas, off the west coast of Africa.

Early in John's reign, in 1483, Abarbanel was accused of conspiracy against the crown and fled to Spain where he entered the royal service. Upon John's death the throne was ascended by Manuel (1495-1521). He nurtured the dream of uniting all of the Iberian Peninsula under one rule and asked for the hand of Isabella, daughter of Ferdinand and Isabella and heiress to the throne of Aragon and Castille, in marriage. One of the marriage terms demanded by the Spanish monarchs was the expulsion of all Jews from Portugal. On Dec. 4, 1496, the king signed a decree ordering all Jews to leave the country before the end of October, 1497, or face death.

The expulsion from Portugal was accompanied with even more cruelty than that from Spain. On the first day of Pesach, without warning, the king had all the Jewish children seized to be forcibly baptized. Many Jews killed themselves together with their families. About 20,000 people were tricked into coming to Lisbon, the capital, with the expectation that they would be allowed to embark from there. Instead they were herded into a big palace and told they were now slaves of the king. Food and water were denied them and priests came to convince them to convert. When all blandishments failed, they were bodily dragged to the baptismal fount. Only a few escaped. When prominent churchmen vehemently protested Manuel's cruel policies, he relented and announced a period of clemency for the new converts. They were not allowed to return to their ancestral religion or leave the country, but would be free from further persecution. In 1531 Pope Clement VII authorized the introduction of the Inquisition into Portugal, and many Marranos left the country. In return for an exorbitant bribe, King Sebastian (1531-78) allowed all the Marranos to leave; many of them went to the Netherlands and established flourishing communities in Amsterdam and the Hague.

Morocco

The origins of the early Jewish settlements in Morocco are shrouded in mystery. The Jewish communities in the Atlas mountains claim to have originated during the reign of King Solomon, but the Amoraim R' Yehudah and R' Chisda (third century) stated (*Menachos* 110a) that west of Carthage 'they do not know [about] Israel and our Father in Heaven.' History records that many of the Berber tribes, the indigenous inhabitants of Morocco and Algeria, practiced Judaism. Indeed the last resistance to the Arab conquerors came from a tribe led by the Jewish princess, "the *Kahina*," who died in the attempt. Remnants of these Jewish Berbers have survived to modern times. During their oppression under Visigothic rule, many Spanish Jews crossed the straits of Gibraltar to the comparative safety of Morocco. A further influx of Jews from the East came with the Arab conquest of Algeria and Morocco (approx. 698). The early Moslem caliphs were tolerant toward Jews, but when Idris I established his dynasty (788) a short period of persecution followed, which abated under his successor Idris II (791-828), who allowed Jews to settle in his newly established capital, Fez. In general the Jews fared well under the following dynasties until the rise to power of the Almohads.

Here were born the early Jewish grammarians, Yehudah ibn Kuraish, Donash ben Lavrat, and Yehudah ibn Chayug, and the great Talmudic scholar R' Yitzchak al-Fasi (of Fez) spent most of his life in Morocco. The beginning of the thirteenth century saw the emergence of the Almohads, and the Jews were forced to accept Islam or be killed. The city of Fez enjoyed a short period of grace, during which R' Maimon and his famed son, Rambam, resided there after fleeing Spain. In 1165 the accession of a new ruler removed even this oasis of peace. The fortunes of the Jews waxed and waned under successive Almohad rulers and their situation varied from bad to worse. Forced conversions and massacres were the order of the day, and many emigrated to Christian Spain and the east.

In 1269 the Almohads were defeated and the succeeding Mernid and Wattasid dynasties were favorable to the Jews. In the year 1391 and the period of persecution following it in Spain, droves of Jews made their way to Morocco. This was repeated during the mass exodus from Spain in 1492 and from Portugal in 1497. In spite of the ruler's permission allowing the Jews into the country, Morocco was not ready to accommodate them, either physically or economically. Multitudes died of hunger and thirst while camping in the open fields surrounding Fez. Many were killed and robbed by bands of brigands and some even fell prey to wild animals. Their suffering was so great that some returned to Spain.

Up to the downfall of the Almohads (1269) the history of Algeria is identical with that of neighboring Morocco. Under the Caliphate and the Almohads, **Algeria** as well as under the intervening dynasties, Algeria was part of the territory dubbed the Maghreb (West; מַעֲרִיב) including it and Morocco. The Jews of this region shared the persecutions of the Almohads together with their brethren to the west. The downfall of the Almohads brought with it the creation of the kingdom of Algeria and the plight of the Jews was somewhat alleviated. The mass exodus of Spanish

Jewry in 1492 brought to Algeria many noteworthy newcomers, who were well received. Among them were Rivash and R' Shimon ben Tzemach, both of whom settled at Algiers (Aljezair; אלגזייר): the latter's descendants occupied the Algerian rabbinate for many generations. The refugees revitalized the economy and in the subsequent exodus from Spain in 1492, Algeria absorbed an additional number (about 5000) of refugees.

The roots of the Jewish community in Tunisia go back to ancient antiquity. The Jews of Djerba (an island off the Tunisian coast) claim to have settled

Tunisia there during the reign of Solomon. Cyrene, in neighboring Lybia, is known to have had a flourishing Jewish community during the time of the Second Temple. Several Amoraim [ר' יצחק, ר' אבא ור' חנא קרטיגנאה,] were native Carthaginians (Carthage is on the Tunisian coast). A number of Jewish captive slaves were settled by Titus in Tunisia and several communities are known to have existed there during the rule of the Roman and Byzantine empires. After the Arab conquest of Tunisia in 643, its history is identical to that of Algeria and Morocco. The Jews were treated leniently by the Caliphate and the succeeding dynasties and enjoyed prosperity and peace until the mid-eleventh century. The flourishing community of Kairouan ('the camp'), founded in 670 by the Arab invaders, developed into an important center for Jewish scholarship whose Sages carried on an extensive correspondence with the Geonim in Babylonia (Iraq). R' Nissim Gaon, R' Chushiel and his son R' Chananel (Rif's mentor) were inhabitants of Kairouan. The Jews of Tunisia suffered with their brethren under the Almohads but were liberated from this yoke earlier when, in 1228, the Tunisian governor revolted against his Almohad overlord. From then on their lot was no worse than elsewhere in the east. It is not known whether large numbers of Spanish Jews emigrated to Tunisia following the persecutions of 1391 and 1492. In any case no distinguished Spanish scholar is known to have settled among them.

The existence of a widespread Jewish community in Egypt during the period of the Second Temple is well known. The exodus to Egypt of some

Egypt victims of Nebuchadnezzar's destruction of Jerusalem and Judea is recorded in Scripture (*II Kings* 25:26) and the Jewish community in Alexandria was one of the most populous in the Old World. In 115 C.E. the Jews of Alexandria, Cyrene (Lybia), and Cyprus, acting in concert with their brethren in *Eretz Yisrael* under the leadership of Shimon bar Kusiva (Bar Kochba), revolted against the oppressive regime of Trajan. The revolt was put down (117) and a terrible massacre wiped out the Jewish settlement.

Scattered references in the pagan and Christian literature of the fourth and fifth centuries attest to a small resettlement. The Arab conquest (640) brought Egypt, as well as the rest of North Africa, an influx of Jews from the east. A significant community was founded in Fostat (Old Cairo, south of the modern city), the new city founded by the conquerors. The scholars of this community carried on an extensive correspondence with the Babylonian Geonim as well as with the roshei yeshivah of the academy in *Eretz Yisrael*. R' Saadyah Gaon (approx. 882-942) was educated in Egypt. The tradition of Talmudic scholarship was furthered by the Italian Sage R' Shmaryah ben Elchanan, one of the "four captives" (see above), who was ransomed by the Jewish community in Egypt and who founded an academy in Fostat that was later headed by his son R' Elchanan. In 969 the Fatimid dynasty seceded from the Abbasid Caliphate in Baghdad and established Egypt as a strong independent kingdom. Their attitude toward Jews was generally a lenient one, and the Jewish community flourished under them and under later dynasties. The Jewish community enjoyed a measure of autonomy and had a representative officially recognized by the rulers called the *naggid* (prince). For many generations this position was held by Rambam's descendants.

The religious persecution of the Almohads in western Africa and Moslem Spain brought many Jews to Egypt, among them Rambam who became physician to Sultan Saladin (1169-93) and his court. Rambam found a strong Karaite community in Egypt whose influence on the customs of traditional Jewry was considerable, but by virtue of the esteem in which he was held and the uncompromising stand he took on this question he succeeded in changing the deleterious trend. Scarcely any Egyptian scholars are known in the period following the death (14th cent.) of Rambam's great-grandson, the *naggid* R' Yehoshua (ben David), the author of a work of responsa. Egyptian Jewry experienced a revival in the period of the Spanish exile (1492), when R' Moshe Alasker and R' David abu Zimra (Radbaz) officiated as rabbis. R' Yitzchak Luria (Arizal) was a native of Cairo and studied under Radbaz and his successor R' Betzalel Ashkenazi.

The history of the Jews in *Eretz Yisrael* after the Roman Emperor Constantine (313) converted to Christianity is one of decline. Religious

Eretz Yisrael persecution increased to an intolerable level and, fearing the abolition of the *semichah* [the classic rabbinic ordination that did, in fact, become abolished], the *nassi* Hillel II (a descendant of R' Yehudah HaNassi the compiler of the Mishnah) instituted the currently used calendar (358) as a substitute for the Scriptural procedure that required witnesses attesting to a sighting of the new moon before a duly ordained *beis din*. With the reaction that set in after the assassination of Julian "the Apostate" (363), the Jewish community was reduced in size

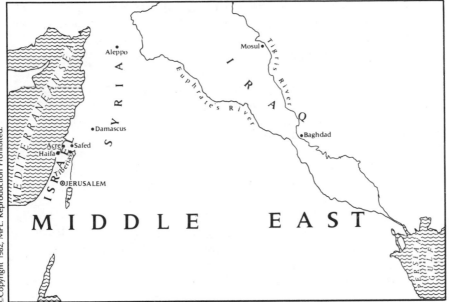

and impoverished. Little is known about the Jewish community from the "sealing" of the Jerusalem Talmud (4th cent.) to the Arab conquest (634), but isolated references in the Geonic literature indicate that religious persecution all but curtailed the public observance of *mitzvos* and the study of Talmud (see *Sefer Halttur, Hilchos Tefillin* sec. 8; *Shibolei HaLeket, Hilchos Tefillin* p. 382). However the Academy, which was the successor of the Sanhedrin, continued to exist and function. The Jewish communities of Christian Europe, to whom continuous contact with the yeshivos of the Geonim in Babylonia (outside of the Roman Empire) was a virtual impossibility, kept up a correspondence with the roshei yeshivah in *Eretz Yisrael.*

Very few scholarly Talmudic writings have come down to us from these academies, but the contribution of *Eretz Yisrael* to the study of Scripture and Hebrew grammar is inestimable. The Sages of Tiberias were known as masters of the Hebrew language and they codified and committed to writing a complex system used to this day — the *mesorah* — which ensured the purity of the Scriptural text. Nonetheless the number of known scholars until the fifteenth century is negligible and it may be assumed that the number of Jews was small. In 1099 the Crusaders conquered Jerusalem and put the members of the Jewish community to the sword. When Ramban settled in Jerusalem in 1267, he found only a handful of Jews. In 1210-11 R' Yechiel of Paris with a significant number of his disciples and others established a Jewish community in Acre (עַכּוֹ), but this too was shortlived. The great persecution of the Jews in Spain in the fourteenth and fifteenth centuries brought an influx of refugees who established important communities in Jerusalem, Safed (צְפַת), Gaza and elsewhere, attracting such personages as R' Ovadyah Bertinoro, Ralbach, R' Yosef Karo, Ramak and scores of others.

Babylonia (Iraq) Iraq, or Babylonia as it was known in antiquity, was the most populous Jewish community for many centuries following Nebuchadnezzar's exile. Even during the entire era of the Second Temple, Babylonia's Jewish population probably exceeded that of *Eretz Yisrael,* and it was the dominant community in the period that gave form to the Talmud, and later, when the Babylonian Geonim with their academies were considered the supreme authorities in the Diaspora. The decline of the Geonate had its roots in two contributing factors. The emirs of the Persian dynasty (Buwayhid), which usurped authority in Babylonia during the last century of the Geonate (945-1055), were extremely xenophobic; under them, all religous minorities were severely persecuted and their rights curtailed. The office of *Resh Galusa* (Exilarch; the Jewish prince who ruled the Jewish community with a certain measure of automony) was abolished. Simultaneously, the dependency of the Diaspora on the Geonim had begun to lessen — Spain and Tunisia now had their own academies — and with this the prestige and economic base of the Geonate academies in Babylonia was eroded. Until then, they had been supported to a large degree by donations from the Diaspora. With the demise of R' Hai Gaon (1038), the Geonic era is considered ended. However, the academy was reestablished in Baghdad and its roshei yeshivah considered themselves the spiritual heirs to the glory that had belonged to the Babylonian Geonate. Among the more famous members of the academy were R' Shmuel ben Eli and R' Daniel HaBavli, who opposed many of Rambam's halachic rulings.

II. France and Germany

The early history of the Jewish communities in France and Germany is so closely intertwined, both politically and culturally, that they can be considered as one. Very little is known about Jewry in these countries before the tenth century, although tradition relates that some Jews arrived here even prior to the erection of the first Temple (see note in Rashi to Judges 20:45) R' Yaakov Levi *(Maharil, Likkutim),* who died in 1427, told his disciples that he had seen an eleven-century old gravestone in the cemetery of Mainz (Mayence; מַגְּנְצָא). Another tradition (cited in *Teshuvos Maharshal* 29; R' Elazar of Magenza, author of *Rokeach,* cited by R' Yosef S.

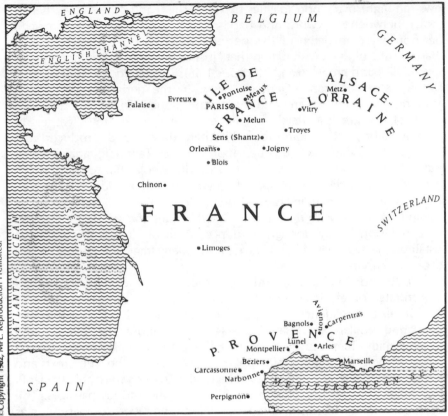

Delmedigo in *Matzref LaChachmah* ch. 12) reports that the great French king Charlemagne (784-814) brought R' Moshe HaZaken and his son R' Klonimos to Mainz from Lucca (Lombardy in Northern Italy), presumably to bolster that ancient Jewish community. It is assumed that the Jews fared well under the rule of the Carolingian dynasty (Charlemagne's descendants), although there is evidence of mounting anti-Jewish feeling nurtured by oral and written diatribes of the clergy.

The tenth century, which ushered in the first persecutions of French Jews, also produced the first known French scholars. R' Gershom Meor HaGolah (the Light of the Diaspora) and the circle of his mentors, colleagues and disciples emerged in this century. The *selichos* (supplications) and *kinos* (dirges) written during that period, especially those by R' Gershom, speak in heartrending terms of frightful persecution. R' Gershom was a seminal figure in two ways. His method of learning became the basis for the major Ashkenazic academies of future centuries, and his *takanos* [religious enactments] safeguarded the halachic and ethical development of Ashkenazic Jewry. During his time, a rumor was circulated that the Jews had joined in a pact with the Moslems. Feeling against the

Jews ran high; many principalities expelled them and others gave them a choice between the sword and baptism. It is probable that a son of R' Gershom was the victim of this persecution. Historically, however, it is characteristic of the Jewish nation that "just as (much as) they oppress it, so it multiplies and grows strong" (*Exodus* 1:15). This paradox manifests itself in the history of Franco-German Jewry. In the period of its greatest suffering, the era preceding and during the bloody Crusades, it achieved some of its greatest heights. This era gave Jewry the "Father of Commentators," R' Shlomo ben Yitzchak (Rashi) and produced the Tosafists, the school of unique approach to Talmudic analysis that established itself as the standard for Talmudic scholarship to this day.

In contradistinction with Spanish Jewry, we meet no philosophers, scientists, and statesmen in Franco-German Jewry. Rather it was marked by a singular and exclusive devotion to Jewish values and scholarship, to the total exclusion of any foreign influence. Probably it was this trait that sustained this segment of Jewry through the many tragic martyrdoms it was forced to endure.

Prior to the Tosafists, Talmudic commentators, including Rashi, had concentrated on elucidating the text of the folio page they were studying. The Tosafists broadened the horizons of scholarship by citing and comparing similar and related passages throughout the Talmud and halachic midrashim and by subjecting the plain meaning of the text to logical analysis. By pointing out apparent discrepancies between texts and demonstrating seeming difficulties in logic, the Tosafists were able to clarify and define the relevant principles underlying the various passages. The result was that seemingly incompatible rulings and rationales were seen as an interrelated tapestry of thought and halachah. As the leader of a later generation of Spanish Jewry — Ramban — expressed it: "The French Sages ... they are the mentors and teachers, it is they who expose the hidden ..." (*Kuntres Dina D' Garmi*).

The genius of Rashi did not develop in a vacuum, for as is apparent in his monumental works, he had received great portions of the material in his commentary from his mentors. To us they are relatively unfamiliar names, but their greatness lingers on in the works of their disciple; thus they never ceased to influence Jewry. The same is true of many of the Tosafists. Many are known only through a few stray quotations in one of the Tosafist glosses, but future generations of Jewish greats stood in awe of these virtually anonymous sages. To a contemporary scholar who had the temerity to draw a parallel between himself and Rabbeinu Tam, Rivash exclaimed "All of the Jewish sages alive today are but as the peel of garlic or a grain of sesame compared to one of his smallest disciples!" (*Teshuvos Rivash* 394). The French segment of the Tosafist school is dominated by the overtowering personalities of Rashi's descendants — Rashbam, Rabbeinu Tam and R' Yitzchak (Ri HaZaken), not to mention many lesser known luminaries. Seldom has one family produced brilliance in such abundance.

In the latter part of Rashi's lifetime, the First Crusade (1056) swept over Europe. Although French Jewry was spared most of the brutality suffered by their German co-religionists, it nevertheless endured great torment. The entire community of Rouen was massacred. Although the Second Crusade (1247) did not cause great loss of Jewish life, nevertheless it left French Jews ruined economically, for they were forced to contribute an exorbitant amount of money to finance the Crusade. The great Rabbeinu Tam was about to be murdered by the Crusaders, but Providence intervened at the last moment when a noble, an acquaintance of Rabbeinu Tam, happened upon the scene and saved him.

The antipathy aroused by the Crusades gave rise to a spate of blood libels. In 1171 the entire community of Blois met a martyr's death as a result of such an accusation. The boy king Philip II (1180-1223), ardently believed in this myth and in 1181, soon after his coronation, had the Jews in Paris arrested and their property confiscated. In 1182 they were banished. The edict, however, was effective only in the fief held directly by the king — Ile de France — Paris and the surrounding area. Because of the weakness of the monarchy, the lords of the other provinces were free to disobey the king. In 1198 the king allowed the Jews to return to his domain, but they suffered greatly under his rule and that of his successors, Louis VIII (1223-26) and Louis IX (St. Louis!; 1226-70). Several dukes independently banished their Jews. Severe restrictions were enacted to hamper the chief occupation left open to them — usury. On occasion, various dukes abrogated Jewish loans.

In 1240, at the instigation of the apostate Donin, an accusation was brought forward that the Talmud contained blasphemies against Christianity and its founder. To answer the accusation, the Jews were forced to send representatives, among them the Tosafists R' Yechiel of Paris and R' Moshe of Coucy. Obviously, the verdict was decided even before the debate began — guilty! In 1242 twenty-four cartloads of Talmud manuscripts were burned in Paris. In those pre-printing days, the destruction of such an immense store of laboriously handwritten manuscripts was a tragedy of major proportions. R' Meir of Rothenburg composed a moving memorial *kinah, Sha'ali Serufah Ba'esh* (recited with the *Kinos* of *Tishah B'Av* in the Ashkenazic custom) to lament this catastrophe. The subsequent prohibition against the study of the Talmud hampered Torah study and was the harbinger of a decline in scholarship. R' Yechiel of Paris, together with three hundred of his disciples, left France and established a yeshivah in *Eretz Yisrael.*

The tradition of persecution was followed by the succeeding kings of France. In 1306 Philip IV (the Fair; 1285-1314), ordered the imprisonment of all Jews and the confiscation of their belongings. By then the kingdom under the monarchs control had been substantially enlarged, so the extent of the suffering was much greater than that under earlier French kings. Jews took refuge in Germany, Spain, and Italy, as well as in French provinces not yet subservient to the crown (e.g., Lorraine). Although Louis X (1314-16) revoked the expulsion edict (1315) and permitted the Jews to return, it appears that not many took advantage of this generosity and the French Jewish community never regained its vigor. The Jews continued to be persecuted, and in 1322 they were again expelled. In 1359 the French government was in desperate need of money and Jews were allowed to come back in return for a huge bribe. In 1394 the Jews were again banished, not to return to France until the seventeenth century.

As mentioned previously, the history of Jewry in Germany is closely bound up with that of France. Even after 843, when Charlemagne's empire was
Germany divided up among his grandsons into parts approximating the modern states of Italy, France, and Germany, the cultural ties between the French and German Jewish communities were not severed. Travel seems to have been unhampered between the academies of the two countries, and the dean of French scholarship — Rashi — studied in the German academies at Mainz and Worms. The development of the French Tosafist academies with their unique approach to Talmud studies was paralleled in Germany, although the work of the German scholars has come down to us in different form than that of the French school. Where the thoughts of the French scholars exist for us largely in the collection of Tosafos, novellae assiduously gathered by generations of scholars, the German scholars' words have come down to us in a more individualized form — in halachic works of individual authors, such as *Even HaEzer* (Ravan), Ra'avyah and *Or Zarua*. These works differ from the French Tosafos not only in individualization, but in content and purpose as well. The goal of the Tosafos is the elucidation of the Talmudic texts *per se,* without attempting to apply the implications of their studies to practical Halachah, whereas the main thrust of the works of the German school is halachic application. To the German scholars the Tosafist method was a vehicle to arrive at halachic conclusions relating to practical questions of law. The father of the German Tosafists was R' Yitzchak ben Asher I (d. 1133), known as Riva. This era came to an end with R' Meir of Rothenburg (d. 1293), the leader of all German Jewry and author of extensive responsa, whose disciples composed such major halachic codes as *Shaarei Dura, Hagahos Maimon,* and *Rosh.* Germany's great era of Talmudic scholarship was cut short by the monarchy's greedy exploitation of its Jewish population, a policy that caused R' Meir to spend his last years in prison and his most prominent disciples to emigrate.

Another trend of great importance that manifested itself in Germany is that of extreme piety as exemplified in the classic works *Sefer Chassidim*

and *Sefer Rokeach*. It is not in vain that the German sages came to be called the *Chassidei Ashkenaz* (Devout Ones of Germany). These works admonished the Jew to live up to the purest ideals of the Torah in his relations with his fellow Jew as well as with the gentile, and also to strive for the strictest observance of the *mitzvos* in all their ramifications. Much attention is given to the prayer service, which is adorned with kabbalistic insights and allusions [רְמָזִים]. In general the world of allusion was assiduously cultivated by the German scholars and was used by them very successfully in Biblical exegesis as exemplified in their works on the Torah *(Perush R' Yehudah HaChassid,* et al.).

The Crusades exacted a terrible toll from German Jewry. They bore the brunt of the persecution, plunder, and massacres perpetrated upon them by the barbarous rabble that was recruited to fight the so-called "holy war," but they endured the fiery trial of martyrdom heroically. The Jewish settlements were concentrated in the Rhine Valley and this is where the undisciplined Crusaders passed in 1096 and vented the fury of their religious hatred upon the defenseless Jews. Entire communities went to a martyr's death rather than acquiesce to baptism. The prestigious communities of Worms, Speier, and Mainz were decimated. A special prayer — *Av HaRachamim* — was inserted into the Sabbath service and a special fast — 20 Sivan — was instituted to commemorate the martyrs.

The tribulations of Jewry did not end with the Crusade, which was merely the precursor of scores of local oppressions and massacres. Jews were accused of using Christian blood in their matzos and of desecrating the bread used in church services. They were severely restricted economically and taxed exorbitantly. In 1241 the entire community of Frankfurt am Main was butchered by a murderous mob and forty-four years later the same fate befell the Jews of Munich. At the close of the thirteenth century, the Jewish communities in southern Germany were devastated by a unruly mob led by a nobleman called Rindfleisch. Taking advantage of the anarchy caused by the civil war (1298-9) between two pretenders to the German crown, Adolph of Nassau and Albrecht of Austria, Rindfleisch annihilated the Jewish communities in Bavaria; only the towns of Ratisbon (Regensburg) and Augsburg were protected by their magistrates and saved. The Jews of Nuremburg, among them R' Mordechai ben Hillel and his family were martyred. More than a hundred communities were destroyed. The hysteria spread to neighboring Austria where it is estimated that more than 100,000 Jews and a hundred communities perished.

Scarcely half a century went by and German Jewry again suffered heavily; it is a miracle that any Jewish life survived in Central Europe. In 1348-51 the so-called Black Death (bubonic plague) swept across Europe, claiming, according to some estimates, half of its population. A malicious rumor was spread accusing the Jews of poisoning the drinking water. The climate was such that any accusation against the Jews, no matter how absurd (the Jews, too, drank the same water), was given credence and the aroused mob pillaged, robbed, murdered and massacred. The communities of Bavaria and the Rhine valley again were the prime victims of this slander. They were massacred en masse and in many cases expelled. One source lists the names of 200 communities in Germany (not counting those in Austria) that were attacked. The only step taken by the emperor was to fine the inhabitants of some towns for the loss of revenue caused him by the murder of the Jews. The catastrophe all but ended Jewish communal life in Germany, and scholarship all but ceased. Maharil explained his reliance on the halachic work *Agudah* by saying that its author "lived before the persecutions."

The Jews emigrated en masse to the East, specifically to Poland whose kings in this period encouraged Jews to settle in their country. Slowly German Jewry recuperated; here and there individual towns admitted Jews and promised them protection. In mid-fourteenth century Vienna we find a community headed by R' Meir HaLevi. He is credited with instituting a system of accrediting rabbis — *semichas moreinu* — to ensure they were qualified to rule on questions of halachah. This institution is in effect to this day. Later we find R' Israel Isserlein *(Terumas HaDeshen)* in Wiener-Neustadt and Maharil in Mainz. Because of the disintegration of the German empire and the absence of a central authority, the Jews were at the whim of the local rulers of each locality. The history of the fifteenth century is replete with examples of local expulsions of the Jews. Here and there the blood libel was revived and resulted in bloodshed. The war between the Hussites and Orthodox Christians (1420-36) caught the Jews of Austria and Bohemia in the middle, causing them great suffering. However, the decentralization of authority had its good side, too. When the Jews were banished from one place, they were able to move to a neighboring town, and thus German Jewry was spared the catastrophe of general expulsion that was the lot of their Spanish and French brethren.

The medieval Jewish community of England was composed mainly of Jews who had crossed the English Channel from France and were French Jews in

England the cultural sense. The English Jews seem to have fared very well financially, and for this they were subjected to punitive taxes by the kings. Concurrent with the coronation of Richard I (the Lionhearted; 1189), anti-Jewish riots broke out in London and spread to other towns. The Jews of York were shut up in a castle and despaired of escape. At the urging of their leader, the Tosafist R' Yom Tov of Joigny, they decided to kill themselves rather than submit to the choice of death at the hands of the mob or baptism. The later history of Jews in England is one of increasing oppression, persecution, and occasional martyrdom. In 1290 Edward I expelled the Jews from all of his dominions including the province of Brittany in France. Such brutal persecution and anti-Semitism is widely evidenced by English literature. They were not permitted to return until 1656, when Oliver Cromwell was convinced by Menashe ben Israel, the rabbi of the Portugese cor· ·iunity in Amsterdam, that it would be to his advantage to revoke the four centuries-old edict of expulsion.

III. Provence

The history of the Jews in this southern region of France is closely tied to that of their brethren south of the Pyrenees, both culturally and politically. In the terminology used by Jewish writers of the period, Provence also includes most of the area in the province of Languedoc. In the early days of the Frankish kingdom, Provence and Languedoc were considered part of France. Jewish tradition records that during a siege of Narbonne a Jewish knight saved the life of King Charlemagne (or another of the many Frankish kings named Charles), and that the Jews were rewarded with special privileges (R' Meir ben Shimon HaMe'ili, *Milchemes Mitzvah* in *Sefer HaMeoros*). Although it was nominally a part of the Frankish kingdom, because of its remoteness from the center of France Provence was actually ruled by local counts or kings.

In 1113 the count of Barcelona (Catalonia, Spain) expanded his rule to annex neighboring Provence. This annexation, and the influx of Jews fleeing Almohad persecution in Andalusia, opened Provencal Jewry to Spanish influence. The study of the sciences and philosophy was greatly encouraged in Provence, as was the discipline of Hebrew grammar and the art of poetry. The scholars of Lunel [חַכְמֵי לוּנֵיל] were among the first adherents of Rambam's *Moreh Nevuchim* ("Guide for the Perplexed"), as well as being avid students of his *Mishneh Torah*. R' Yonasan HaKohen corresponded at length with Rambam on halachic topics, and R' Shmuel ibn Tibbon and R' Yehudah al-Charizi rendered the "Guide" and part of the *Commentary to Mishnah* from Arabic into Hebrew. It was Provence that sparked the great Maimonist controversies (see below) and paradoxically it was probably this country where the study of Kabbalah, under Ravad II, was given its first development in southern Europe.

In 1229 Languedoc was divided. The eastern part, including the important Jewish communities of Carcassone, Beziers (Badrash), Montpellier, Peripignan, et al., was annexed by the French crown, and its Jews shared the fate of their brethren in France proper. They were expelled in 1306, but some were readmitted in 1315 and reestablished some of the old communities, notably Carcassone. They suffered greatly from the excesses of the *Pastoreaux* in 1320 and were finally evicted in 1394, when, however, the communities of Narbonne and Montpellier were spared. The expulsion of Jews from France in 1306 spared the Jews of Provence and the rest of Languedoc, but they suffered greatly during the Black Plague (1348) when they became the scapegoats and were accused of poisoning the population. In 1482 Provence was incorporated into France, but the Jews were not banished. Shortly afterward (1484), however, anti-Jewish riots broke out and in 1498 Louis XII ordered their expulsion. The edict was finally enforced in 1501.

An ideological war which was to have far reaching consequences was sparked as soon as Rambam's works were disseminated in southern Europe.

The Controversy Concerning Rambam's Writings Even before Rambam there had been Jewish rationalists, but the sensation caused by the appearance of his comprehensive *Mishneh Torah* and the impetus given the rationalists by philosophical works were a cause of apprehension among the more traditionalist Torah scholars. Already in Rambam's lifetime (approx. 1202), R' Meir HaLevi Abulafia [Ramah] was astonished that Rambam *(Hilchos Teshuvah* ch. 8) failed to refer explicitly to the future resuscitation of the dead. Instead, Rambam describes the World to Come (עוֹלָם הַבָּא) — the ultimate reward promised to those who fulfill G–d's word on this world — as being totally incorporeal and as being reserved only for the souls, not living human beings. Ramah (and Ravad III) protested that Rambam omitted the resurrection of the dead as a vital factor in the Divine scheme of reward and punishment. Rambam's supporters were quick to point out that the great codifier had indeed mentioned the tenet of resurrection elsewhere, and had branded those who deny this tenet as heretics who were not worthy of the World to Come. Likewise Rambam had classified this tenet as one of the thirteen fundamental beliefs (י"ג עִיקָרִים) in his commentary to the Mishnah *(Sanhedrin* ch. 10). However Ramah refused to be mollified by these attempts to justify Rambam, arguing that the belief in reward for the body as well as for the soul was central to Judaism and well founded in Scripture and the Talmud. R' Meir aroused Jewish world opinion, going so far as to contact the Tosafists in northern France and ask for their opinion in this matter. Also, he disputed many decisions in Rambam's code and sought to prevent its acceptance as the last word in Halachah. The Sages of Provence, Rambam's greatest admirers (among them R' Aharon ben R' Meshullam, a former mentor of Ramah), were scandalized and countered R' Meir's attack with a barrage of open letters refuting his charges and berating him for his audacity in casting aspersions upon someone of Rambam's stature.

R' Meir did not relent. He reiterated his view-point at length in his novellae *(Yad Ramah)* on tractate Sanhedrin (beginning of ch. 11). However, although he differed sharply from Rambam on matters he considered fundamental, this did not prevent him from recognizing Rambam's greatness and the service his code had performed for Judaism. When at a later date he was asked to intervene in the dispute surrounding Rambam's *Moreh Nevuchim*, R' Meir wrote to Ramban that he shared the views of Rambam's opponents (R' Shlomo of Montpellier, et. al.), however he lavished unstinting praise on *Mishneh Torah* and its author, calling him "a G–dly man."[3]

---

3. Ramah's correspondence has been published under the title *Iggaros HaRamah* (Paris, 5631; Jerusalem, 5727). Ramban treats this topic at length in his *Toras HaAdam* toward the end of the

It was probably the furor caused by Ramah's ideological attack that prompted Rambam to write his essay on the topic of resurrection — *Ma'amar Techiyas HaMeisim* — reiterating and clarifying the stance adopted by him in *Mishneh Torah,* and at the same time reasserting his belief in the resurrection.

A similar but more comprehensive attack on Rambam was made by a Provencal scholar, Ravad III. This had as its main focus, not Rambam's ideology — Ravad differed sharply on this too — but *Mishneh Torah's* authority as a halachic text. Basic to Ravad's criticism was his umbrage that decisions were rendered in the Code without the presentation of sources, and his apprehension that acceptance of the Code would sound the death knell to individual Talmudic scholarship. He set out to demonstrate in hundreds of *hasagos* (criticisms) where Rambam had erred in his understanding of the Talmud. Although these criticisms often are concluded in acerbic language, Ravad acknowledged that the code was a superb work and that its author had performed "a supreme task."

Sharp though it was, this first stage of the conflict ended amicably compared with what followed in the next few generations.

In the year 1232, R' Shlomo of Montpellier *(min HaHar)* became alarmed at the spread of Rambam's rationalist views and at the study of philosophy in general. Together with his disciples R' Yonah (the famed author of *Shaarei Teshuvah)* and R' David ben Shaul, R' Shlomo pronounced a ban upon those who study Rambam's philosophic works and any secular disciplines. Soon the communities of Aragon pronounced a counter ban against R' Shlomo. Although he was already advanced in years, R' David Kimchi again traveled to Spain to gain adherents for Rambam's views. However, although many of the leaders of Spanish Jewry were unwilling to endorse the extreme position of R' Shlomo, they expressed their dismay at the trend that was developing in the Maimonist camp. R' Yehudah Alfakhar, himself a doctor and thoroughly educated in secular studies, stated that those who wish to live in luxury and to ease the yoke of the Torah point to the "Guide" as the rationale and ideological basis for their deeds.

The combatants turned to Ramban, already the recognized leader of Spanish Jewry, to arbitrate the dispute. Although Ramban's answer revealed an ideological affinity with the attackers, it stopped short of a censure of Rambam's views and his works. He insisted that consideration must be given to Rambam's great stature as a Talmudist, and the utmost

---

part called *Sha'ar HaGemul,* and basically endorses Ramah's position. He greatly softens the debate saying that basically it is a disagreement over definitions, namely over the meaning of the term *Olam Haba,* the World to Come, rather than one over whether or not the dead will be resuscitated. He adds, however, that the question of whether the risen dead will again die to return to their incorporeal reward is a point of departure for the two sides. Ramban concludes with proofs from earlier sages, especially the Gaon and philosopher R' Saadiah, endorsing his and Ramah's view.

respect was due to him because of his services to Jewry and his unblemished and saintly personality. It is told that in the end even R' Yonah, one of the original pronouncers of the ban, did penance for this defamation of the great Torah Sage and traveled to *Eretz Yisrael* to beg forgiveness at Rambam's grave.

Another half century passed. Again a furor arose, and again Provence sparked the controversy. Alarmed at the heretical tendencies he perceived in the youth of his country who were addicted to the study of philosophy, R' Abba Mari of Montpellier appealed to R' Shlomo ben Aderes (Rashba) in Barcelona to pronounce a ban against the study of metaphysics before the age of twenty-five.

Rashba answered with a responsum endorsing R' Abba Mari's views and, together with the *beis din* of Barcelona, he signed a decree prohibiting the study of Greek philosophy and science (except for medicine) to anyone under twenty-five years of age.[4]

By this time Rambam's own reputation was already unassailable and his works were not directly involved. In fact, when the French R' Shlomo Petit, a recognized Talmud scholar and kabbalist in the community of Acre, endeavored to pronounce a ban upon Rambam and his works in 1285, he tried in vain to find supporters among the scholars of France and Italy. The leaders of the Jewish communities in Damascus and Mosul, R' Yishai ben Yechezkel and R' David ben Daniel, and the Rosh Yeshivah of Bagdad, R' Shmuel ben Daniel, excommunicated R' Shlomo Petit for his temerity (see *Minchas Kenaos*, pp. 182-4).

IV. Italy

The Italian Jewish community is one of the oldest in the Diaspora. The Hasmonean rulers of *Eretz Yisrael* in the Second Temple era had contact with the Jewish community of Rome. Here and there this community is referred to in the Mishnah and Talmud. In the days of Julius Caesar (first century B.C.E.) large numbers of Jews lived in Rome and a part of the city was called the Jewish Section. In defending someone accused of swindling Asian Jews, the famous lawyer and orator Cicero complained that too many Jews were present in the courtroom.

Of the 95,000 captives taken during Titus' destruction of the Temple (Josephus, *Wars* 6:11), no doubt many were sold as slaves and brought to Rome. According to one version in *Yossipon* (ch. 95) 16,000 Jews were brought to Rome. According to an ancient tradition four distinguished

---

4. Rashba's correspondence on this topic is in his responsa, part I, sec. 414-8. R' Abba Mari's correspondence encompassing 101 letters on this topic have been published as *Minchas Kenaos*, Pressburg, 1838.

Italian familes were originally brought to Italy by Titus: (delMansi, dePommes, delVecchio, and deRossi). Many later Italian scholars (notably R' Nassan, author of *Aruch)* traced their descent to these families. From Rome the Jews eventually branched out southward, founding communities in port cities such as Brindisi, Naples, Pompeii and others. The island of Sicily also had a Jewish community in that era.

From the time of Constantine the Great's conversion to Christianity (312), the Jewish community in the Roman Empire began to suffer from restrictions placed upon it by increasingly intolerant emperors. Jews were prohibited from employing non-Jewish slaves, thus shutting them out of the prime labor market in that age, and they were not permitted to erect new synagogues. It is ironic that in Italy, the seat of the papacy, Jews generally fared better than in the rest of Europe. We hear of no expulsions and wholesale massacres perpetrated by Italian rulers, although the Jews were restricted in many ways.

Next to nothing specific is known about the state of Jewish scholarship in Italy in the post-Talmudic era, but it is known with certainty that a high level of scholarship prevailed there. The Spanish tradition attesting to the exportation of Talmudic scholarship from Italy to Spain, Tunisia, and Egypt has already been mentioned. German traditions speak of a similar transplant of Torah from Lombardy (northern Italy) to Germany, and Rabbeinu Tam spoke of a tradition which attributed great authority and scholarship to the Sages of Bari and Otranto (southern Italy). Although no Talmudic works of these scholars have come down to us, many of the liturgical compositions *(piyutim)* composed by Italian sages are found in the Ashkenazic *machzor.* The compositions of the ninth century sages Amitai, Shefatyah, and Zevadyah occupy an important place in the *selichos* liturgy.

R' Shefatyah established a yeshivah at Oria and headed the local *beis din.* A distinguished scholar and kabbalist, R' Aharon (Abu Aharon) ben Shmuel was compelled to leave his native Baghdad, the seat of one of the geonic academies in Babylonia and instructed a member of the famous Klonimos family of Lucca. Already in the sixth century, parts of southern Italy containing significant Jewish populations (specifically the 'tip' and 'heel' of the Italian 'boot') were annexed by the Byzantine Empire, which imposed the harsh anti-Semitic restrictions of the Justinian Code, but not until much later did the persecutions become unbearable. In the mid-ninth century, the Byzantine emperor Basil I promulgated a decree bidding all Jews to convert or face death. The chronicle *Megillas Achimaatz,* by R' Achimaatz ben Paltiel, a descendant of R' Shefatyah, tells how the Jewish community was saved. R' Shefatyah traveled to Constantinople to intercede with Basil. There, he found the emperor's daughter deathly ill, but the Jewish sage was able to effect a miraculous cure. He asked that as his reward, the decree be annulled. However, half a century later (932) the Byzantine emperor Romanus Lecapenus (919-44) banished the Jews. The fanatical mob

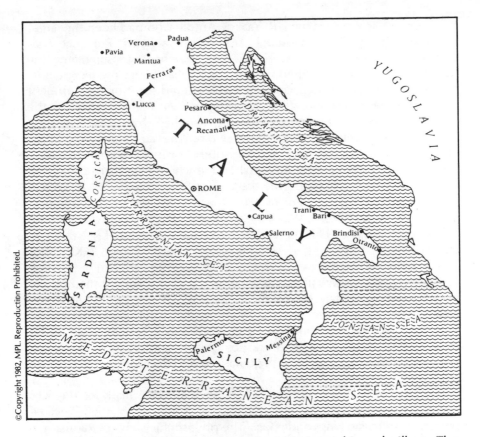

understood the cruel decree as an invitation to murder and pillage. The prestigious communities Bari and Otranto were virtually eradicated. Chisdai ibn Shaprut, the powerful Spanish Jewish leader, was able to exert pressure on the co-emperor, Constantine VII, to revoke his edict, but the damage had already been done.

Although it is likely that many Jews migrated to northern Italy to escape the persecutions, the southern communities remained larger even centuries later as related in the chronicle of the Spanish Jew, R' Benjamin of Tudela, who visited Italy (1160-73).

In the middle of the ninth century the Moslem rulers of Kairouan (Tunisia) conquered Sicily and ruled it until the Norman conquest in 1061. This exposed Italian Jews to the same influences that were affecting Eastern and Spanish Jewry, and these, too, began to study the sciences, specifically medicine and astronomy, and to delve into the intricacies of Greek philosophy. During the Norman occupation of the island, many Jewish scholars occupied a prominent place in the courts of the culture-loving Norman kings. Many scholarly works were translated from Arabic into Latin by Jewish scholars at the behest of the kings. The fervent adherent of

Rambam's philosophic system, R' Yaakov Antoli, who had been the target of a campaign against philosophic studies in his native Provence, was summoned to settle in Sicily. The Arabic influence also stimulated the development of Hebrew poetry, in which the Italian Jews were second only to the Spaniards. The Angevine kings who ousted the Normans brought with them the intolerance then prevailing in their native France. As the result of a blood libel in 1290, the Jews in southern Italy were given the familiar choice between baptism or death. The communities of Bari, Naples, et al., ceased to exist, and the south lost its predominant role.

Even in the generation of Rashi, when French and German scholarship was already firmly established, the academy at Rome, headed by R' Yechiel and his son R' Nassan (author of *Aruch)*, was consulted on a question of halachah by Rashi himself. When the traveler R' Benjamin of Tudela visited Rome (second half of 13th century) he found a descendant of R' Nassan, R' Daniel, heading the academy. An otherwise unknown scholar, R' Klonimos of Rome, is cited with great respect by Rashi *(Beitzah* 24b) and his opinion accepted without reservation. The emergence of the Tosafist method did not fail to influence Italy. One of the Italian Sages, R' Eliezer of Verona, was a disciple of Ri HaZaken, and the foremost Italian scholar of his day, R' Yeshayah ben Mali of Trani (Rid), is unmistakably a Tosafist, albeit in his own original way. Halachic works by Italian authors (e.g., *Shibbolei HaLekket, Tanya)* are replete with quotations and decisions of the German and French masters.

The relative freedom allowed Italian Jews induced many of them to occupy themselves with secular studies, and a number of them became physicians to Italian kings and popes. The philosophic views of Rambam in his "Guide" found one of its staunchest defenders in R' Hillel of Verona. However the proponents of the Kabbalah were also well represented in Italy, the tradition having been introduced and taught by R' Shefatyah's colleague, R' Aharon ben Shmuel of Baghdad. One of the most important early kabbalistic commentaries to the Torah was written by an Italian scholar, R' Menachem Recanati. Subsequent migrations of German Jews to Italy in the fifteenth century established a strong Ashkenazic community in Italy. The German Jews brought their Talmudic scholarship with them; R' Yehudah Mintz established a large Talmudic academy in Padua and R' Yaakov Landau settled in Naples. One of the greatest scholars of this age, R' Yosef Colon (Maharik), was the son of a French Jew. Still later, Italian Jewry was further strengthened with the arrival of many Spanish Jews, among them the venerable Don Yitzchak Abarbanel, making Italy one of the foremost centers of Torah scholarship in Europe.

❧ The Sephardic Lands

The Sephardic Lands

R' Yitzchak HaYisraeli I

ר' יִצְחָק (בֶּן שְׁלֹמֹה) הַיִּשְׂרְאֵלִי

b. Egypt, c. 832
d. Kairouan, Tunis, c. 932

Scholar.

Although very little of his writings have come down to us, we know that R' Yitzchak greatly influenced his contemporaries. His disciple, *R' Donash ben Tamim, tells us that R' Saadiah Gaon (892-942), while still living in Egypt (before 928), often addressed questions in various areas of knowledge to R' Yitzchak.

After moving to Kairouan, R' Yitzchak served as physician in the court of the caliph, at whose request he composed several medical treatises in Arabic. Being well received, they were translated into Latin, Spanish, and Hebrew. *R' Avraham ibn Chisdai, at the request of *R' David Kimchi, translated R' Yitzchak's Arabic *Sefer HaYesodos (Drohobycz, 1900),* a medical-philosophical work dealing with the elements, into Hebrew.

R' Yitzchak's lengthy Torah commentary (including an entire two volumes on the first chapter of Genesis alone) has been lost. *R' Avraham ibn Ezra quotes fragments of this work and sharply disagrees with R' Yitzchak's method of interpretation. However, in the introduction to his commentary on the Torah, in which Ibn Ezra outlines the methods of other commentators and explains his own, he states: "... This is the path followed by great men who are the sages of the yeshivos in the Arabian kingdoms, such as R' Yitzchak ..." A commentary on *Sefer Yetzirah* has also been ascribed to R' Yitzchak, although many entries were the work of his disciple, R' Donash.

R' Yitzchak lived almost one hundred years. However, for reasons not known to us, he never married.

R' Yehudah ben Kuraish

ר' יְהוּדָה בֶּן קוּרֵישׁ

Tahort, Tunis, late 9th-early 10th cent.

Grammarian.

One of the earliest grammarians to teach that Hebrew, Aramaic and Arabic words all stem from similar roots. Although different in their development, these languages are strongly related, and therefore exhibit the same grammatic forms. Thus, the *Targum* provides a clear translation of the Bible. R' Yehudah admonished the Jews of Fez not to disregard the reading of the Aramaic Targum together with the reading of the Torah in Hebrew. In a letter to Fez, he cites proofs from the Talmud and *Sefer Halachos Gedolos (Behag)* to substantiate this view.

R' Yehudah strongly rejected the literal interpretation of verses that assign human qualities to the Creator. He uses the maxim "the Torah speaks in the language of man" to explain all anthropomorphic and anthropopathic (the attribution of human characteristics and feelings to non-human beings or creatures or even, as in this case, to G—d Himself) verses of Scripture.

*R' Avraham ibn Ezra praises R' Yehudah's work, *Sefer HaYachas,* also called *Sefer Av VeEim,* a dictionary of Semitic tongues which has been lost, and counts R' Yehudah among the "Elders of the Holy Tongue." R'

Yehudah also composed liturgical hymns for Yom Kippur.

R' Donash ben Tamim

ר' דּוֹנָשׁ בֶּן תָּמִים

b. Iraq
d. Kairouan, Tunis late 9th cent.
Grammarian.

Known for his view that Aramaic and Arabic are merely corrupt derivatives of Hebrew, and not separate languages with their own rules, R' Donash was also a philosopher, physician, astronomer, and prolific author.

Only one of his works — a commentary to *Sefer Yetzirah* — has survived. In it, R' Donash relates that many early manuscripts of R' Saadiah Gaon (892-942), written while the latter was still a resident of Egypt (before 928), reached his teacher *R' Yitzchak HaYisraeli. R' Yitzchak, in turn, instructed R' Donash, then twenty years old, as to which parts of R' Saadiah's works he agreed with and which parts he disputed. In his commentary, R' Donash also mentions some of his other books, including a treatise on astrology written in honor of the caliph, and one on astronomy written at the request of *R' Chisdai ibn Shaprut. *R' Avraham ibn Ezra quotes R' Donash in his commentary to Scripture, often disagreeing sharply with him and his method of philology. Yet, in the introduction to his *Moznaim*, Ibn Ezra places R' Donash alongside R' Saadiah Gaon and *R' Yehudah ben Kuraish among those whom he categorizes as "Elders of the Holy Tongue."

R' Chisdai ibn Shaprut

ר' חִסְדַּאי (בֶּן יִצְחָק) אִבְּן שַׁפְרוּט

b. Jaen, Spain, c. 915
d. Cordova, Spain, c. 990
Statesman, Patron of Jewish scholarship.

Trusted physician to the caliph Abd al-Rahman III and his successor, al-Hakim II, R' Chisdai is reputed to have discovered a remedy called *al-faruk*, which was effective for many maladies. A linguist who even mastered Latin, a language then known only to the higher clergy of Spain, he translated the Latin editions of some Greek works into Arabic. He was also familiar with philosophy.

R' Chisdai had extraordinary skill as a diplomat. Although not titled vizier, he was de facto minister of foreign affairs and arranged alliances between his caliph and other rulers, among them the Byzantine emperor Constantine VII (949).

Convinced that his lofty stature and diplomatic prowess were granted him not for personal aggrandizement, but as tools with which to help his oppressed brethren, R' Chisdai spared no effort in responding to the requests he received from far and near to intervene on behalf of Jewish causes. Thus, Jews from many countries viewed R' Chisdai as their protector. He would always question travelers as to the condition of the Jews in their homeland. Accordingly, among his correspondence is a letter addressed to Joseph, king of the Khazars, whose ancestor Bulan had converted to Judaism along with many of his subjects. (This kingdom and its conversion are the subjects of *R' Yehudah HaLevi's *Kuzari*.) In his letter R' Chisdai asks the monarch for details concerning the origin of his tribe and its political and military structure, and expresses his desire to visit that land.

R' Chisdai supported the Torah academies of Babylon, which gratefully conferred upon him the honorary title *Resh Kallah* ["Chief of the Assembly"]. He also encouraged and supported grammarians and *paytanim*.

Among those who benefited from his beneficence were *R' Menachem ben

Saruk, who also served as his private secretary, and *R' Donash ben Lavrat. As president of Cordova's Jewish community, he installed *R' Moshe ben Chanoch as rabbi of that city, helped him found a Torah academy there, and upheld his authority on all religious matters concerning the community.

R' Chisdai was also instrumental in procuring copies of important works for use by Spanish scholars. At his request, R' Dosa, son of R' Saadiah Gaon, wrote a detailed biography of his illustrious father, and *R' Donash ben Tamim sent him his treatise on astronomy and calendar intercalation.

R' Menachem ben Saruk

ר' מְנַחֵם (בֶּן יַעֲקֹב) בֶּן סָרוּק

b. Tortosa, Spain, c. 920
d. Spain, c. 980

Poet, Grammarian.

At an early age, R' Menachem was brought to Cordova by his patron, R' Yitzchak ibn Shaprut. Upon learning of his parents' deaths, R' Menachem returned to his native Tortosa for a short period. He was soon recalled to Cordova by R' Yitzchak's son, *R' Chisdai ibn Shaprut, who recognized the great talents of his father's protege, and appointed the youth his personal secretary. In this position, R' Menachem wrote important documents of state, as well as R' Chisdai's famous letter to Joseph, king of the Khazars, one of whose ancestors (along with many of his subjects) had converted to Judaism.

R' Menachem wrote many poems honoring his benefactors. When R' Yitzchak died, R' Menachem composed the eulogies and lamentation that were later inscribed on the walls of the synagogue R' Yitzchak had built in Cordova.

At R' Chisdai's request, R' Menachem compiled Machberes, a dictionary of the Hebrew language. R' Menachem wrote this work in Hebrew, thus departing from the accepted practice among Babylonian and North African grammarians who generally composed such books in Arabic. He also abandoned their practice of deriving the definition of Hebrew words from phonetically similar ones in Arabic and Aramaic; by so doing he stirred much criticism.

Among R' Menachem's foremost opponents was *R' Donash ben Labrat, who wrote an extensive criticism of the Machberes, prefaced by a laudatory dedication to R' Chisdai. R' Menachem himself, on the other hand, was opposed to R' Donash's introduction into Hebrew poetry of Arabic verse forms and meters. Nevertheless, he did not reply to R' Donash's criticisms. His pupils, including *R' Yehudah ibn Chayug, the father of the suptematic Hebrew grammar, defended their master by compiling an entire treatise in which they eloquently refuted all of R' Donash's arguments. The controversy did not end there, for R' Donash's disciple, R' Yehudi ben Sheshes, in turn, compiled a treatise defending his master's opinions. About two hundred years later, the Tosafist *Rabbeinu Tam composed Sefer Hachraos to vindicate R' Menachem. It was followed by *R' Yoseph Kimchi's Sefer HaGalui, defending R' Donash. Thus, the original controversy between R' Menachem and R' Donash was instrumental in promoting an entire literature of philology in Spain, and later in France.

Despite all the formidable opposition, the Machberes became very popular among Jewish scholars residing in Christian countries, who, because they were not fluent in Arabic, could not use the earlier books on word roots. *Rashi, *Rashbam and Rabbeinu Tam frequently quote from Machberes as a basis for Biblical commentary.

At a later date, R' Menachem aroused R' Chisdai's displeasure to the extent that the latter ordered that he be forcibly removed from the community. It has been conjectured that R' Menachem's sometimes vitriolic exchange with R' Donash and his disciples were the cause of R' Chisdai's actions, but there is no evidence for this and it seems highly unlikely. R' Menachem addressed two touching letters to R' Chisdai complaining of the wrong done to him, but whether they achieved their desired effect is not known.

R' Donash ben Labrat

ר' דּוֹנָשׁ בֶּן לַבְרָאט

b. Baghdad, Iraq, or Fez, Morocco, c. 920
d.c. 990

Grammarian, Paytan.

He was the scion of an illustrious family, as attested to by his disciple R' Yehudi ben Sheshes. At an early age, R' Donash left his native Fez to study under R' Saadiah Gaon in Baghdad. Some scholars believe that R' Donash was closely related to his teacher.

Expert in defining the rules of Hebrew grammar and the meaning of obscure Hebrew terms, R' Donash often disagreed with R' Saadiah and even wrote *Teshuvos al R' Saadiah Gaon* in which he disputes many of his teacher's definitions. This work is not extant in its entirety, and has been published in an incomplete form.

*Rashi frequently quotes R' Donash in deciphering a difficult word or passage. *R' Yoseph Kimchi and *R' Avraham ibn Ezra praise him. His treatise, listing two hundred instances in which his understanding of word roots and definitions clashed with those given in the *Machberes* of his colleague *R' Menachem ben Saruk, set the stage for a debate that continued through the centuries. First, R' Menachem's disciples, including *R' Yehudan ibn Cha-

yug, refuted R' Donash's arguments against their teacher. This was followed by the treatise of R' Yehudi ben Sheshes, R' Donash's student, defending his master's opinions. Two hundred years later, the dispute was renewed when the Tosafist *Rabbeinu Tam wrote *Sefer Hachraos* to vindicate R' Menachem, and *R' Yoseph Kimchi wrote *Sefer HaGalui* to defend R' Donash. Eighty of his arguments against R' Menachem are included in R' Donash's poetic lyric *LaDoresh HaChochmos.*

The main differences between the two grammarians were in deriving the true roots of various words, thus altering their meaning. They did not differ, however, on the accepted grammatical rules of their day, such as recognizing two- and even one-letter word roots.

R' Donash's main contribution in song and poetry was his introduction to Hebrew verse of specific forms of meter borrowed from Arabic poetry. In this system, the sequence of vowels (i.e. syllables) are broken up at regular intervals with pauses [נָע שְׁוָא] termed *yeseidos* [יְתֵידוֹת], thus ensuring a certain rhythm and symmetry. He was criticized for this innovation by the disciples of R' Menachem ben Saruk, who pointed out that the construction of words differed in Hebrew to the extent that the usage of the Arabic system was an impossibility unless new grammatical forms were improvised. Nevertheless, R' Donash's method was adopted by all of the following generations of poets, making it the hallmark of Sephardic poetry. He seems also to have been the first Hebrew poet of note to use Hebrew verse for secular topics, emulating the Arabs both in his choice of themes and modes of expression. Although R' Donash is surely not considered to be the greatest Sephardic poet, he is recognized as the father of Spanish-Hebrew verse. Some of his compositions have become popular liturgical hymns, including the Sabbath hymn *Dror Yikra,* and *Dvai Haseir,* the preface to *Bircas HaMazon* at wedding feasts.

R' Chushiel ben Elchanan

ר' חוּשִׁיאֵל בֶּן אֶלְחָנָן

b. Italy
d. Kairouan, Tunisia
c. 1000

Talmudist, Teacher.

One of the "Four Captives" (see *Historical Introduction), R' Chushiel was ransomed along the African coast. From there he repaired to Kairouan, a flourishing community in Tunisia, which appointed him its rabbi. In Kairouan, R' Chushiel headed a prominent Talmudic academy, which produced outstanding halachists and Talmudists for several generations.

R' Chushiel was acclaimed far and wide. R' Hai Gaon (939-1038), last and greatest of the Geonic line of Babylon, wrote of him; "We have heard that in Kairouan there is to be found a great scholar, an expert halachist, named R' Chushiel ben R' Elchanan." In 1006 R' Hai encouraged the prominent Kairouan scholar, *R' Yaakov ben Nissim, who had previously addressed all his inquiries to the Gaon, to direct all his future questions to R' Chushiel, and to forward the responses to the Babylonian academy so that its scholars could benefit from R' Chushiel's knowledge. In recognition of his greatness, the Babylonian academy bestowed upon R' Chushiel the title *Rosh Bei Rabbanan* ["Chief Rabbinic Authority"]. In R' Chushiel's academy, the Jerusalem Talmud was studied side by side with its Babylonian counterpart. Although none of R' Chushiel's writings remain, his approach can be discerned in the writings of his son, *R' Chananel, and of his disciple, *R' Nissim ben Yaakov.

Upon R' Chushiel's demise, *R' Shmuel HaNaggid ordered that memorial services in his honor be held in Granada, Lucena, and Cordova. R' Shmuel also addressed a personal letter of condolence to R' Chushiel's son and successor, R' Chananel.

R' Shmaryah ben Elchanan

ר' שְׁמַרְיָה בֶּן אֶלְחָנָן

b. Italy
d. Cairo, Egypt, 1011

Talmudist, Halachist.

One of the "Four Captives" (see Historical Introduction), R' Shmaryah was sold by his captors at Alexandria, where he was later ransomed by wealthy members of the Jewish community. R' Shmaryah thereupon made his way to Fostat (Old Cairo), where his father, R' Elchanan, had been one of the leading rabbis. There he founded a flourishing academy.

Recognized as an outstanding Talmudist and Halachist he was called *Av Beis Din Shelechol Yisrael* ["Chief Judge of all Israel"], a title that was rarely bestowed upon scholars dwelling outside the Holy Land or Babylon.

R' Shmaryah was consulted by rabbis from distant countries, and *R' Donash ben Lavrat wrote a poem praising him and his scholarship. Unfortunately, none of his responsa have survived. He corresponded with his teacher R' Sherira Gaon (d. 1000) and the latter's son R' Hai Gaon (939-1038) in Babylon, and with the academies of Eretz Yisrael.

His son R' Elchanan succeeded him to the Fostat rabbinate.

R' Moshe ben Chanoch

ר' משֶׁה בֶּן חֲנוּךְ

d. Cordova, Spain, c. 1000

Talmudist, Halachist.

Of the "Four Captives" (see Historical Introduction), R' Moshe's lot was the most bitter. He had been captured together with his wife and young son, Chanoch. Beholding the extraordinary beauty of R' Moshe's wife, their captor, Ibn Rumahis, began making advances to her. She asked her husband in Hebrew whether those who drowned were destined to rise at the resurrection. R' Moshe replied by quoting the Psalmist (68:23): "I shall bring back from Bashan; I shall bring back from the depths of the sea." Hearing this she immediately flung herself into the sea and was drowned.

R' Moshe and his small son were ransomed by the wealthy Jewish community of Cordova, which appointed him its rabbi and accorded him great honor. It is told that when R' Moshe first came to Cordova he found his way to the study hall where the local *dayan* (head of *beis din*), the saintly R' Nassan, was lecturing on a difficult passage of Tractate *Yoma*. When R' Nassan was unable to answer the questions and objections raised by his students, R' Moshe asked permission to reply. Noting his thorough knowledge of the topic and clear response to every question, his audience presented many other difficulties which neither they nor their rabbi had been able to resolve. When R' Moshe had finished clarifying all the issues, R' Nassan declared before all who had assembled to have their cases adjudicated, "Henceforth I am no longer *dayan* here. This impoverished captive will be your teacher and I will be his disciple." The community leaders accepted this recommendation and appointed R' Moshe to the post of *dayan*.

Upon learning the true identity of his erstwhile captive, Ibn Rumahis petitioned Caliph Abd-el-Rachman to allow him to demand a greater ransom. *R' Chisdai ibn Shaprut interceded and convinced the caliph that R' Moshe's arrival would herald the ascension of Cordova as a city of Torah scholarship, thus ending the need for Spanish Jewry to be subject to Jewish authorities living in an alien kingdom. Although the study of Talmud was widespread in Cordova at that time, the level of expertise was limited, and all difficulties in comprehension had to be sent to the far-off Babylonian academies for clarification. The caliph accepted this argument and rejected Ibn Rumahis' petition.

With the arrival of R' Moshe, a new Torah epoch began for the Jews of Spain. R' Moshe was thoroughly versed in the entire Talmud, its interpretation, and its application to Halachah. No question seemed too difficult for him to answer. He founded an important academy in Cordova, which drew many disciples. In consequence, Spanish Jewry became independent of the Babylonian Geonim, and remained an important Torah center until the expulsion of the Jews from that country half a millennium later.

R' Moshe's son, *R' Chanoch, succeeded him as Rabbi of Cordova.

R' Chanoch ben Moshe

ר' חֲנוֹךְ בֶּן מֹשֶׁה

d. Cordova, Spain, 1025

Talmudist, Halachist.

As a child, R' Chanoch and his father, *R' Moshe ben Chanoch, were captured by pirates (see Historical Introduction). After being redeemed by the Jewish community of Cordova, R' Moshe was appointed its rabbi, and upon his death, R' Chanoch succeeded him.

As R' Chanoch's fame grew, many inquiries were sent to him from all corners of the globe. Some of his responsa can be found in collections of the Geonic responsa of Babylon. He had numerous disciples, among them *R' Shmuel HaNaggid. R' Chanoch's Arabic commentary to the entire Talmud is mentioned in the translator's preface to *Rambam's commentary on *Nezikin*, but some scholars doubt whether such a commentary existed. Despite R' Chanoch's wealth and the royal treatment accorded him by his followers and admirers — including *R' Chisdai ibn Shaprut, the wealthy president of the community, — he led an ascetic life, depriving himself for the benefit of the poor and needy.

R' Chanoch was not destined to continue undisturbed in his post. Although no one dared oppose him during the lifetime of his patron, the powerful and influential R' Chisdai ibn Shaprut, upon the latter's death, R' Chanoch's authority was challenged by *R' Yosef ibn Avisur, a principal disciple of R' Chanoch's father. The community was split in a great conflict between the two scholars. To halt the strife which threatened the very existence of the community, R' Chanoch pronounced a ban against R' Yosef, whereupon R' Yosef set out to find a community which would appreciate his great scholarship and piety.

So highly respected was R' Chanoch, however, that even R' Hai Gaon (939-1038) honored his ban and refused R' Yosef ibn Avisur an audience. A drastic change seemed to be imminent when R' Yosef's follower, Yaakov ibn Go, was appointed by the caliph as supreme head of the Jewish community of Cordova. He threatened to imprison R' Chanoch on an unmanned ship and let his fate be left to the winds. At the same time he sent for R' Yosef to make a triumphant return as rabbi of the city. The exiled R' Yosef, having seen the great respect accorded his adversary by scholars around the world, replied with a letter that extolled R' Chanoch very highly. He wrote, "I bring the heavens and earth as my witnesses that there is none equal to R' Chanoch — from

Spain to the academies of Babylon." Thus the rabbi of Cordova completely regained his former authority.

Another incident (related by *Ravad I in *Sefer HaKaballah*) attests to R' Chanoch's saintly character. When his son-in-law came bearing the "good news" that his vicious opponent Yaakov ibn Go had died, R' Chanoch wept bitterly, saying, "Yaakov was a very charitable man and supported many of the indigent. Numerous paupers received their daily bread at his table. Who will tend to their needs now that Yaakov is gone?"

It is related that on Simchas Torah, R' Chanoch would ascend the *bimah*, together with all the other scholars of the congregation, for the special Torah readings of that festival. One year their weight proved too heavy and the old woodwork of the platform caved in. R' Chanoch died from injuries sustained in that accident.

R' Yosef ibn Avisur

ר' יוֹסֵף אִבְּן אֲבִיתוּר

b. Merida, Spain, c. 940
d. Damascus, Syria, c. 1020

Talmudist.

A disciple of *R' Moshe ben Chanoch, in Cordova, R' Yosef felt he should succeed R' Moshe as rabbi of the city. When the position was given to R' Moshe's son, *R' Chanoch, R' Yosef mounted an acrimonious struggle for the position, with the result that he was banned by R' Chanoch. As recorded in *Sefer Hakabbalah* of *Ravad I, the caliph told R' Yosef, "If the Ismaelites would reject me as the Jews reject you, I would run away from them. And now you must run away!"

Embittered, R' Yosef went abroad to seek vindication, but R' Chanoch's ban proved so powerful that no other rabbinical authority would agree to see him. R' Yosef had expected support from the Babylonian Gaon R' Hai (939-1038), because R' Chanoch and his father R' Moshe had shifted much halachic authority from the Geonim to Spain, thus causing a decrease in the Geonic revenues, but even R' Hai denied R' Yosef an audience, in deference to R' Chanoch.

Eventually, a silk manufacturer of Cordova, Yaakov ibn Go, was appointed by the caliph as supreme head of the Jewish communities, with the right to appoint his own rabbinical candidates. Ibn Go, a close friend and supporter of R' Yosef, threatened R' Chanoch with abandonment on an unmanned ship if he persisted in maintaining his position as rabbi. At once, Ibn Go sent for R' Yosef to fill R' Chanoch's seat. In a remarkable display of humility, R' Yosef declined the invitation. Instead he lauded R' Chanoch, stating that his equal could not be found from Spain to Babylon. R' Yosef remained in exile in Damascus, never to return to Spain.

Of his works, just a few responsa and fragments of a commentary on Psalms have survived. A prolific liturgical composer, R' Yosef is the first known Sephardic poet to compose a complete Ma'amad, i.e. liturgy for all of the prayers, Avodah, Selichos etc. He composed much liturgy for the Sabbath and festivals, some of which is incorporated in the Provencal, Catalonian, and African prayer books. The liturgy HaYom Yikaseiv, which appears in the Ashkenazic Machzor for the morning service of Yom Kippur, is ascribed to him by some scholars. He is reported to have translated the Talmud into Arabic for Caliph al-Hakim II of Cordova, but no copies of this work are extant.

R' Yehudah ibn Chayug

ר' יְהוּדָה (בֶּן דָּוִד) אִבְּן חַיּוּג

b. Fez, Morocco, c. 950

d. Cordova, Spain, c. 1020

Grammarian.

A pupil of *R' Menachem ben Saruk, R' Yehudah defended his master's grammatical theories against the criticisms of *R' Donash ben Lavrat and his followers. In later years, R' Yehudah became the undisputed authority in this field, and developed his own grammatical theories. R' Yehudah also corresponded on this subject with the sages and scholars of the Holy Land, especially Tiberias.

Whereas earlier scholars recognized roots of two letters, or even one, Ibn Chayug offered proof that all words are derived from three-letter roots, and showed that even words consisting of only two letters stem from a three letter root, with one letter dropping out in the conjugation. For this discovery he was widely and elaborately acclaimed, and *R' Shlomo ibn Parchon, author of Machberes HaAruch, writes of him, "The Almighty revealed to R' Yehudah that which was hidden even from R' Saadiah Gaon ... Upon seeing his book, the scholars of Babylonia proclaimed, 'We have yet to see anything this good come from the west. It is the best in the entire world!' "

Ibn Chayug composed four works: Sefer HaNoach, also called Sefer Osios HaNoach VeHameshech, concerning "weak" verbs (which drop letters in conjugation) and their roots; Sefer Poalei HaKeifel concerning verbs which have doubled root letters; Sefer HaNikud, on vowelization; and Sefer HaRikchah. The first three of these were translated from their original Arabic into Hebrew, first by *R' Moshe ibn Gikatilla and subsequently by *R' Avraham ibn Ezra. The last work was not published and is known to us only because Ibn Ezra cites it in his Sefer Moznayim.

*R' Yonah ibn Janach disputed Ibn Chayug on many points, but *R' Shmuel

HaNaggid, who studied grammar under Ibn Chayug, defended his teacher against these attacks. Despite the criticism, all later Hebrew grammarians — even Ibn Janach — based their work on that of Ibn Chayug.

R' Nissim ben Yaakov

ר' נִסִים בֶּן יַעֲקֹב

d. Kairouan, Tunisia, 1050
Talmudist, Teacher.

A disciple of his father R' Yaakov ben Nissim, to whom the famous *Epistle of R' Sherira Gaon* (d. c. 1020), listing the chain of tradition of the Oral Torah, was addressed, and of *R' Chushiel. R' Nissim maintained an active correspondence with R' Hai Gaon (939-1038), whose opinion he sought on all Talmudic and halachic points. R' Nissim also corresponded with *R' Shmuel HaNaggid, and served as the medium through which R' Shmuel absorbed R' Hai's teachings. The Naggid became a staunch supporter of R' Nissim's academy and the ties between them were further strengthened when R' Shmuel's son, *R' Yosef, married R' Nissim's daughter. When R' Nissim traveled to Spain for the wedding festivities, he remained there for some time, lecturing on the Talmud and gaining many adherents.

*R' Menachem Meiri lists R' Nissim, his Kairouan colleague *R' Chananel ben Chushiel, and R' Shmuel HaNaggid as the first generation of *Rabbanim,* in the era following the Geonic period.

R' Nissim's *HaMafteach* refers cross-referenced Talmudic statements to the Talmudic source that elaborates most fully upon them. Originally written in Arabic, the work was subsequently translated into Hebrew. Most of the extant segments appear in the Vilna edition of the Talmud on tractates *Berachos, Shabbos,* and *Eruvin.* He also compiled notes on Halachah, Aggadah,

and related responsa which were titled *Megillas Sesarim.* Although this manuscript was lost in later generations, its influence is felt in the works of *Rif and *Rambam. R' Nissim is quoted extensively in *Aruch* and in the works of early authors.

R' Nissim's treatise on the commandments, and his composition tracing the various personalities who carried the chain of tradition from Moses onward, were also lost over the centuries.

When his grandson died, R' Nissim sought to comfort his daughter and son-in-law by sending them *Chibur Yafeh MehaYeshuah* (also called *Sefer HaMaasiyos),* a collection of anecdotes from the Talmud and Midrash, portraying Divine Providence and the reward reserved for the righteous. The work was originally written in Arabic and later appeared in a free Hebrew translation.

Although his only son died at an early age, R' Nissim was survived by his daughters.

R' Chananel

ר' חֲנַנְאֵל בֶּן חוּשִׁיאֵל

d. Kairouan, Tunisia, c. 1055
Talmudic commentator, Teacher.

As the light of the Geonic period of Babylon began to flicker, before ending with the passing of R' Hai Gaon (939-1038), a new era was beginning in other countries. R' Chananel, his friend and associate in the academy of Kairouan, *R' Nissim ben Yaakov, and their Spanish colleague, *R' Shmuel HaNaggid, formed the vanguard of the era of *Rishonim* [early authorities].

R' Chananel studied under his father, *R' Chushiel [one of the "Four Captives" who had sailed from Bari, Italy (see Historical Introduction), whom he succeeded as dean of the great Torah academy of Kairouan. Although the Tosafist *R' Tam refers to R' Chananel as a pupil of R' Hai Gaon, he probably does not mean that R' Chananel studied personally under R' Hai, but that he carefully studied and was influenced by his writings.

R' Chananel is best known for his extensive Talmud commentary, which incorporates the interpretations transmitted through the centuries by the illustrious academies of Babylon and Italy. It provides a lucid and abridged rendering of both the Babylonian and the Jerusalem Talmudic texts, and interweaves novel interpretations in the review of the Talmudic dialogue. In many instances, he closes with halachic decisions flowing from the subject matter discussed in the Talmud. In succeeding generations, R' Chananel's commentary was used extensively by almost all commentators, especially *Rif and *R' Nassan of Rome, author of *Aruch*. R' Chananel's commentary was not available to *Rashi, but the French and German Tosafists often cite R' Chananel, sometimes preferring his interpretation to Rashi's.

Owing both to his Italian lineage and his frequent use of the traditional interpretations of the Italian Talmudists, R' Chananel has been called *Ish Romi* (the Roman).

His commentary to most of the orders *Moed* and *Nezikin* appear in the Vilna edition of the Talmud. Fragments of his commentary to the order *Nashim* and Tractates *Berachos* and *Chullin* have also been printed in various collections. A commentary on Tractate *Zevachim*, found in the Oxford library, and subsequently published as the commentary of R' Chananel, was probably written by R' Chananel ben Shmuel (early 13th cent.).

R' Chananel also composed a commentary on Torah, which is cited by *Ramban, *R' Bachya, and *Ibn Shuiv. Various collections of the remaining fragments together with quotations by

other authors have appeared. *Sefer HaMiktzo'os*, an unpreserved text, is also ascribed to him, as is a compilation of dietary laws. Some of his responsa appear in *Even HaEzer* of *Ravan.

R' Chananel was exceedingly wealthy, for many of the merchants of Kairouan gave him shares in their businesses. R' Chananel had no sons, but was survived by nine daughters.

R' Shmuel HaNaggid

ר' שְׁמוּאֵל (בֶּן יוֹסֵף) הַנָּגִיד

b. Cordova, Spain, 993
d. Granada, Spain, 1055

Talmudist, Statesman.

From early youth, R' Shmuel was educated in both religious and secular studies. His master in Talmud was *R' Chanoch ben Moshe, and his teacher in Hebrew grammar was *R' Yehudah ibn Chayug. Under Arab mentors he studied sciences, mathematics, calligraphy, Arabian poetry, and languages. Although he had thoroughly mastered all these fields, R' Shmuel was quite poor. He owned a small variety store from which he barely earned a living. This, however, did not deter him from studying.

In 1012, Cordova was torn by civil war, and when the Berber chieftain Suleiman was victorious, R' Shmuel and many other Jews were compelled to emigrate, because they had supported Suleiman's rival, Mohammed ibn Chashim (see Historical Introduction). R' Shmuel found refuge in Malaga, which was under the peaceable rule of the Berber kingdom of Granada. There he maintained a small business, while devoting as much time as possible to his studies.

The following story is related by *Ravad I about R' Shmuel's rise from small shopkeeper to a position of aristocracy. R' Shmuel's store was located near the courtyard of Ibn al-Arif, vizier to King Chabus of Granada. One day, when al-Arif was away, the vizier's chambermaid asked R' Shmuel to compose some letters to her master. Upon reading the letters, al-Arif was highly impressed with the author's wisdom and style of expression. When he came home and learned the identity of the author, al-Arif immediately engaged R' Shmuel as his private secretary. The vizier was so impressed by his new secretary's talents that he allowed himself to be guided by R' Shmuel in all affairs of state. When al-Arif became sick and was near death, he was visited by King Chabus who was openly disturbed by the prospect of losing his trusted vizier. At this time, al-Arif disclosed the identity of the true advisor, and after the vizier's death, R' Shmuel was appointed his successor. It was because of this position that he was called *HaNaggid* ["the Prince"] by the Jews of Granada and *ibn Nagdela* by the Arabs.

The Naggid's ascendancy was not universally appreciated, however. The jealousy engendered among the Arab nobility by the appointment of a Jew to such a high post gave rise to a variety of plots and accusations. The king, however, paid no heed to the conspirators and R' Shmuel's position remained secure. Despite their attempts to denigrate him in the king's eyes, the Naggid showed great reserve in dealing with his detractors. One popular story about R' Shmuel's forbearance tells of a stroll on which he accompanied the king through the streets of Granada. An Arab shopkeeper, who was a religious fanatic, began hurling epithets and sharp curses at "ibn Nagdela." The incident so angered the king that he ordered his vizier to have the man's tongue cut out. However, instead of sending armed police to carry out the king's orders, R' Shmuel sent a gift to the shopkeeper. Sometime later, the king and his vizier were again strolling past the same shopkeeper's stall. This time, the Arab came out and began showering R' Shmuel with all sorts of blessings and praise. When the king demanded to know why his orders to cut out the man's tongue had not been obeyed, R' Shmuel replied, "Your majesty's command has been fulfilled! I have cut out his evil tongue and replaced it with a good one."

Upon the death of King Chabus in 1037, a controversy arose among influential parties within the royal court as to which of the king's sons should succeed him. R' Shmuel sided with a minority party that favored the elder son, Badis. When the latter's bid was successful, R' Shmuel not only retained his previous post, but was entrusted with even more responsibilites, as the pleasure-seeking king paid little attention to affairs of state. Thus, R' Shmuel became virtual ruler of Granada. In addition to administering the domestic affairs of the kingdom, R' Shmuel also served as commander-in-chief of the armies, and personally took part in Granada's many wars with neighboring states.

In Granada, R' Shmuel established a magnificent synagogue, which included a Talmudic academy. A proficient Talmudist, he himself delivered the daily lecture and provided for the material needs of the many poor students as well. His huge library included many Talmudic and halachic works, in addition to compendiums on Hebrew grammar, poetry, and philosophy. He also spent enormous sums for copies of books, which he then presented to indigent students.

R' Shmuel carried on a halachic correspondence with *R' Nissim ben Yaakov of Kairouan, who conveyed to him the decisions and Talmudic comments of R' Hai Gaon (939-1038).

Their friendship grew and they eventually became related when the Naggid's son *R' Yehosef married R' Nissim's daughter.

The Naggid donated large sums of money for the upkeep of the ancient Babylonian academies of Sura and Pumpedisa as well as for the yeshivah in Kairouan and the synagogues of Eretz Yisrael. In his hometown of Granada, every poor person turned to the charitable Naggid for assistance.

Despite his heavy schedule, R' Shmuel wrote many important works. Mavo HaTalmud describes the logic and terminology of the Talmud; it is included in most editions of the Talmud following the tractate Berachos. His digest of Talmudic laws, Hilchasa Gevurta, was designed to teach Halachah to the layman. The book, which has been lost, is quoted by Baal HaMaor, *Ramban, Sefer Halttim, Eshkol, *R' Yitzchak ibn Gias, and others. These quotes have been collected and published as Hilchos HaNaggid (Jerusalem, 1962). Recently found fragments of a work by the Naggid suggest that he wrote a treatise containing criticisms of Geonic commentaries to the Talmud. *Meiri lists R' Shmuel, R' Chananel and R' Nissim as the patriarchs of the Rabbinic [Rishonic] era, which followed that of the Geonim.

R' Shmuel was also an accomplished poet. He separated his poems into three categories: Ben Tehillim ["Sequel to Psalms"] is a collection of devotional poems; Ben Mishlei ["Sequel to Proverbs"] contains maxims; and Ben Koheles [Sequel to Ecclesiastes"] is a philosophical work. Fragments of these poems first appeared in print in 1879 (St. Petersburg), but the full works were not published until 1934 (Oxford). R' Shmuel also composed grammatical works, none of which are extant. Two of his responsa appear in Pe'er HaDor (Amsterdam, 1765).

As a father, R' Shmuel displayed such a great interest in his children's education that he sent them lessons even from the battlefield and corresponded with them concerning their progress.

R' Shmuel was succeeded by his son R' Yehosef who also assumed the title HaNaggid.

R' Yehosef HaNaggid

ר' יְהוֹסֵף (בֶּן שְׁמוּאֵל) הַנָּגִיד

b. Granada, Spain, 1030
d. Granada, Spain, 1067 (9 Teves, 4827)
Statesman, Talmudist.

Like his father, *R' Shmuel HaNaggid, R' Yehosef was an accomplished Talmudist and linguist. He succeeded his father as dean of the prominent Granada academy and as grand vizier of all territories in the kingdom of the Berber king, Badis.

There was, however, one difference between R' Yehosef and his father. Through his modesty, tolerance and sensitivity, R' Shmuel had defused the antagonism of the Arab population, which resented having a Jew in such an exalted position. R' Yehosef, however, who had grown up in royalty and luxury, was not as tactful as his father had been in dealing with his envious subjects, much less his enemies. His strict orders and aristocratic manner aroused the jealousy and fury of the Arab citizens, whom he further enraged by installing only Jews in high government posts. Although King Badis had implicit confidence in his Jewish vizier, and dismissed all complaints and accusations brought against him, the hostility of the Arab population cost R' Yehosef his life.

A powerful Arab enemy arranged to portray R' Yehosef as a traitor. Infuriated Arab mobs stormed the Naggid's elegant mansion on the Sabbath. They brutally murdered him and hung his body from the city gate. Then they dispersed through the city to wreak havoc on the Jewish population, which fled in terror.

They even destroyed the priceless library of R' Shmuel HaNaggid, which had been open to Torah scholars for many decades. Thus ended the era of Granada as an illustrious Torah center.

R' Yehosef's wife, a daughter of *R' Nissim ben Yaakov of Kairouan, escaped with their infant son, Azariah, to Lucena, where the Jewish community welcomed the remnants of the Naggid's family with love and honor. In Lucena, *R' Yitzchak ibn Gias raised Azariah as if he were his own son, predicted a great future for the lad, and looked forward to proclaiming him Rabbi of Lucena. These aspirations were not realized, however, for Azariah died in his twentieth year.

R' Shlomo ibn Gabirol

ר' שְׁלֹמֹה (בֶּן יְהוּדָה) אִבְּן גַּבִּירוֹל

b. Malaga, Spain, c. 1021
d. Valencia, Spain, c. 1058

Paytan, Philosopher, Ethician.

*R' Moshe ibn Ezra said of R' Shlomo, "By subduing his natural instincts and inclinations in order to purify his body and soul, he achieved sublime holiness and ascended to heights unparalleled by his contemporaries." From this purity of soul welled poems and hymns which have been incorporated into the festival liturgy. (However, many, if not most, of the Selichos in the Ashkenazic rite signed Shlomo ben Yehudah are not by Ibn Gabirol, but by his namesake, R' Shlomo ben Yehudah HaBavli.) One of his outstanding compositions is the lengthy hymn Keser Malchus recited in some communities on Yom Kippur following the evening services. In this poem, Ibn Gabirol presents some of his views about G–d's essence and attributes, the astronomical system of the world and the vastness of the universe, and, finally, man's insignificance and the resulting realization of his sin, his confession, and his profession of his worthlessness. The poem concludes with prayers for forgiveness and compassion from G–d.

One of Ibn Gabirol treatises, Mekor Chaim, which outlines his philosophical views in prose, underwent a remarkable metamorphosis. In the twelfth century, it was translated from the original Arabic into Spanish and Latin while the treatise itself was lost. Even the author's real name was forgotten, probably through a corruption of Ibn Gabirol's Arabic name Abu Ayub Suleiman, the book was attributed to an unknown "Avicebron." In its new form the book became a philosophic tract (titled Fons Vitae, "The Foundation of Life") eagerly studied by intellectuals of the Catholic Church. Its views became the subject of a controversy between the Dominicans and the Franciscans. Of course, the Jewish identity of the author was unknown to his readers and admirers. Indeed, *Ravad I had condemned this work as being devoid of any mention of Judaism. Only in modern times (1846) did a Jewish Arabist (S. Munk) discover, by comparing the Latin book with the fragmentary remains of a translation of an Arabic treatise known to be by Ibn Gabirol, that the Latin book was really the long lost philosophical tract composed by the great Jewish poet and thinker. Subsequently, the entire book was translated into Hebrew, and published (Jerusalem, 1926) under the name Mekor Chaim, together with the fragments of the translation leading to its rediscovery.

Known from childhood as a genius, Ibn Gabirol's uncompromising views and criticism of contemporaries who did not meet his standards brought him great anguish. He seemed to be followed by envy and strife wherever he set foot and continually wandered in search of a place where he could live in peace and contentment. Only in his religious and philosophic endeavors did Ibn Gabirol find the solace he was seeking.

In his early years, he spent some time in Saragossa, a center of Jewish culture and learning, evidently to learn and teach. Soon, however, his rigid standards brought him many opponents. He gained a friend and supporter in the person of *R' Shmuel HaNaggid but later a controversy arose between the two and Ibn Gabirol felt compelled to criticize the Naggid bitterly.

His other works include Tikkun Middos HaNefesh, in which he takes a unique approach to ethics, arranging the virtues and vices in relation to the five senses, with every sense becoming the instrument of two virtues and two corresponding vices. Some are of the opinion that this book influenced *R' Bachya in writing Chovos HaLevavos. Composed in Arabic, Tikkun Middos HaNefesh was translated into Hebrew by *R' Yehudah ibn Tibbon.

A popular collection of proverbs and aphorisms, Mivchar HaPeninim is sometimes attributed to Ibn Gabirol, but no conclusive proof exists for this claim. Some specimens of his exegetical method are to be found in the commentaries of *R' Avraham ibn Ezra.

R' Bachya (Bechaye) ibn Pakudah

ר' בְּחָיֵי (בֶּן יוֹסֵף) אִבְּן פָּקוּדָה

Saragossa, Spain, early 11th cent.
Ethician, Philosopher, Paytan.

In the introduction to his monumental classic, Chovos HaLevavos ["Duties of the Heart"], R' Bachya explains that the purpose of his work is to present the ethical teachings of Judaism and its fundamental beliefs in a systematic pattern. He argues that the "duties of the heart," i.e. the intellect and emotions, should receive priority over the mitzvos performed with only "the limbs." Furthermore, even the mitzvos performed primarily with the limbs are dependent in no small degree upon the participation of the heart. Therefore, the study of the fundamentals of Judaism and the intellectual imperatives deriving from them, plus the Torah's ethical teachings, are of the utmost importance, and should take precedence over other studies. R' Bachya made it a practice to base every tenet presented in his work on a trio of sources (a) Scripture, (b) the traditional teachings of the Sages, and (c) the intellect. The work is divided into ten parts called She'arim [Gates]:

(1) Shaar HaYichud ["Gate of Unity"] — an elaboration upon the author's contention that belief in the existence and unity of G—d should rest not solely on faith, but should be buttressed by conviction based on rationalistic investigation. R' Bachya proceeds to present many examples of arguments proving G—d's existence and goes on to elaborate upon the meaning of Divine unity and oneness.

(2) Shaar HaBechirah ["Gate of Recognition"] — the recognition of G—d's wisdom and goodness as it manifests itself in the universe.

(3) Shaar Avodas HaElokim ["Gate of the Service of G—d"] — the obligation to accept upon oneself the service of G—d. Two types of service are delineated, one based upon the precepts of the Torah and the other rooted in rationalistic thought. The differences between the two types of service are discussed at length and arguments are given for the necessity of both types.

(4) Shaar HaBitachon ["Gate of Faith"] — the meaning of trusting in G—d.

(5) Shaar Yichud HaMaaseh ["Gate of Dedication of Purpose"] — the obligation to divorce service of G—d from any

extraneous intentions — the various forms of humility before G−d.

(6) *Shaar HaKeniah* ["Gate of Humility"].

(7) *Shaar HaTeshuvah* ["Gate of Repentance"].

(8) *Shaar Cheshbon HaNefesh* ["Gate of Accounting of the Soul"] — self examination and meditation.

(9) *Shaar HaPerishus* ["Gate of Abstinence"].

(10) *Shaar Ahavas Hashem* ["Gate of Love of G−d"].

Of the geonim and commentators who preceded him, R' Bachya refers most frequently to the works of R' Saadiah Gaon (892-942), and often exhorts his readers to study that Gaon's brilliant writings.

R' Bachya's treatise is a classic in Jewish thought and considered by many as a fundamental textbook of religious ideology. In a later era, R' Yisrael, the famed Maggid of Kozhnitz, would declare that *Chovos HaLevavos* was the foundation upon which his faith stood, and *Chasam Sofer* would preface his daily Talmud lecture with a reading from this work. It was to become a primer of the *mussar* movement founded by R' Yisrael Salanter. *Chovos HaLevavos* is diligently studied by Jews the world over to this day; age has not dated it nor has the passage of time blunted its appeal and force. Jewish thinkers in later generations have used R' Bachya's principles as the nuclei about which to form their ethical writings. Chida describes R' Bachya and *Chovos HaLevavos* in the following terms: "One who reads his treatise and its preface will realize (the author's) extreme holiness. His words live on ..."

Chovos HaLevavos was written in Arabic for the benefit of the masses in the author's time. It was translated into Hebrew by *R' Yehudah ibn Tibbon in 1161, and later by *R' Yosef Kimchi. Of the latter's translation, which is not as literal as ibn Tibbon's, only one section has survived. In modern times a number of new translations into Hebrew have been made. Due to its popularity, *Chovos HaLevavos* has been reprinted numerous times (first ed., Naples, 1490) and has been translated into many other languages, including English. Several commentaries have been written to it.

R' Bachya also composed *Borchi Nafshi*, a poem devoted to self-reflection, printed in the *Machzor Roma* and some siddurim (e.g., *Otzar HaTefillos*), and a *Viduy* (confession). Some of his liturgical compositions (discussed in *Amudei HaAvodah;* Berlin, 1857) are still in manuscript.

Very little of R' Bachya's personal life is known, except that he served as Dayan of Saragossa, and wrote *Chovos HaLevavos* circa 1040.

R' Yonah ibn Janach

ר' יוֹנָה אִבְּן גַ'נָאח

b. Cordova, Spain, c. 990
d. Saragossa, Spain, c. 1055

Grammarian.

Nothing is known of R' Yonah's early years, not even his family name. The name Ibn Janach is Arabic for "winged one" and is a loose translation of the Hebrew word *Yonah* ["dove"]. His Arabic given name was Marwan which is why *R' Avraham ibn Ezra and others refer to him as R' Marinos.

His major instructors during his youth were the grammarian R' Yitzchak ibn Gikatilla, a disciple of *R' Menachem ben Saruk, and R' Yitzchak ben Mar Shaul of Lucena. R' Yonah dedicated himself to intense study of the Bible and Hebrew grammar, and credited his success in Torah learning and his concomitant grammatical discoveries and innovations to diligence and perseverance. He offered the maxim that the most important factor in the attainment of knowledge was the distance one placed between himself and laziness. As an example of his diligence, he reported that he spent twice as much on oil (to keep the lamps burning late into the night) as most people spent on wine. He also studied Aramaic and acquired great expertise in Arabic.

R' Yonah earned his livelihood as a physician and composed a medical treatise. He was acquainted with Catholic claims concerning the interpretation of certain Biblical verses, from which the Church sought to prove the authenticity of Christianity. In his grammatical treatises he refuted such exegeses on philological grounds; in a similar manner he rebutted the arguments of the Moslem clergy.

When the Jews were expelled from Cordova in 1012 (see Historical Introduction), Ibn Janach settled in Saragossa, where he joined a group of scholars studying Hebrew grammar. *R' Shlomo ibn Gabirol, who was living in Saragossa at the time, staunchly supported Ibn Janach's work.

Although it is not known for certain whether R' Yonah actually was a student of *R' Yehudah ibn Chayug, he does call that great grammarian by such titles as the exalted teacher and the perfect leader. His first published book on Hebrew grammar, Sefer HaHasagah, also called Sefer HaTosafos, points out numerous roots about which Ibn Chayug was either unaware or mistaken. Although Ibn Janach praised Ibn Chayug for his erudition, acknowledging that much of his own knowledge of grammar was derived from the latter's books, and considering his own work as an extension of Ibn Chayug's, his critical analysis of the latter's works aroused the indignation of many leading scholars who had personally studied under the grammarian and who considered their teacher's rules flawless.

The most notable of Ibn Janach's adversaries was *R' Shmuel HaNaggid, with whom he was acquainted from their mutual birthplace, Cordova. While he was at the home of a friend, Abu Sulaiman ibn Taraka, a stranger from Granada revealed that the Naggid was preparing attacks on Sefer HaHasagah and enumerated fourteen criticisms which he remembered. R' Yonah answered these arguments in Sefer HaHashva'ah, claiming that his contemporaries had no basis for criticising him, other than jealousy of his knowledge. This treatise inaugurated a great controversy between the two scholars.

Although by nature peaceful and forgiving, R' Shmuel was outraged by Ibn Janach's attitude. In Igros HaChaverim ["The Letters of Friends"], a no longer extant series of pamphlets, the Naggid vehemently attacked Ibn Janach's work. In replying to these attacks, Ibn Janach was no milder in his treatment of the respected Naggid. Ibn Janach's four subsequent treatises refuting his opponent were sharply worded and very critical. Although their controversy remained unresolved in their lifetimes, it proved very beneficial to the furtherance of Hebrew linguistics, for each scholar revealed new insights. The books and pamphlets mentioned above have never been translated into Hebrew, but they have been printed in the original Arabic with a French translation (Paris, 1880).

Ibn Janach's chief work, completed towards the end of his life, was Sefer HaDikduk, comprising two parts: Sefer HaRikmah, a compilation of rules governing the Holy Tongue; and Sefer HaShorashim, an alphabetical encyclopedia of the roots of all words found in the Bible. For his discovery and translation of roots, R' Yonah drew on similar words found in Targum or Rabbinic literature, and on his knowledge of Aramaic and Arabic. This work is of great value in Biblical exegesis. Like all his works, they were written in Arabic, thus effectively blocking their use in the Ashkenazic academies, nor was R' Yehudah ibn Tibbon's subsequent (1214) Hebrew translation widely disseminated. Consequently, when Arabic ceased to be the language of Jewish scholars, Ibn Janach's fame rested only on random citations in the commentaries and grammars of *R' Avraham ibn Ezra and *R' David Kimchi. Only in recent times have the Hebrew translations of *Sefer HaRikmah* and *Shorashim* become available (Frankfort, 1856; Berlin, 1896).

R' Yehudah ibn Balam

ר' יְהוּדָה (בֶּן שְׁמוּאֵל) אִבֶּן בַּלְעָם

b. Toledo, Spain, c. 1000
d. Spain, c. 1070

Bible commentator.

Written in Arabic, R' Yehudah's interpretations of Scripture were extremely popular with his and succeeding generations. His work greatly influenced *R' Avraham ibn Ezra, who quotes Ibn Balam on numerous occasions and lists him among the fifteen "elders of the Holy Tongue." Although his commentary on Torah has not been preserved in its entirety, the one on Prophets seems to have survived intact. Besides his own unique and original explanations, he incorporates many Talmudic and Midrashic interpretations. He frequently quotes other commentators, and with penetrating analysis refutes their opinions. Many of his strongest polemics are aimed at his colleague, *R' Moshe ibn Gikatilla.

An implacable opponent of Karaism, a sect that accepted only the Written Torah but not the Mishnah and Talmud, he often engaged in vehement debate with the Karaites and labeled them heretics.

An expert in Hebrew language and

grammar, Ibn Balam composed various works in this field as well, including *Sefer HaPoalim; Osos HaInyanim; Sefer HaMeyasheir;* and *Sefer HaTzamid,* devoted to word roots and usage. In this realm, he followed *Ibn Chayug and *Ibn Janach, expanding and applying their rules. The works *Taamei HaMikra* (Paris 1566; partially found in R' W. Heidenheim's *Mishpetei HaTa'amim*) and *Horo'as HaKoreh* have also been attributed to him, but without sufficient evidence.

In his later years, Ibn Balam, also known by his Arabic name, Abu Zechariah Yachya, spent much of his time in the study of Halachah. He also composed liturgical poems, some of which have survived in the Sephardic and Italian *Selichos* services

R' Moshe ibn Gikatilla

ר' מֹשֶׁה (בֶּן שְׁמוּאֵל) אִבֶּן גִּיקַטְלְיָא

Spain c. 1050

Grammarian, Bible exegete, Paytan.

R' Moshe translated *Ibn Chayug's principal grammatical works, *Sefer Poalei HaKeifel* and *Sefer Osios HaNoach VeHameshech* into Hebrew. Most of his compositions have not been preserved, but numerous citations are found in the works of other commentators, especially *R' Avraham ibn Ezra on Prophets and Psalms. R' Moshe's contemporary, *R' Yehudah ibn Balam, criticized him for basing his interpretations — even those concerning miracles recorded in the Bible — on a rationalistic approach. *R' Moshe ibn Ezra considered Ibn Gikatilla among the greatest masters of prose and poetry in Hebrew and Arabic.

R' Yitzchak al-Fasi (Rif)

ר' יִצְחָק (בֶּן יַעֲקֹב הַכֹּהֵן) אַלְפָסִי (רי"ף)

b. Kila Chamad, Algeria, 1013
d. Lucena, Spain, 1103

Talmudist, Teacher, Codifier.

Born in a small village in Algeria, R' Yitzchak moved to the major city of Fez in Morocco, hence his surname al-Fasi and his acronym Rif (Rabbi Yitzchak of Fez). There he headed a large academy whose best known student was *R' Ephraim of Kila Chamad. Rif was considered the successor to the famous teachers, *R' Nissim ben Yaakov and *R' Chananel.

At the age of seventy-five, Rif was slandered to the government on some unknown charge, and was forced to flee to Spain. He spent a short time in Cordova where he was cordially received. From there he moved to Lucena, a two-century old stronghold of Torah, which was under the leadership of *R' Yitzchak ibn Gias. When Ibn Gias died just a few months later in 1089, Rif was chosen rabbi of Lucena and head of its great Talmudic academy. Among the numerous disciples who attended his discourses was *R' Yosef ibn Migash.

A collection of 320 of Rif's responsa exists (Leghorn, 1821), and additional collections of responsa have been printed more recently (Bilgorai, 1934; New York, 1975). He left his deepest imprint on future generations, however, with his magnum opus *Sefer HaHalachos,* an abridged version of the Talmud that deals strictly with halachic applicable discourses and their practical application. The work reviews the vital points of the Talmudic text and provides a clear picture of the halachic conclusion. In it, Rif excerpts from the Talmud only those passages pertinent to the practical halachah, omitting the lengthy discussions of the Amoraim. His arrangement generally follows that of the Talmud, thus facilitating additional research in the source. However, Rif also assembles from throughout the Talmud all the scattered discourses pertaining to one subject so that the reader can obtain a broad un-derstanding without searching through all tractates. This type of arrangement was not original to Rif; it had already been introduced by the first post-Talmudic halachah text — *Halachos Gedolos.* The feature which distinguishes Rif is that his work incorporates most of the body of halachah developed by the Geonim. As a result, his work "suffices for them all" (*Rambam, preface to his Mishnah commentary). Rif's decisions form the basis for Rambam's code; Rambam himself reports that he has deviated from Rif's view in only approximately thirty instances. When we consider that R' Yosef Karo's *Shulchan Aruch* is based primarily upon Rambam's code, we realize how formidable is Rif's influence on contemporary halachah. In ruling, Rif usually follows the view of the Babylonian Geonim. However, in instances where he differs with the Geonic opinions, Rif elaborates on the difficulties arising from their explana-tion, and then offers the Talmudic interpretation on which he bases his original halachic decision. Many times he quotes at length from the commen-tary of his mentor — R' Chananel — and, where he disagrees, presents the arguments that caused him to do so.

Confining itself only to halachos applicable to his time, *Sefer HaHalachos* omits all laws governing sacrifices, ritual purity, and agriculture in *Eretz Yisrael.* The work therefore covers only three of the six orders of the Mishnah — *Moed, Nashim* and *Nezikim* — and tractates *Berachos* and *Chullin.* Laws discussed in orders *Kodashim* and *Taharos* but also applicable today (e.g., tefillin, mezuzah) were gathered by R' Yitzchak under the title *Halachos Ketanos,* and are printed after Tractate *Menachos* in most full editions of the Talmud.

Many commentaries were written on *Sefer HaHalachos,* among them, *R'

Zerachiah HaLevi's *HaMaor* which disputes Rif on many decisions, and *Ramban's *Milchamos HaShem,* written to refute the criticisms of *HaMaor* as well as those of *Ravad III. The later commentators *R' Yehonasan of Lunel, *Ran and *R' Yosef Chaviva *(Nimukei Yosef)* also wrote commentaries on *Sefer HaHalachos.*

*Meiri refers to Rif as the greatest of the halachic authorities; Rambam writes of him that he superseded all his predecessors in his great work; and Ravad III, who was most critical in his evaluation of other authors, states in regard to Rif, "I would adhere to the words of the rabbi even if he were to decide that right was left." The Ashkenazic scholars also lauded him. The Tosafist *Ri states, "It is impossible for a mortal to compose such a work unless the Divine Presence rests upon him."

R' Yitzchak Alfasi represents a departure from the prototype of the Sephardic scholar as generally known until his time. Whereas most, if not all, recognized scholars before him cultivated the study of the Hebrew language and its grammar, composed poetry, mastered secular sciences, and delved into the complexities of Greek philosophy as interpreted by the Arabic scholars, Rif seems to have devoted all of his time, talent and energy to the study of the Talmud. It can perhaps be said that Rif's example set in motion (in Spain) a gradual shift in emphasis from other intellectual pursuits to a more intense and exclusive study of Jewish texts. In doing so, Sephardic Jewry noticeably shifted toward the views held by their French and German counterparts, and created the climate for the subsequent acceptance of this school's authority in matters of Talmudic interpretation. This shift is evidenced by the works of *Ramban, *Rashba, *Ritva

and *Ran, and by the acceptance of *Rosh as the supreme halachic authority in some provinces of Spain.

Before his death, Rif appointed *R' Yosef ibn Migash as his successor, even though his own son R' Yaakov was an accomplished Talmudic and halachic scholar.

R' Ephraim of Kila Chamad
ר' אֶפְרַיִם מִקִּלְעָה חַמַּד
Kila Chamad, Algeria, c. 1075

A principal disciple of *Rif, R' Ephraim studied under him in Fez. R' Ephraim was the first scholar to add notes and refutations to Rif's *Sefer HaHalachos* and is frequently quoted in *Sefer HaMaor, Milchamos HaShem, Tamim Deim* and many other works. A collection of his works was recently published (Jerusalem, 1976). *R' Shlomo ibn Parchon was a disciple of R' Ephraim.

R' Yitzchak Ibn Gias
ר' יִצְחָק (בֶּן יְהוּדָה) אִבְּן גִּיאַת
b. Lucena, Spain, c. 1020
d. Cordova, Spain, 1089
Talmudist, Halachist, Paytan.

R' Yitzchak maintained close ties with *R' Shmuel HaNaggid, under whom he is thought to have studied, and with R' Shmuel's son, *R' Yehosef HaNaggid. When the latter was murdered, Ibn Gias took R' Yehosef's young son Azariah into his home and raised him as his very own son, hoping to have him appointed rabbi of Lucena eventually. Azariah, however, died at the age of twenty, and Ibn Gias himself was subsequently proclaimed rabbi. Under his leadership the community thrived as a center of learning and culture.

Ibn Gias began many works, but never had time to complete them, for his role as the principal educator of his generation was very demanding. Pupils from all over Spain flocked to his academy to hear his lectures. Among his most prominent disciples were *R' Yosef ibn Sahal, who later was a *dayan* in Cordova; his own son R' Yehudah ibn Gias; and *R' Moshe ibn Ezra.

From among R' Yitzchak's numerous unfinished manuscripts, only parts of his halachic compendium *Meah Shearim* have survived. Unlike his contemporary *Rif, Ibn Gias arranged his halachic data and analysis according to topics rather than according to the Talmudic sequence. In adopting this method, he followed the lead of R' Saadiah Gaon, R' Hai Gaon and other Geonim. This work was cited by virtually all authorities from his contemporaries to *R' Yaakov ben Asher, author of *Arba'ah Turim*, who frequently quotes it.

Ibn Gias' halachic work differs from Rif's, however, not only in its external structure, but in its manner of presentation, choice of sources, and choice of subject matter. Rif's method formulates the halachah in the words of the Talmud itself, by quoting the passage reflecting the accepted view and leaving the reader to draw his own conclusion. Ibn Gias first formulates the laws in his own words, and then offers a review of the sources, engaging the reader in a discussion of the pros and cons of the respective positions. While Rif generally restricts his code to the statements of the Babylonian Talmud, Ibn Gias makes extensive use of the Jerusalem Talmud and refers constantly to the Geonic responsa and halachic codes. Indeed his work is an abundant treasury of Geonic literature. Finally, Rif rules only upon matters discussed in the Talmud and rarely discusses halachic matters not found in the Talmud. Ibn Gias does not restrict himself in this way, and chooses topics at his own discretion.

Ibn Gias also wrote an Arabic translation and commentary on Ec-clesiastes, but it is known to us only through quotations in the works of later authors. His liturgical compositions convey a deep sense of faith, and inspire the worshiper to spiritual heights. These prayers captured the hearts of most of Spain and North Africa, and were quite popular in Italy. Many of them are printed in the Tripoli *Machzor*.

After becoming ill, Ibn Gias journeyed for medical treatment to Cordova, where he passed away. His body was brought to Lucena to be buried with his forefathers.

R' Yitzchak Alballah

ר׳ יִצְחָק (בֶּן בָּרוּדְ) אַלְבַּאלְיָה

b. Cordova, Spain, 1035
d. Granada, Spain, 1094

Talmudist.

Legend has it that after Titus destroyed the Second Temple (68 C.E.), the governor of Spain bade the Roman general to send him some of the famous craftsmen of Jerusalem. Titus fulfilled his request and sent, among others, a Jew named Baruch, who used to weave curtains for the Temple. Baruch, who settled in the Spanish city of Merida, was the progenitor of R' Yitzchak's line. In later years the family relocated in Cordova, where it lived in prosperity for many centuries.

Even as a child, R' Yitzchak was quite studious. He studied Torah under the French scholar, R' Prigoras, who had emigrated to Spain, and also under *R' Shmuel HaNaggid, who took a special liking to the youth and kept a watchful eye over his progress. R' Shmuel supplied him with books and showered him with gifts. After R' Shmuel's death, R' Yitzchak continued to maintain very cordial relations with the Naggid's son and successor, *R' Yehosef. On the day of the great Arab uprising in Granada, in which R' Yehosef was savagely murdered (9 Teves, 1066), R' Yitzchak had been visiting the Naggid's home, but miraculously escaped the mobs.

In 1069, King al-Mutamid of Seville appointed R' Yitzchak as his advisor and chief astrologer, and also as rabbi and leader of the Jews in his realm. In this capacity he was able to influence the king's treatment of the Jews.

His official post did not distract R' Yitzchak from his studies and his devotion to Torah, and he headed a large academy. He also undertook a work titled *Kupas HaRochlim* dealing with the interpretation of difficult Talmudic passages. The book, which, according to his grandson *Ravad I, was never completed, was eventually lost. As a gift to R' Yehosef HaNaggid, he also composed a treatise explaining the complexities of calendar intercalation and its cognate astronomical problems.

One of his responsa, in which he differs with *Rif concerning *tzitzis*, is recorded in *Ravad III's *Tamim Deim* (224). In his responsa (Jerusalem, 1934, no. 4), *Rambam refers to R' Yitzchak's decision but asserts that Rif's opinion is correct.

Although R' Yitzchak and Rif were bitter opponents (the basis of their controversy is unknown), R' Yitzchak, on his deathbed, sent an apology to Rif through his seventeen year old son, Baruch, beseeching Rif to teach the youth Talmud. Rif accepted both the apology and the task. He taught the lad the entire Talmud, and R' Baruch later became a *dayan* in Cordova.

R' Yitzchak of Barcelona

ר' יִצְחָק (בֶּן רְאוּבֵן) אַלְבַּרְצְלוֹנִי

b. Barcelona, Spain, 1043
d. Denia, Spain

Talmudist, Halachist.

R' Yitzchak served as *dayan* in the important community of Denia in southern Spain.

At the age of thirty-five, he translated

R' Hai Gaon's (939-1038) *HaMekach VehaMimkar,* from Arabic into Hebrew, to make it accessible to Jews residing in Christian dominions, who were unacquainted with Arabic.

R' Yitzchak wrote a commentary on various chapters of Tractate *Kesubos.* He also composed liturgical hymns, many of which were incorporated into the prayers of North African Jews. Most famous of these is his *Azharos,* which enumerates the 613 commandments of the Torah in poetic form.

Some historians mistakenly credit R' Yitzchak with authorship of *Shaarei Shevuos,* a work which may have been written by a later scholar of the same name, R' Yitzchak ben Reuven. Although *R' Yehudah of Barcelona is reputed to have been his disciple, the latter never mentions R' Yitzchak in any of his works.

*Ramban was a descendant of R' Yitzchak.

R' Yosef ibn Sahal

ר' יוֹסֵף (בֶּן יַעֲקֹב) אִבְּן סָהֵל

d. Cordova, Spain, 1124

Halachist, Paytan.

A disciple of *R' Yitzchak ibn Gias, R' Yosef served as *dayan* of Cordova from 1113 until his death. He is reputed to have translated many of the responsa of *Rif from Arabic into Hebrew, but his translation has not survived. *R' Moshe ibn Ezra praises his colleague, R' Yosef, as a keen-minded and expert halachist, and as an eminent *paytan.*

R' Baruch Albaliah

ר' בָּרוּךְ (בֶּן יִצְחָק) אַלְבַּאלְיָה

b. Cordova, Spain, 1077
d. Cordova, Spain, 1126

Dayan.

In his youth, R' Baruch studied under his father, *R' Yitzchak Albaliah; however, just before the latter died, he instructed his seventeen year old son to travel to Lucena and become a disciple of *Rif, with whom R' Yitzchak had been feuding for several years. When R' Baruch conveyed to Rif his father's apology and his request to receive his son as a disciple, Rif was greatly moved and promised to be a father to the young man. R' Baruch remained with Rif until the great halachist taught him the entire Talmud. R' Baruch also excelled in the study of philosophy.

After Rif's death, R' Baruch was chosen *dayan* by the Jewish community of Cordova, where he also taught Talmud. Among his many pupils was his nephew, *Ravad I.

R' Baruch is praised in the poetry of *R' Yehudah HaLevi and *R' Moshe ibn Ezra for his excellent character traits and great erudition. His sudden death at the age of forty-nine brought much grief to all of Spanish Jewry.

Other than a few scattered quotations, none of his writings are extant.

R' Yosef ibn Migash (Ri Migash)

ר' יוֹסֵף (בֶּן מֵאִיר הַלֵּוִי) אִבְּן מִיגַּשׁ

b. Seville, Spain 1077
d. Lucena, Spain 1141

Talmudist, Teacher.

At a tender age, R' Yosef displayed great talents and sharp wit. *R' Yitzchak Albaliah predicted that the child would become a great luminary in the Torah world and implored Yosef's father to provide him with outstanding teachers and to dedicate all of the youth's time to learning. R' Meir, the child's father, readily complied, and young Yosef began his studies under R' Yitzchak.

At the age of twelve, R' Yosef traveled to Lucena, where he studied under *Rif for fourteen years. Rif's praise of R' Yosef was unbounded, and although his own son R' Yaakov was an eminent sage, Rif designated the youthful R' Yosef to be his successor.

As head of the famous academy at Lucena, R' Yosef taught numerous disciples including R' Maimon, father of *Rambam.

Rambam's praise of R' Yosef is uncharacteristically ecstatic. "The depth and scope of his wisdom astound all who study his words, so that it may be said of him (Scripture's description of King Josiah), 'And equal to him there was no king who preceded him'". Having absorbed R' Yosef's teachings from his father, R' Maimon, Rambam refers to R' Yosef as "my teacher." Such references have led many to believe that Rambam personally studied under R' Yosef. This is impossible, however, since Rambam was only six years old at the time of Ri Migash's passing.

R' Yosef also replied to halachic inquires sent to him from all the Sephardic communities, and his sharp intellect was apparent in correspondence as well as in his discourses. A small portion of his extensive responsa has been published under the title *Sheilos U'Teshuvos HaRi Migash* (Salonika, 1791).

Ri Migash composed commentaries to many Talmudic tractates, of which only those to *Bava Basra* (Amsterdam, 1702) and *Shevuos* (in *Oriyon T'lisa'a*, Solonika, 1759) have been published. His *Megilas Sesarim*, containing a critical analysis of Rif's *Sefer HaHalachos* and quoted in *Sefer HaMaor*, has not survived.

R' Moshe ibn Ezra

ר' מֹשֶׁה (בֶּן יַעֲקֹב) אִבְּן עֶזְרָא

b. Granada, Spain, c. 1070
d. Spain, c. 1140

Paytan, Linguist.

Although born into one of Spain's wealthiest and most prominent families, Ibn Ezra did not lead a serene life. Due to a dispute with one of his brothers, he was forced to leave his native Granada and sojourn in Portugal and Seville.

While spending some time in Christian Spain, he was imprisoned for a short while for an unknown reason. As is evident from his writings, he was married and had children, but nothing more is known of his family life.

From his youth, this pupil of *R' Yitzchak ibn Gias excelled in poetry. Because the greater part of his 220 sacred compositions, found in the Sephardic *Machzorim*, are mainly *Selichos* ["penitential poems"] for the High Holy Days, he has been called *HaSalach* ["the supplicant"]. His *Kinnos* ["laments"] are also well-known, particularly his poetic eulogy for *Rif, which was inscribed on the halachist's tombstone. (The full text appears in the publisher's preface to Rif on *Berachos*.)

R' Moshe was also a distinguished philosopher and linguist, who specialized in the Hebrew language. While the *paytan* *R' Yehudah HaLevi sojourned in Granada, he was R' Moshe's guest, and their friendship continued even after R' Yehudah returned to his native land.

In his later years, R' Moshe composed *Shiras Yisrael,* which discusses the development of Hebrew poetry in Spain, analyzes the different styles and meters, and gives his critical assessment of the various poets and their work. This work is a treasury of information about the early Spanish scholars. R' Moshe also wrote a philosophical work *Arugas HaBosem,* concerning the relationship between the Creator and the universe. In this treatise, of which only fragments are extant, he quotes R' Saadiah Gaon and *R' Shlomo ibn Gabirol. Both books were written in Arabic and later translated into Hebrew.

In his earlier years, R' Moshe also wrote secular poetry, but about this period he writes *(Shiras Yisrael):* "In my youth, in the dawn of my life, I also valued poetics as a worthy vehicle to perpetuate my memory. Subsequently, however, I abandoned poetry as a deer leaves its shadow, for I became eager to fill the days of my life with more worthy pursuits."

An accomplished linguist, R' Moshe was fluent in Hebrew, Aramaic, Arabic, Latin and probably Greek, and was often drawn into disputation and debate with gentile scholars.

R' Yehudah HaLevi

ר׳ יְהוּדָה (בֶּן שְׁמוּאֵל) הַלֵּוִי

b. Tudela or Toledo, Spain, c. 1080
d. Eretz Yisrael, c. 1145

Paytan, Philosopher.

A disciple of *Rif, R' Yehudah continued his studies under *Ri Migash, and remained close with his fellow student *R' Baruch Albaliah until the latter's premature death. In addition to studying Talmud, R' Yehudah became a master of literary style in Hebrew and Arabic and studied science and medicine. Although he earned his livelihood as a practicing physician, R' Yehudah credited neither himself nor his profession with the ability to heal the sick. In his own words: "Not on my own cure do I rely, but to Your cure do I aspire."

Like other Spanish scholars of his era, he composed lofty Hebrew poetry and liturgical hymns; the Sabbath *zemer* "Yom Shabbason" and the *kinnah* for the Ninth of Av, "Zion Hallo Sishali," are examples. His older colleague, *R' Moshe ibn Ezra, had the greatest praise for the younger man, and invited him to settle in his hometown, Granada, where he came in contact with many of the nobility, who admired his wisdom and knowledge. Although R' Yehudah HaLevi is considered one of the greatest Hebrew-Spanish poets, in his later years he regretted having written secular poetry in his youth. In the *Kuzari* he writes: "One wishing to purify his soul and his thoughts will do harm to his goal by occupying himself with romantic song!"

His greatest contribution to Torah knowledge was *Kuzari,* a philosophical work telling of the King of the Khazar tribe, who sought to determine the true religion by questioning a Christian, a Moslem and a Jewish scholar. In a deep and penetrating analysis, R' Yehudah describes the Jew's lessons with the Khazar king in a question-and-answer dialogue. The king becomes convinced of the authenticity of Judaism, which he, together with his entire kingdom, embraces as the true religion.

Originally written in Arabic, the *Kuzari* was later translated into Hebrew by *R' Yehudah ibn Tibbon, and still later into Latin, Spanish, German, and English. A popular classic, it has been reprinted numerous times (first ed. Fano, 1506) and has exercised great influence on subsequent Jewish thinking.

In this work, R' Yehudah examines most of the tenets and fundamentals of the Jewish religion. He argues that a system of truths known by tradition is infinitely more trustworthy than one based on philosophical speculation. Surely the arguments for creation *ex nihilo* are at least as persuasive as those against. The philosopher's decision to accept arguments to the contrary are due to his conviction that nothing in his experience demonstrates creation, thus allowing his espousal of the view (accepted by Aristotle and his followers) ascribing eternity to the universe. Tradition can play the role of arbiter between these intellectually balanced views. He touches upon the sin of the 'golden calf' explaining that it did not, as commonly understood, constitute blatant idol worship. Much space is devoted to a discussion of the names or attributes with which the Deity is

described. R' Yehudah's discussion concerning the excellence of *Eretz Yisrael* includes arguments culled from the author's knowledge of geography and astronomy. A passage from this discussion looms large in the recent dispute (involving such notable authorities as Radbaz, *Shoel U'Meishiv* and *Chazon Ish*) concerning the exact halachic location of the date line in regard to the Sabbath and Festivals. This classic work includes, among other topics, discussions on Hebrew grammar, punctuation, the oral tradition, reward and punishment, the Tabernacle, refutation of the Karaite heresy, astronomy, and a short commentary on *Sefer Yetzirah.* A host of super-commentaries have been written on *Kuzari,* and, in recent times, there have been new translations into Hebrew and other languages.

To escape the Moslem persecution that was prevalent in southern Spain, R' Yehudah set out for the Christian north. There he lived in various places until, late in his life, he decided to settle in *Eretz Yisrael.* Reaching Egypt, he was enthusiastically received and beseeched to remain in that land, which was free of religious oppression and had many thriving Jewish communities, but he insisted on continuing his journey to *Eretz Yisrael.* R' Yehudah is known to have reached Damascus, Syria, but no further documentation of his journey has come down to us. Tradition has it that he finally reached Jerusalem where he fell to the ground in a state of ecstasy. As he was kissing the soil of the Holy City, he was trampled and killed by an Arab horseman.

According to legend, *R' Avraham ibn Ezra was R' Yehudah HaLevi's son-in-law, but this is not probable. He did, however, have an intimate friendship with R' Avraham, and many of R' Yehudah HaLevi's exegetic comments are to be found in Ibn Ezra's commentary. Some believe that the two were buried near each other in the Upper Galilee.

R' Yosef ibn Tzaddik

ר' יוֹסֵף (בֶּן יַעֲקֹב) אִבְּן צַדִּיק

b. Southern Spain, c. 1075
d. Cordova, Spain, 1149

Author of Olam Katan.

As dayan of Cordova for the last eleven years of his life, R' Yosef served on a beis din which included such illustrious members as R' Maimon, father of *Rambam.

R' Yosef, a disciple of *R' Yitzchak ibn Gias, delved deeply into philosophy and his fame rests upon his religious philosophical work Olam Kattan ["Microcosm"] (Leipzig, 1854), in which man is portrayed as a miniature world. Originally written in Arabic, Olam Kattan was translated into Hebrew by *R' Moshe ibn Tibbon. The work is cited by *R' Yedayah HaPenini. Rambam, in a letter to *R' Shmuel ibn Tibbon, wrote, "Although I have not see Olam Kattan, I am familiar with the man and his work, and I recognize both his and his book's value." R' Yosef also wrote a book on logic, which is quoted in Olam Kattan but has been lost.

*R' Yehudah al-Charizi acclaimed R' Yosef's poetry, of which only a few pieces, besides some liturgical compositions appearing in North African machzorim, have been preserved.

R' Chiya al-Daudi

ר' חִיָּיא אַלְדָאוּדִי

d. Castille, Spain, 1154

Paytan.

In 1040, R' Chizkiyah Gaon, the Babylonian exilarch who had been appointed to succeed *R' Hai Gaon as dean of the Academy of Pumpedisa, was tortured and killed. Fearing additional persecution at the hands of the Babylonian government, R' Chizkiyah's family fled to Spain, where they found refuge in the home of *R' Yehosef HaNaggid. R' Chiya was a descendant of R' Chizkiyah and his surname al-Daudi alludes to his descent from the royal house of King David. R' Chiya's greatest contribution was in the field of liturgy. However, most of his works have been lost.

R' Avraham ibn Ezra

ר' אַבְרָהָם (בֶּן מֵאִיר) אִבְּן עֶזְרָא

b. Tudela, Spain, 1089
d. c. 1164

Bible commentator, Paytan.

R' Avraham's early life was spent in Spain, mainly Cordova, where he devoted his time to studying Torah. He also acquired proficiency in science, philosophy, mathematics, astrology, and Hebrew grammar. Despite his extraordinary capabilities, Ibn Ezra never succeeded in his various financial ventures, and lived in poverty. His friendship with *R' Yehudah HaLevi (Ibn Ezra often quotes the latter in his commentary to Scripture) has given rise to many popular, but undocumented, stories. According to one of these, R' Avraham was married to R' Yehudah's daughter.

Among Ibn Ezra's misfortunes was the untimely death of his wife, who left him with a small son, Yitzchak, their other children having died in infancy.

During the Almoravid uprising of 1135 (see Historical Introduction), R' Avraham went into exile with his brothers. After an arduous journey, he arrived in Rome, where he began to compose his Bible commentary, beginning with Ecclesiastes. During the next four years, he moved from place to place in Italy, devoting himself to Biblical exegesis, writing on most, if not all, the Books of Scripture. Some of these exist in both lengthy and abridged versions.

During the course of his wanderings, Ibn Ezra's son Yitzchak had departed for Baghdad, where after a time he converted to the Moslem faith. Subsequently, he repented and returned to Judaism. In a poem which he composed to vindicate himself, R' Yitzchak asserts that he never transgressed the Torah; he merely made an unwilling profession attesting to the prophethood of Mohammed (Rambam in his *Igeres HaShmad* rules that such a profession may be made under duress). A short time afterward, R' Yitzchak died. When R' Avraham became aware of the events some three years later, he was stricken with unending grief because of the double tragedy and from that time on he was unable to settle in a permanent home. From Italy he traveled to Provence, and then on to northern France, where he spent several years.

Wherever he journeyed he was enthusiastically received, and the illustrious Tosafist, *Rabbeinu Tam, accorded him great honor. He is mentioned in Tosafos *(Rosh Hashanah 13a).*

In 1158, Ibn Ezra traveled to London, where he composed *Yesod Mora,* explaining the reasons for the various commandments; and *Igeres HaShabbos,* proving that the Sabbath is to be observed from sundown Friday until nightfall Saturday, and not from dawn on Saturday to Sunday morning, as implied by another commentator. The year 1160 found him once again in Narbonne, Provence, but the place of his death and burial are uncertain. Among the guesses are Calahorra, in northern Spain, Rome, and London. Some say that Ibn Ezra traveled to the Holy Land and his grave is next to R' Yehudah HaLevi's in the Upper Galilee.

A colorful personality whose brilliance extended to almost every field of knowledge, R' Avraham was recognized in his youth as a paytan of rare caliber. *Ravad I calls him "the last of the great men who formed the pride of Spanish Judaism and who strengthened Israel with songs and words of comfort."

Of his poems, *R' Yehudah al-Charizi states, "They provide help in time of need and bring refreshing rain in time of drought. All his hymns are lofty and admirable in their content." So greatly did *Chasam Sofer* (1762-1839) regard Ibn Ezra's *zemer, Tzamah Nafshi,* that he sang it every Friday evening upon arriving home from the synagogue service, even before reciting the *Kiddush.*

Ibn Ezra chose to interpret the Scriptures in their plainest meaning, and not according to aggadic homily. Although his views with regard to Biblical interpretation are controversial, in defining the performance of the precepts he scrupulously and zealously adheres to the views of the Sages of the Talmud, and does not hesitate to reprimand anyone straying from this path — even the most recognized scholar. His sharp wit and keen understanding of human nature are apparent in the many proverbs and riddles he uses to make his point. He has no patience for those who propose interpretations of Scripture which he considers false. For such comments and their authors, he had barbs and biting satire. Specially targeted for such treatment are the Karaite commentators, such as Ben Zuta, whom Ibn Ezra dubs "the one stricken with blindness." In one instance, *Exodus* 21:35, where Ben Zuta mistranslates "if one man's ox shoves his fellow ox" (instead of the correct "if one man's ox shoves his fellow man's ox"), R' Avraham makes short shrift of the Karaite: "An ox has no fellow, save Ben Zuta himself!"

Due to its immense popularity, Ibn Ezra's Bible commentary has been the object of more that fifty supercommentaries, many of which exist only in manuscript.

In addition, Ibn Ezra is reputed to have written novellae on tractate *Kiddushin*. He wrote many grammatical works, the most famous of which is *Moznayim*, and he translated *R' Yehudah ibn Chayug's books on grammar into Hebrew. Ibn Ezra also wrote books on mathematics, astronomy, and astrology, one of the better known being the *Sefer HaIbbur* (Lyck, 1874).

R' Maimon ben Yosef HaDayan

ר' מַיְמוֹן (בֶּן יוֹסֵף) הַדַּיָן

b. Cordova, Spain, late 11th cent.
d. Eretz Yisrael 1165/1170

Talmudist, Teacher.

R' Maimon is best known as the father of *Rambam, but he was a great scholar and leader in his own right. One of the leading students of the illustrious *R' Yosef ibn Migash, R' Maimon became a *dayan* in Cordova, following a generations-long family tradition. He was an accomplished Talmudist and teacher, as well as an astronomer, mathematician and philosopher. Rambam frequently quotes his father's Talmudic and halachic commentaries and *R' Avraham ben HaRambam quotes extensively from R' Maimon's Torah commentary. He also wrote on the laws of festivals, prayer, ritual purity, and many responsa. As was customary in his time, his books were written in Arabic. Unfortunately, only a few fragments of his writings are extant. Among the teachings cited by Rambam is R' Maimon's family tradition regarding the value of a *perutah,* the smallest coin of Talmudic times. The exact value of the coin has halachic implications,

and R' Maimon's ruling has been accepted by the Halachah to this day.

The closing years of R' Maimon's life were filled with suffering and tragedy, but he remained a source of courage and inspiration not only to his family but to many Jewish communities. The troubles began when the Almohads conquered Cordova in 1149 [see Historical Introduction]. They forced the Jews under their sway to choose between conversion, death, and exile. R' Maimon and his family left Cordova and began a long period of rootless wandering in the face of hostility and persecution that lasted for the rest of his life. After perhaps ten years of wandering in Spain, R' Maimon took his family to Fez, Morocco, where they found an appalling situation. There, too, Jews were forbidden to practice Judaism publicly. What is more, there was a false Jewish Messiah who was misleading the people. R' Maimon forbade the people to heed the Messianic blandishments of the imposters. The spiritual state of the Jews was depressed, however, for many of them had come to feel that G—d had indeed abandoned Israel and chosen another nation in its place. R' Maimon wrote the lengthy *Iggeres HaNechamah* ["Letter of Consolation"] in Arabic, strengthening the people's faith in G—d and the eventual redemption and exhorting them to hold fast to the *mitzvos,* to whatever degree possible, even if they could bring themselves to do so only secretly. He compared the victims of Moslem persecution to a drowning man and the Torah to a rope from heaven. Whoever grasped it — even with his fingertips — had a hope of survival; whoever let go would surely drown.

After writing this defiant letter, R' Maimon could no longer remain in Fez. With his family he traveled to *Eretz Yisrael,* but the Land had not recovered from the ravages of the Second Crusade. Life was poor and dangerous. R' Maimon encouraged his family to go on to Egypt. As for him, he was already an old man and chose to live out his remaining days in *Eretz Yisrael*. He died not long after, probably in Jerusalem, although some say he is buried in Tiberias, near Rambam.

R' Avraham HaNassi (Rabach)

ר' אַבְרָהָם (בֶּן חִיָּיא) הַנָּשִׂיא (רַאבַּ"ח)

Barcelona, Spain, early 12th cent.

Ethician.

R' Avraham's *Hegyon HaNefesh* is a profound religious work which deals with morals and penitence. In it, he constantly cites Scripture to substantiate his ethical views. Indeed, *Hegyon HaNefesh* contains many of his original interpretations of Biblical verses. He also devoted a treatise, *Megillas HaMegaleh*, (Berlin, 1924) to a calculation of the year of the Messianic redemption.

R' Avraham carried on a running debate with his contemporary, *R' Yehudah of Barcelona, regarding the validity of astrology. In an epistle addressed to R' Yehudah, Rabach attempts to prove that astrology is not proscribed by Torah law. R' Yehudah, on the other hand, forbade it as a form of sorcery.

R' Avraham was a scientist of great renown, writing books on geometry, astronomy, and intercalation. His treatise on astronomy was of interest to Jewish scholars because of its relevance to the calculation of the Jewish calendar. His *Tzuras HaAretz* (Basel, 1546) was a popular text on this complex subject. R' Mordechai Yafeh, author of *Levush,* wrote a commentary to this treatise (*Beur'ei Yafeh,* Lublin, 1595). Other works by R' Avraham are *Halbbur* (London, 1856) on calculating the times for the new moon, the beginning of the

years, months, and seasons, and the intercalation of months; and *Chibur HaMeshichah VehaTishbores* (Berlin, 1892) on geometry and surveying.

R' Avraham is unique among Spanish authors of his era in his use of Hebrew instead of Arabic even in his scientific treatises. The author intimates that he did so because he intended them for study by French Jews too.

R' Avraham played an important role in transmitting Greek science to Christian Europe by translating basic texts from Arabic into Latin. Some of R' Avraham's own works were translated into Latin and other European languages.

Owing to his influence in royal circles, R' Avraham was called *Nassi* ["prince"].

R' Yehudah of Barcelona

ר' יְהוּדָה (בֶּן בַּרְזִילַי) אַלְבַּרְצְלוֹנִי

Barcelona, Spain, early 12th cent.

Halachist.

*Ramban states that R' Yehudah was an expert in all Geonic works, which he kept before him while studying. *Ravad II is reputed to have been his disciple.

Tradition records that R' Yehudah studied Talmud and Halachah under *R' Yitzchak of Barcelona; however, R' Yitzchak is never mentioned in any of R' Yehudah's extant works.

Following in *Rif's footsteps, R' Yehudah composed a work that offers the reader a clear halachic decision based upon the Talmud, citing only as much from this source as is necessary for the halachah. However, whereas Rif eliminated a great deal of Geonic data, R' Yehudah supplies not only the Geonic opinions and interpretations on each topic, but also quotes the commentators and codifiers preceding him, including Rif, thereby developing each subject into an elaborate and thorough thesis. The halachos are arranged according to subject matter, and do not follow Talmudic sequence.

This extensive work, cited by most of the early codifiers, was divided into three major sections: *Sefer HaIttim* (published in part, Cracow, 1903), encompassing all laws governing daily religious observance, such as prayers, *Tefillin*, the dietary laws and regulations of the Sabbath and the holy days; *Yichus She'air Basar* (not extant), dealing with the laws of marriage and divorce; and *Sefer HaDinim*, encompassing all matters pertaining to civil law. A small segment of this part has been published as *Sefer HaShtaros* (Berlin, 1898). It discusses the legal requirements pertaining to documents in Jewish law, with the text of each document examined in the light of halachah and its validity proven according to sources in the Talmud.

Sefer HaEshkol, a halachic compendium composed by R' Yehudah's disciple *Ravad II, is based, to a great extent, on information found in *Sefer HaIttim*.

*R' Menachem HaMeiri places R' Yehudah alongside *Rif, *Rashi, and *Ravad III as "the patriarchs of the Talmud ... from whom the entire world [of Talmudic commentary] sprang."

R' Yehudah's running commentary on the kabbalistic *Sefer Yetzirah* from a scientific and philosophic point of view has been published (Berlin, 1885). In this work, the author makes mention of his *Sefer HaZmanim*, but this is not extant.

Because of his prestigious lineage, he was sometimes referred to by the honorary title *Nassi* ["prince"].

R' Avraham Ibn Daud (Ravad I)

ר' אַבְרָהָם (בֶּן דָּוִד הַלֵּוִי) אִבְּן דָּאוּד
(רַאב"ד הָרִאשׁוֹן)

b. Cordova, Spain, c. 1110
d. Toledo, Spain, c. 1180

Author of *Sefer HaKabbalah*.

A grandson of *R' Yitzchak Albaliah, R' Avraham studied under his uncle, *R' Baruch Albaliah.

Although a proficient Talmudist, physician, and philosopher, Ravad I is best known for his *Sefer HaKabbalah*, in which he lists chronologically all important events and personalities from Adam until his own time.

The book's division of Jewish history into periods of *Zugos, Nesiim, Tannaim, Amoraim, Rabbanan Savurai, Geonim,* and *Rabbanim* became the norm for all future Jewish historic chronicles. Of special importance is his account of the Torah renaissance which took place in Spain in the two centuries preceding him. The two appendices — a history of the Roman empire; and a history of the Jewish nation during the period of the Second Temple, as adapted from Josephus — are of doubtful authorship.

The purpose of *Sefer HaKabbalah* was to refute Karaitic beliefs by delineating the unbroken chain of tradition from Moses down to the rabbinical authorities of his own day, thereby proving the authenticity of the Oral Law. Another work containing a polemic against Karaites has been lost.

His philosophical treatise *Emunah Ramah* on the topics of free will, prophecy, and Divine omnipotence and eternity cites *Emunos Ve'Deios* of R' Saadiah Gaon (892-942) and *MeKor Chaim* of *R' Shlomo ibn Gabirol, harshly criticizing the latter. *R' Shlomo ben Labi translated *Emunah Ramah* from Arabic into Hebrew (Frankfurt, 1853). *R' Shmuel Motot's translation, entitled *Emunah Neseah*, exists in manuscript. Several other works of Ravad, including a treatise on astronomy, have not survived.

He died a martyr, hanged by the King of Toledo for refusing to leave the Jewish faith.

R' Shlomo ibn Parchon

ר' שְׁלֹמֹה (בֶּן אַבְרָהָם) אִבְּן פַּרְחוֹן

b. Aragon, Spain
d. Salerno, Italy, mid-12th cent.

Grammarian.

When the Almoravid upheaval (see Historical Introduction) forced R' Shlomo to flee Spain, he settled in Italy. Finding the people there entirely ignorant of the grammatical works of the Spanish scholars written in Arabic, and acquainted only with *R' Menachem ben Saruk's Hebrew Machberes, R' Shlomo compiled Machberes HaAruch. This lexicon, which traces words to their origin in Scripture and lists their roots and the rules governing them, is a synthesis of the works of *R' Yehudah ibn Chayug, *R' Yonah ibn Janach, and other grammarians. Machberes HaAruch also includes Talmudic discourses, halachic analyses, ethics, as well as discussions of medicine, astrology, and astronomy. In this work R' Shlomo quotes as his "teachers" the Geonim R' Saadiah (892-942) and R' Hai (939-1038), as well as *R' Ephraim of Kila Chamad, *R' Yehuda HaLevi, *R' Avraham ibn Ezra, *R' Shlomo ibn Gabirol and *Rashi.

R' Binyamin of Tudela

ר' בִּנְיָמִין (בֶּן יוֹנָה) מִטּוּדֵּילָא

Tudela, Spain, c. 1175

Celebrated traveler.

Setting out from Tudela, Spain, about 1160, this keen observer journeyed through southern France, Italy, Greece, Syria, and Eretz Yisrael, to Baghdad. His return trip took him through the Indian Ocean and the Red Sea to Egypt. He arrived home by way of Sicily in 1173.

His sojourns in the countries through which he traveled gave him ample time to collect and record information in his diary, published under the title Masaos shel R' Binyamin (Constantinople, 1543).

This important chronicle depicts the Jewish community of each city and describes the writings of scholars and leaders, some of whom are still famous and others who are known only thanks to R' Binyamin. Schools of learning are listed, along with the occupations engaged in by the Jewish populace, its civil status, population census and, perhaps most importantly, customs peculiar to that area. In addition, there is also a wealth of political history and geography. R' Binyamin also seems to be the first European author to mention China. At the end of the book there are notes concerning the Jews of Germany, the Slavic lands east of Prague, and northern France. Although R' Binyamin did not personally visit these places, he received his information about them from reliable sources. Thus R' Binyamin's work encompasses all the Jewish centers of his day.

It seems that he was also a Talmudic scholar. The anonymous editor who wrote a short preface to Masaos calls R' Binyamin, "A wise and understanding man, a master of Torah and Halachah."

R' Shmuel ben Eli

ר' שְׁמוּאֵל בֶּן עֵלִי (הַלֵּוִי)

d. Baghdad, Iraq, 1195

Talmudist, Halachist, Teacher.

R' Eli HaLevi, R' Shmuel's father and a descendant of the prophet Samuel, was one of the early deans of the illustrious Gaon Yaakov academy of Baghdad, a restoration of the ancient Babylonian academies, Sura and Pumpedisa. In 1164, his son, R' Shmuel, succeeded R' Shlomo ben Shmuel as Rosh Yeshivah.

Under R' Shmuel's leadership, the academy flourished and established itself as the premier Torah institution in Iraq. As many as two thousand students would flock to his lecture, which was delivered through an intermediary.

Nine subordinate deans formed a panel which decided all questions of ritual law and litigations in Baghdad. In all of Syria, Persia, and Iraq, no *dayan* was appointed without explicit authorization from R' Shmuel, and his halachic decisions were law, even in *Eretz Yisrael*. Because of his position he dressed in gold, resided in a palace, and was attended by sixty servants who enforced his rulings, but he remained humble and righteous.

Regarding only one matter did the populace refuse to follow R' Shmuel. In 1190, R' Shmuel moved that the office of exilarch be abolished, on the grounds that Jews were bound to serve the king of the land and had no need of an exilarch, but only of scholars who could teach them the ways of Torah and decide matters of Halachah. He also regarded the heavy taxes paid to the exilarch as an encroachment on the academy's income. However, R' Shmuel was unable to sway the public, which was unwilling to forsake the Davidic lineage personified by the exilarch, and the office of exilarch was retained.

In 1191, *Rambam issued a reply to the Jewish community of Yemen clarifying certain aspects of the resurrection of the dead. R' Shmuel disagreed with Rambam's approach, which he considered philosophical, and offered his own reply on the matter. He was also strongly opposed to Rambam's philosophic treatise *Moreh Nevuchim*. R' Shmuel and his disciples (among them *R' Daniel HaBavli) generally did not accept some of Rambam's halachic decisions either; for instance, Rambam permitted traveling on rivers on the Sabbath whereas R' Shmuel forbade it.

R' Shmuel wrote some responsa and pastoral epistles (Jerusalem, 1970) which shed light on Jewish life in Iraq and Syria in his times.

He and his only child, a daughter who is reputed to have been well learned in Scripture and Talmud, passed away on the same day.

R' Moshe Ben Maimon (Rambam) [Maimonides]

ר' מֹשֶׁה בֶּן מַיְימוֹן (רמב"ם)

b. Cordova, Spain, 1135
(14 Nissan 4895)
d. Cairo, Egypt, 1204
(20 Teves 4965)

Halachist, Commentator, Philosopher.

Rambam's first teacher was his father *R' Maimon, a disciple of *Ri Migash [referred to by Rambam as "my teacher R' Yosef HaLevi"] and a *dayan* in the *beis din* of Cordova alongside *R' Yosef ibn Tzaddik. The family traced its ancestry through an illustrious chain of Torah luminaries stretching back to R' Yehudah HaNassi, compiler of the Mishnah, and King David. [Rambam's signature at the end of his Mishnah commentary lists seven generations of forebears: five bearing the title *dayan*; one, the title *chacham* (sage); and one, *rav*.] Rambam occasionally cites his father and in the introduction to his Mishnah commentary writes, "I have gathered all that has come to my hands from the commentaries of my master, my father of blessed memory, and others ..."

A popular tradition relates that when Ri Migash lay fatally ill, R' Maimon brought his son Moshe to his mentor's bedside for a blessing. Fully aware of the child's unusual qualities and potential, Ri Migash kissed the young Moshe and blessed him. Many years later, Rambam reportedly ascribed all his Torah wisdom to the venerable scholar's blessing.

When Rambam was only thirteen, Cordova fell to the rule of the fanatical Almohad Moslem sect (see Historical Introduction), which forced the Jewish population to choose between Islam and exile. R' Maimon and his entire family left for Christian Spain, where they wandered from place to place for almost twelve years. They then emigrated to Fez in Morocco, the residence of many Jews who had been forcibly converted to Islam. Since anyone caught there observing Judaism was sentenced to death, they left for *Eretz Yisrael* at the earliest opportunity. At that time, the Holy Land, still torn by the Crusades, was not safe for Jews. In 1165 they finally settled in Cairo, Egypt, which afforded asylum and religious freedom to oppressed Jews. There, Rambam flourished and became [in *Meiri's play on the wording of *Psalms* 48:3]: "The beauty of Nof [Egypt], joy of all the earth."

Despite his wanderings, at the age of twenty-three Rambam began writing a Mishnah commentary, *Sefer HaMaor,* popularly known as *Peirush HaMishnayos.* As he said in his afterword, he wrote under extreme difficulty, during "the Divinely decreed exile which caused us to wander among the lands, from one end of the heavens to the other; some of it written while traveling over land, some on board ship ..." This work thoroughly analyzes the various opinions mentioned in each Mishnah. He embellishes this commentary with valuable introductions which clarify some basic fundamentals of the Jewish faith and trace the chain of transmission of the Oral Law. A philosophical analysis in the introduction to tractate *Avos* is popularly known as *Shemonah Perakim.* This work discusses the nature of the soul, its afflictions and their cures, man's purpose in the world, prophecy, and the problem of free will versus Divine omniscience.

Even in the commentary proper, Maimonides sometimes delves into the tenets of Judaism. In his commentary to *Sanhedrin* 10:1 [on the passage, "All of Israel has a portion in the world to come ..."] he outlines the differing views as to the nature of the Divine scheme for reward and punishment, presents the correct approach, and discusses the need for reward. In a tangential discussion, he sets forth his opinion that the Agaddah, specifically that relating to the ultimate reward and punishment, must generally be interpreted allegorically. He argues that human language cannot describe what has not been experienced. We lack terms that are adequate to describe the joys and pains of the World to Come. Consequently, the Sages describe the World to Come by means of allegories taken from life on earth. Nevertheless, the Garden of Eden is a lush and fertile area on this globe.

Rambam describes the resuscitation of the dead and the 'Days of the Messiah' but avers that the ultimate reward is not intended to be dispensed in the latter two eras, but in the spiritual World to Come. This view, which is reiterated in his code, later created a great furor among Jewish thinkers, and induced *R' Meir Abulafia to fight an ideological war against Rambam. Finally, Rambam outlines his famous thirteen fundamental tenets of Judaism. A whole literature has sprung up around Rambam's classification of these tenets as fundamentals (*R' Yosef Albo in his *Ikarrim* is one of the many who disputes Rambam's view). R' Yitzchak Abarbanel devoted an entire work *(Rosh Amanah)* to defending Rambam. These fundamentals were set in prose as the *Ani Maamin* recited by many Jews every day, and in poetry as the popular hymn *Yigdal* which prefaces the daily morning prayer service. Clearly, the multitudes of Israel have decided for Rambam.

The commentary to Mishnah, which took seven years to complete, was written in Arabic. The translation into

Hebrew was done piecemeal, having been started by *R' Yehudah al-Charizi and continued by various others. First printed in 1492 in Naples, Italy, this work has recently been retranslated from the Arabic by R' Yosef Kafich (Jerusalem, 1964).

During his early years in Egypt, Rambam experienced many misfortunes: His father, R' Maimon, died, leaving his younger son David to support the family by trading in gems, while Rambam devoted his entire time to study. However, David, and with him the family fortune, perished when his ship sank in the Indian Ocean. Devastated by the loss of David, Rambam succumbed to a protracted illness.

Upon recovering, he was faced with the responsibility of supporting both his own family and his brother's. Opposed to earning a livelihood through the rabbinate, Rambam became a physician. His medical reputation grew and Sultan Saladin appointed him doctor to the royal court. Rambam composed many treatises on medicine, and his fame brought so many patients to his door that his professional duties occupied most of his day and sometimes parts of his night. Nevertheless, Rambam found time to write and to manage the religious affairs of the Cairo community.

As physician to the royal court, Rambam used his influence for the welfare of his brethren. He was named Naggid ["prince"] of Egyptian Jewry, a title held by his son, *R' Avraham, and five generations of Rambam's descendants. The Naggid appointed the dayanim for all Egyptian communities and arbitrated all disagreements arising between the dayanim and their flocks.

In about 1170, Rambam began his monumental Mishneh Torah, a comprehensive halachic compendium derived from the Talmud and the works of the Geonim. The work comprises fourteen books [hence its popular title Yad HaChazakah, "Mighty Hand" — the word יד, "hand," having the numerical value of fourteen], each arranged systematically according to topics. The work, which took ten years to write, was unique in its format as well as its content. Unlike his predecessors, who discussed only halachic topics relevant to the time of the exile, Rambam included laws pertaining to Eretz Yisrael in the Temple era, such as sacrifices, contamination and purity. Mishneh Torah is concisely written in pure, lucid Hebrew. However, in his concern for brevity, Rambam omitted the source of each decision, and thereby evoked much criticism, since it was almost impossible to verify the halachic decisions. Rambam himself later regretted that he had not composed a separate work citing the source of each decision, and resolved to do so, but unfortunately never had time to write it.

Mishneh Torah immediately gained extraordinary popularity, and even *Ravad III, who composed critical notes, Hasagos HaRavad, printed alongside the text in most editions, acknowledged that the work was a magnificent contribution. The scholars of Lunel, Provence, known for their sharp erudition, also studied the code zealously, and addressed their questions to Rambam himself, who replied to their satisfaction.

Mishneh Torah became a pillar of Halachah and over 325 commentaries were written on it. Some of the most famous are Maggid Mishneh, Kesef Mishneh, Lechem Mishneh, Mishneh LaMelech, Hagahos Maimonios, Mirkeves HaMishneh and Or Sameach. Most of the responsa and Talmudic novellae written through the centuries discuss relevant rulings in Mishneh Torah.

Another work, *Sefer HaMitzvos*, composed in Arabic, traces the 613 Torah precepts. Since many differing views existed as to which of the precepts were to be counted among the 613, Rambam set down principles clarifying the matter. This book, which was intended as an independent prologue to *Mishneh Torah,* also inspired a host of commentaries, among them *Hasagos HaRamban,* and R' Yitzchak Leon ibn Tzur's *Megillas Esther.*

Moreh Nevuchim ["Guide for the Perplexed"], Rambam's philosophical treatise, was written in Arabic about 1185, and translated into Hebrew by *R' Shmuel ibn Tibbon. The purpose of this work was to guide persons who, having studied philosophy, were perplexed by seeming contradictions between the teaching of the Torah and philosophical theory. Rambam demonstrates that there is no contradiction between the two and that all difficulties arise from the misinterpretation of the true fundamentals of either and from the false conclusions drawn from them. Although this work was written when Rambam was about fifty years old, he had already envisioned such a volume more than two decades earlier.

A major part of *Moreh Nevuchim* dispels the anthropomorphic notions that G–d is corporeal or that He has such human attributes as wrath, jealousy etc. Indeed Rambam holds the incorporeality of G–d to be so central to Judaism that to think otherwise is heretical.

In the first section of the *Moreh,* Rambam explains that such Scriptural terms as "eyes" or "hand" of G–d are used figuratively and he explains their true definitions. He goes on to a related subject: the uniqueness and absoluteness of G–d's unity. Rambam argues that Scripture's multiplicity of Names to designate the Deity does not suggest that He is multiple or changing. Rather they describe how G–d appears to man. When we perceive His deeds as compassionate, we describe Him as the Compassionate One, although it is only our perception of Him, not He, that has changed. Then Rambam proves G–d's existence and that He is the Creator of the universe. Rambam goes on to explain prophecy and its varying degrees; revelation; and the balance between G–d's omniscience and man's free will.

Rambam's view, like that of his predecessors *Rabbeinu Bachya *(Chovas HaLevavos)* and R' Saadiah Gaon, was that the quest for a rational understanding of G–d and His creation is a Divine precept that is incumbent upon everyone who is intellectually capable of it. Thus, in Rambam's view, *Moreh Nevuchim* was not an exercise in "secular studies" but the most exalted brand of study enjoined by the Torah — delving into the secrets of the Deity and His creation.

Although the book was not meant for scholars educated exclusively in Torah, it sparked a confrontation on the rabbinical scene. *R' Shlomo of Montpellier fought bitterly against the study of philosophy in general and *Moreh Nevuchim* in particular, and he was joined by many other scholars. The polemic was renewed more than fifty years later by *R' Shlomo Petit (see Historical Introduction). Despite the bitterness of the controversy, Rambam has remained a pre-eminent figure in Jewish thought, no matter what the school.

During a period of religious persecution and the rise of a false Messiah in the Jewish community of Yemen, Rambam wrote a letter of encouragement, *Iggeres Teiman* (Basel, 5389), which greatly inspired the masses and kept them from forsaking their faith. So indebted did the Yemenite community feel to Rambam for the inspiration of his letter, that during Rambam's lifetime their version of the Kaddish prayer included, "... during your lifetime and during your days and during the lifetime of R' Moshe ben Maimon ..."

Rambam's other works include *Maamar Techias HaMeisim* (Constantinople, 1569) on the resurrection of the dead; *Milos HaHegayon* (Venice, 1552) on the terminology of logic; responsa (Constantinople, 1536), which were republished with addenda as *Pe'er HaDor* (Amsterdam, 1765) and as *Teshuvos HaRambam* (Jerusalem, 1934; 1958-61), and a Talmud commentary, mentioned in the Mishnah commentary but extant only on tractate *Rosh Hashanah* (Paris, 1865). Fragments of Rambam's digest of the halachic material found in the Jerusalem Talmud, written in the same style as *Rif's* halachic digest of the Babylonian Talmud, have been published (New York, 1948).

Rambam's reputation as a brilliant physician was widespread in the Orient and he is frequently quoted in the medical literature of his day. Some of his medical treatises have been recently translated into Hebrew.

When Rambam died, both Jews and non-Jews of Cairo officially mourned him, and in Jerusalem a fast was decreed. Rambam's body was taken to Tiberias, and his tomb is a place of pilgrimage to this day. The Rambam's greatness is expressed in the popular maxim (inscribed on his tomb), "From Moshe [Moses] till Moshe [Rambam], none arose like Moshe."

R' Yehudah Alfakhar

ר' יְהוּדָה (בֶּן יוֹסֵף) אַלְפַכַּאר

d. Toledo, Spain 1235
Talmudist.
Although R' Yehudah, who served as

personal physician to King Ferdinand III, was knowledgeable in philosophy and revered *Rambam greatly, he joined *R' Shlomo of Montpellier in his fight against Rambam's *Moreh Nevuchim* (see Historical Introduction). R' Yehudah saw a great danger to tradition in the dissemination of philosophy, because Torah is predicated on a belief in G−d, creation and a Divine concern and intervention in the affairs of man, culminating in miracles — concepts which tend to be rationalized or even negated in standard philosophical systems. His opinion was so highly regarded that when the French supporters of the *Moreh* sought to gain the support of the Spanish camp, *Radak (who journeyed to Spain for this cause), wrote several letters to R' Yehudah in an attempt to enlist his support. R' Yehudah replied in the negative, and in the sharpest terms denounced the philosophical theories expressed in *Moreh Nevuchim,* stressing the differences between the Torah and secular philosophy.

R' Yehudah later apologized for slighting Radak with his strong words, but remained steadfast in his opposition to the *Moreh.*

R' Yaakov Ben Sheshes

ר' יַעֲקֹב בֶּן שֵׁשֶׁת (מִגֵּירוֹנָה)

Gerona, Spain, early 13th cent.
Kabbalist.

A colleague of *R' Ezra, *R' Ezriel, and *Ramban, R' Yaakov opposed the study of philosophy, including Rambam's philosophical works.

R' Yaakov is reputed to be the author of *Shaar HaShamayim* also known as *Likutei Shem Tov* (Warsaw 1798 and attributed to *R' Shem Tov ibn Gaon) which expounds the doctrines of Kabbalah, and *Meishiv Devarim Nechochim* (Jerusalem, 1969), a defense of Kabbalah against philosophy. In this work he frequently quotes from R' Ezra's commentary on Aggadah. The work *Sefer HaBitachon,* generally attributed to Ramban, is thought by some scholars to have been composed by R' Yaakov.

R' Azriel of Gerona

ר' עֲזְרִיאֵל (בֶּן מְנַחֵם) מִגִּירוֹנָה

b. Gerona, Spain, c. 1160
d. Gerona, Spain, c.1238

Kabbalist.

A disciple of *R' Yitzchak Sagi Nahor, R' Azriel did much to spread Kabbalah in Spain.

He wrote *Ezras Hashem,* an explanation on the ten *Sefiros* [Emanations], in question and answer form which was printed as *Sh'elos U'Teshuvos L'Rabbi Azriel* (Warsaw, with *Likutei R' Hai Gaon* and as *Perush Esser Sefiros,* Berlin, 1850 with *Derech Emunah*). His commentary on *Sefer Yetzirah* was erroneously ascribed to *Ramban, and his kabbalistic interpretation of the prayers is usually ascribed to his senior colleague, *R' Ezra, whose commentary on Aggadah of the Talmud R' Azriel greatly enlarged, clarifying the ideas and simplifying the language (Jerusalem, 1943).

Colleagues, disciples of the same master, living in the same city, and bearing similar names, R' Azriel and R' Ezra have often been confused by historians and scholars of later generations. Some mistakenly took them to be one person. The laudatory poetry of R' Meshullam ben Shlomo de Piera, a contemporary and fellow critic of the study of philosophy, ["I have Ezra and Azriel to aid me!"] clearly identifies them as two people. Some have taken R' Meshullam's poetic description of the two as "brothers" in a literal sense, although he probably used the word metaphorically. [R' Ezra's father's name was Shlomo, while R' Azriel's father was Menachem.] Still other historians maintain that R' Azriel married R' Ezra's daughter.

R' Meir HaLevi Abulafia (Ramah)

ר' מֵאִיר (בֶּן טוֹדְרוֹס) הַלֵוִי אַבּוּלַעְפִיָא (רמ"ה)

b. Burgos, Spain, c. 1180
d. Toledo, Spain, 1244

Talmudist, Kabbalist.

At a young age, Ramah, an erudite Talmudist whose opinion *Ramban sought on halachic issues, moved with his family to Toledo, where his father, R' Todros, was named rabbi and given the honorary title *Nassi* ["prince"].

During his father's tenure, R' Meir was appointed as a *dayan,* along with *R' Avraham HaYarchi, on the *beis din* of Toledo, and after his father's death he was named Rabbi of Toledo and also assumed the title *Nassi.*

He strongly opposed the study of philosophy, seeing in it a danger to the wholesome belief in Judaism, which is based (a) on faith and not on philosophical speculation, and (b) on the Talmud and tradition, not on the works of Aristotle and other non-Jews. In 1200, he sent a letter to the scholars of Lunel in Provence expressing criticism of certain philosophical views expressed in *Rambam's writings, and asking the sages there to prohibit their study before a designated age. His plea was unsuccessful, and met with the strong opposition of *R' Aharon ben Meshullam. His correspondence with R' Aharon and other French scholars is to be found in *Sefer Igros HaRamah* (Paris, 1871).

R' Meir composed a Talmud commentary titled *Pratei Pratin,* of which only the portions on *Bava Basra* (Salonica, 1790) and *Sanhedrin* (Salonica, 1798), bearing the title *Yad Ramah,* are extant. Some of his responsa appear in *Or Zadikim* (Salonica, 1799). His *Masores Seyag LaTorah* (Florence, 1750) contains alphabetically arranged Masoretic notes on the Torah. His kabbalistic commentary on *Genesis, Ginas Bisan,* is still in manuscript.

R' Yitzchak ben Yisrael

ר' יִצְחָק בֶּן יִשְׂרָאֵל

d. Baghdad, Iraq, 1247

Talmudist, Teacher.

Dean of the renowned Baghdad Talmudic academy from 1221 until his death, he was highly respected for his erudition. Even *R' Avraham, son of *Rambam, addressed him with exalted titles.

R' Yitzchak was also an astronomer and a composer of liturgical hymns, some of which may be found in the North African *Machzor.*

R' Yehudah Almadari

ר' יְהוּדָה (בֶּן אֶלְעָזָר הַכֹּהֵן אִבְּן) אַלְמַדָּארִי

Syria, mid 13th cent.

Talmudist.

R' Yehudah wrote a running commentary on *Rif's halachic compendium. Of this work only the portions on *Sanhedrin, Makkos, Avodah Zarah, Yevamos, Kesubos, Gittin,* and *Kiddushin* have been printed.

R' Yehudah al-Charizi

ר' יְהוּדָה (בֶּן שְׁלֹמֹה) אַלְחַרִיזִי

b. Spain, c. 1165
d. c. 1234

Translator, Poet.

In about 1190, R' Yehudah left Spain and journeyed to Provence, in southern France, where at the request of *R' Yehonasan of Lunel, he undertook to translate *Rambam's Mishnah commentary from Arabic into Hebrew. R' Yehudah's lucid translation is easy and enjoyable reading, thanks to his clarity of expression and precision of phrase. Only Rambam's introduction and the first five tractates of order *Zeraim* have

come down to us from this translation, and it is doubtful whether R' Yehudah translated other tractates.

Upon his return to Spain, al-Charizi translated Rambam's *Moreh Nevuchim* from Arabic into Hebrew. In this endeavor he had been preceded by *R' Shmuel ibn Tibbon, whose work remained the authorative translation despite al-Charizi's simpler and more vibrant language. Scholars felt that the original thought was conveyed more accurately and completely by Ibn Tibbon.

He also translated Rambam's *Maamar T'chias HaMeisim* on the resurrection of the dead. Al-Charizi himself wrote a commentary on Job and *Sefer HaMavo LiLashon HaKodesh* which, as the name implies, was an introduction to the Holy Tongue. He was fluent in languages and wrote in such mellifluous idiom that he earned his livelihood as a translator of all genre of literature; poetry, medicine, philosophy and law. He also composed original Hebrew poetry.

From 1216 to 1230, he traveled through Egypt, *Eretz Yisrael,* Syria, Iraq, and Greece, and he subsequently shared his experiences with readers in the epic poem *Techakmuni.* As with his other works, *Techakmuni* is dedicated to sponsors who helped support the author with their benevolent gifts.

R' Avraham ben HaRambam

ר' אַבְרָהָם בֶּן הָרַמְבַּ"ם

b. Cairo, Egypt, 1186
d. Cairo, Egypt, 1237 (18 Kislev 4998)

*Rambam personally instructed his only son, named for the Patriarch Abraham, and divulged to him many new insights which he had not recorded in his works.

At the age of nineteen, R' Avraham, who had been born in his father's fifty-first year, succeeded his father as personal physician to the Sultan and his royal court, and assumed leadership of Egyptian Jewry as the *Naggid,* a position which placed all Jewish courts under his jurisdiction and made him responsible for appointing suitable rabbis and *dayanim.*

The new *Naggid* enacted major improvements in communal affairs. He halted the common practice of bans of excommunication and counter bans being pronounced by every minor functionary against his real or supposed adversaries for the most insignificant slights to his prestige. R' Avraham forbade bans to be pronounced by any but a panel of three *dayanim* of the authorized *beis din* of the city. To reverse the lust for honor and prestige which ensnared many public officials, he instituted a rule forbidding anyone from sitting in the synagogue with his back to the ark, facing the congregation, considering this posture disrespectful to the Torah.

Like his father before him, R' Avraham received inquiries on religious practice from *Eretz Yisrael,* Yemen, Provence, Baghdad, Syria and, of course, Egypt. Only about 130 of his numerous responsa have been preserved in manuscripts and in the halachic works of other authors. Some of them have been published (Jerusalem, 1938 and as an appendix to *Mishneh Torah,* New York, 1947). Brief, concise, and always to the point, his answers trace the problems to their Talmudic principles and solve them through logical reasoning.

Some of his responsa deal with biblical exegesis, ethical matters, and defense of Rambam's decisions in his code. Two other collections of R' Abraham's responsa are devoted to a rebuttal of *R' Daniel HaBavli's arguments against *Mishneh Torah (Birkas Avraham,* Lyck 1860; with *Mishneh Torah,* New York, 1947) and *Sefer HaMitzvos (Ma'aseh Nissim,* Paris, 1867). When R' Avraham heard of the great polemic against his celebrated father's philosophical views, he rose to the challenge with a spirited defense in an essay entitled *Milchamos Hashem* (in *Kovetz Teshuvos HaRambam* Leipzig, 1859; separately, Jerusalem, 1953), in which he reports that many of the French scholars (among them Tosafists) who had visited Egypt were able to understand the *Moreh Nevuchim* in *R' Yehudah al-Charizi's translation and 'rejoiced in its discussions.'

Only a few chapters remain of his magnum opus, *HaMaspik L'Ovdei Hashem* ["Sufficient (instruction) for servants of G—d"]. Presumably this work was a large compendium endeavoring to show the correct way to those who strive for excellence in their service of G—d. It probably contained halachic sections too. The extant chapters enable us to catch a glimpse of the author's intimate thoughts and nobility of character. The elegance of expression, loftiness of thought, and force of style serve to confirm Rambam's characterization of his young son — in a letter to his disciple, *R' Yosef ibn Aknin — as, "one of the most humble of people, in addition to his other noble character traits. With G—d's help, he will unquestionably become famous among the great." R' Avraham makes a strong case for austerity and asceticism and delineates the advantages of introspective solitude. In the section on *Bitachon* (trust in G—d), he anticipates the thought enunciated by many later thinkers that the degree of trust one must have depends upon the spiritual level of the individual and his closeness to G—d. With practical examples, he demonstrates how this trust should be used to guide the true believer's actions. The remaining fragments of this work have been translated from the original

Arabic into English (The High Ways to Perfection of Abraham Maimonides, I New York, 1927; II Baltimore, 1938) and into Hebrew (Jerusalem, 1973).

In his Bible commentary, of which only the books of Genesis and Exodus have survived (London, 1958), R' Avraham stresses the plain meaning and disregards homiletic interpretations. His commentary preserves gems of exegesis by his father — Rambam — and grandfather — R' Maimon, besides scores of quotations from the works of the Geonim R' Saadiah, R' Shmuel ben Chofni, and others. An essay on the approach to the Aggadah, known as Ma'amar al HaDerashos, attributed to R' Avraham has been printed many times.

R' Avraham also began a commentary to Mishneh Torah which would cite the source of each decision, and a similar commentary to Moreh Nevuchim, but unfortunately died before he was able to complete them.

He was succeeded as Naggid by his son, *R' David.

R' Shlomo of Montpellier (Min HaHar)

ר' שְׁלֹמֹה (בֶּן אַבְרָהָם) מִן הָהָר
(מוֹנְטְפֶּלְיֶיר)

b. Barcelona, Spain
d. Montpellier, France c. 1240

Talmudist, Halachist, Teacher.

R' Shlomo's contemporaries *Ramban, *Ramah, and *R' Yehudah Alfakhar, referred to this eminent Talmudist with great respect and admiration, and *Rashba quotes his halachic decisions. Although his novellae are often cited by R' Betzalel Ashkenazi in Shitah MeKubetzes, none of his works are known to be extant.

Fearing that *Rambam's philosophical works, Moreh Nevuchim and Sefer HaMada, would endanger the people's pure faith in Torah, R' Shlomo and his two pupils, *R' Yonah of Gerona and R

David ben Shaul, pronounced a sentence of excommunication on these books and on those who studied them, in 1232. Although he did not gain much support from the scholars of Provence, many rabbis of northern France concurred with his view. The fierce controversy (see Historical Introduction) between the Rambam's and R' Shlomo's camps continued unabated even after the latter's death.

R' Yonah of Gerona (Gerondi)

ר' יוֹנָה (בֶּן אַבְרָהָם) גֵּירוֹנְדִי

b. Gerona, Spain c. 1180
d. Toledo, Spain 1263
(8 Mar Cheshvan 5024)

Author of Shaarei Teshuvah.

A disciple of *R' Shlomo of Montpellier, R' Yonah was one of the most active participants in the controversy instigated by his teacher over *Rambam's philosophical works. However, when twenty-four wagon loads of Talmud were burned by the church at the same spot in Paris where Rambam's Moreh Nevuchim had been burned some nine years earlier, R' Yonah, seeing in this a Divine reproach, regretted his previous actions against Rambam's works. As related by his devoted disciple, R' Hillel of Verona, R' Yonah declared publicly that he had been wrong, and vowed to travel to Tiberias to Rambam's tomb, where he would beg the forgiveness of the deceased before a minyan of ten people.

R' Yonah began his journey, but was detained for three years in Barcelona where he lectured, always quoting Rambam's halachic decisions and Talmudic interpretations with great reverence. After three years, he again set out to fulfill his vow, but was detained in Toledo, where the community implored him to stay for a while and give them Talmudic instruction. He died there suddenly, never completing his journey to *Eretz Yisrael*. He was mourned by all of Spanish Jewry, and *Ramban — whose mother was a sister to R' Yonah's father, and whose son R' Shlomo was married to R' Yonah's daughter — composed a eulogy in his honor.

R' Yonah is most famous for his classic ethical work, *Shaarei Teshuvah* ["Gates of Repentance"]. He also wrote a commentary to *Rif's *Sefer HaHalachos*, edited by his disciples, but printed only on tractate *Brachos*. R' Yonah's Talmudic novellae, cited by many halachists, were subsequently lost. Only those to *Sanhedrin* and *Bava Basra* have been printed. His *Megillas Sesarim*, mentioned by *Rashba and *Ran, is no longer extant. A commentary on Tractate *Avos* cited by later commentators has been published (Berlin, 1848; and in the Vilna ed. of the Talmud). His commentary on the Book of Proverbs (Berlin, 1910) is lauded by *R' Bachya, who said, "He has set his words with tiers of sapphire to illuminate the eyes. I have placed his words as a crown of fine gold upon my head, to enliven my soul ..."

R' Yonah's halachic treatise on *Chanukah* is cited by *Rashbatz (this may have been a part of *Megillas Sesarim*). *Iggeres HaTeshuvah* (Cracow, 1586), *Sefer HaYirah* (Cracow, 1612) and *Shaarei Teshuvah* are probably parts of an unpreserved extensive work titled *Shaarei Zedek*, cited by *R' Chisdai Crescas, which contained treatises on such topics as fear of G—d, Torah study, and prayer.

A work, entitled *Sha'arei HaAvodah*, reputed to have been composed by R' Yonah as part of *Shaarei Tzedek*, has been printed recently (Bnei Brak, 1967). A work of homilies on the Torah entitled *Derashos U'Peirushei R' Yonah* (Jerusalem, 1980) has also been attributed to R' Yonah, albeit without sufficient substantiation.

Among his pupils were *Rashba, R' Shlomo ben Eli of Sirai, who wrote a treatise of Talmudic novellae gleaned from R' Yonah's teachings, and R' Hillel ben Shmuel of Verona [who recorded much of the biographical information about his master].

R' Yosef ibn Aknin

ר' יוֹסֵף (בֶּן יְהוּדָה) אִבְּן עַקְנִין

b. Ceuta, Morocco c. 1160
d. 1226

Disciple of *Rambam.

Due to the oppression of the Almohad conquerors (see Historical Introduction), R' Yosef was forced in his youth to practice the laws of the Torah in secrecy, while outwardly giving no indication of his religious beliefs. He therefore moved to Alexandria, Egypt, where he could practice Judaism openly. From Alexandria, R' Yosef corresponded with Rambam, who detected in R' Yosef's words a sincere desire for knowledge. Rambam invited R' Yosef to visit him in Cairo, and the latter gladly complied, becoming a zealous student. When the great master lectured him on the Books of the Prophets, R' Yosef was disturbed by the conflict between their teachings and philosophy. For the benefit of R' Yosef, Rambam wrote the *Moreh Nevuchim* ["Guide for the Perplexed"]. R' Yosef did not complete his course of study, but traveled to Aleppo, Syria, in 1186 where he married and earned his livelihood as a physician. He continued to study Torah in his spare time, pursuing his lessons with Rambam through frequent correspondence.

When *R' Shmuel ben Eli of Baghdad opposed the halachic decisions of Rambam's *Mishneh Torah*, R' Yosef wished to move to Baghdad to establish an academy where he would teach

Talmud according to the Rambam's views, and thus defend his master against his adversaries in their own territory. Rambam, however, dissuaded him from such an undertaking as he would be forced to give up his medical profession and depend on a salary obtained by teaching Torah, an act of sacrilege in Rambam's eyes. R' Yosef did, however, begin to lecture and spread Rambam's teachings in Allepo.

R' Yosef compiled the halachic work *Chukim U'Mishpatim* in the spirit of *Mishneh Torah* written in Arabic; *Sefer HaMussar* (Berlin, 1911), a commentary in Arabic on Tractate *Avos*; a commentary on Song of Songs *Hisgalus HaSodos VeHofaos HaMeoros* (Jerusalem, 5724), and *Refuas HaNefashos* (parts were printed in *Kovetz Teshuvos HaRambam*, Liepzig, 5619 and various publications). Since his philosophical treatise *Maamar BeChiuv HaMetzius* (Berlin, 1906) does not mention the *Moreh Nevuchim*, it was probably written by R' Yosef before the *Moreh* was sent to him.

R' Daniel HaBavli

ר' דָּנִיאֵל (בֶּן סְעַדְיָה) הַבַּבְלִי

d. Damascus, Syria, c. 1230

Torah Scholar.

Like his teacher *R' Shmuel ben Eli, R' Daniel was an opponent of *Rambam's works. He once sent forty-seven questions on *Mishneh Torah* and thirteen questions on *Sefer HaMitzvos* to Rambam's son, *R' Avraham, demonstrating great Talmudic knowledge and piercing analysis. Despite R' Avraham's replies (*Bircas Avraham*, Lyck, 1870; *Maaseh Nissim*, Paris, 1867), R' Daniel continued his vehement criticism, especially in his commentary to *Koheles* ("Ecclesiastes") in which he sharply attacked Rambam's philosophical views. Rambam's supporters, led by *R' Yosef ibn Aknin,

requested R' Avraham to pronounce a ban of excommunication against R' Daniel, but the latter declined on the grounds that R' Daniel was an eminent Torah scholar, who lectured and exhorted his audiences to true repentance. The opposition did not rest however, and brought their case before R' David, the exilarch at Mosul, who pronounced the ban against R' Daniel. R' Daniel was forced to repent his actions, and only then was the ban lifted. He thereafter left Baghdad and made his home in Damascus, where his erudition attracted many disciples.

R' Yehudah ben Yakar

ר' יְהוּדָה בֶּן יָקָר

b. Provence, France, c. 1150
d. Spain, c. 1225

Kabbalist.

After having learned Talmud under the famed Tosafist *R' Yitzchak ben Avraham, R' Yehudah was guided in the study of Kabbalah by *R' Yitzchak Sagi Nahor. R' Yehudah and his two colleagues, *R' Ezra and *R' Azriel, both of Gerona, undertook to spread the teaching of Kabbalah in Spain. Arriving there about 1173, R' Yehudah influenced many disciples, the most famous among them being *Ramban.

R' Yehudah composed a complete commentary on the Jerusalem Talmud, which is cited and lauded in the works of the codifiers, but was unfortunately lost in later generations. Recently, *Mayan Ganim,* his interpretations of the prayers and the Passover *Haggadah,* was published (Jerusalem, 1979). The interpretations, frequently quoted by both the French and Spanish schools, convey the plain meaning and the origin of each prayer while ignoring its kabbalistic implications. *R' David Abudraham used this work as one of his major sources.

R' Ezra of Gerona

ר' עֶזְרָא (בֶּן שְׁלֹמֹה) מִגִּירוֹנָא

Spain, c. 1225

Kabbalist.

Disciple of the famed kabbalist *R' Yitzchak Sagi Nahor, R' Ezra and his colleague *R' Azriel of Gerona were among the first to introduce kabbalistic teachings in Spain. Unlike R' Azriel, however, R' Ezra disseminated the secrets transmitted to him by his teacher in their original form, without furnishing any additional explanatory principles. In accordance with the dogma of his masters, he strongly opposed the study of philosophy.

He greatly influenced *Ramban to study the secrets of the mystical lore, and, according to some, was the latter's mentor in this field.

For a long time R' Ezra's commentary on Song of Songs, which includes discourses on the mysteries of creation and the deeper significance of the commandments, was erroneously ascribed to Ramban. Much of it was later incorporated by Radbaz in his own commentary *Migdal David.* Only parts of R' Ezra's commentary on the *Aggadah* of the Talmud were published, the rest remaining in manuscript.

R' Shmuel HaSardi

ר' שְׁמוּאֵל (בֶּן יִצְחָק) הַסַּרְדִי

b. Spain (or Sardinia), c. 1190
d. Spain, c. 1256

Halachist.

R' Shmuel was a contemporary of *Ramban, and *R' Nassan ben Meir of Trinquetaille, whom he consulted extensively on halachic matters. R' Shmuel's correspondence with Ramban provided him with much material for his *Sefer HaTerumos* (Salonica, 1596) on the laws of loans and debts. R' Azariah Figo composed a commentary on this work entitled *Gidulei Terumah* (Venice, 1643).

In his introduction to *Sefer HaTeru-*mos, R' Shmuel tells us that he also wrote *Sefer HaZichronos,* novellae on the Talmudic tractates dealing with financial matters, but it has not survived.

R' Shmuel was a wealthy landowner who actively supported community projects. He even bequeathed his house to the community.

R' Moshe ben Nachman (Ramban) [Nachmanides]

ר' מֹשֶׁה בֶּן נַחְמָן (רמב"ן)

b. Gerona, Spain 1194
d. Eretz Yisrael 1270
[11 Nissan 5030]

Talmudist, Kabbalist, Teacher.

Scion of a prominent Rabbinical family and a relative of *R' Yonah Gerondi, Ramban was a disciple of *R' Yehudah ben Yakar and *R' Nassan ben Meir of Trinquetaille, and received kabbalistic instruction from *R' Ezra and *R' Azriel, both of Gerona. He also studied medicine, which later became his profession.

At the age of fifteen, Ramban compiled *Hilchos Nedarim* and *Hilchos Bechoros* in the style of *Rif's *Sefer HaHalachos,* because Rif had omitted these two tractates from his code.

Most of Ramban's life was spent in Gerona disseminating Torah to his many disciples. He was acknowledged as the foremost halachic authority in all of Spain, and his decisions were respected in other countries as well.

In 1238, Ramban was called upon to voice his opinion concerning the great controversy regarding *Rambam's works. In response, he praised the scholarship of *R' Shlomo of Montpellier, who headed the opposition to Rambam, and severely chastised all who would insult this great Talmudist for his zeal. At the same time, Ramban also sought to still the vehemence of Rambam's opponents by pointing out that *Mishneh Torah* shows no leniency in interpreting Halachah, and is sometimes quite strict. As to *Moreh Nevuchim*, Ramban explained that it was not intended for public use, but only for those who had been led astray by philosophy. He also pointed out that while *Moreh Nevuchim* might be unnecessary and even injurious to the Jews of France and Germany, it was of vital necessity to the philosophically oriented Sephardic community of Spain. Accordingly, he beseeched the promulgators of the ban to revoke it, permitting the study of the *Moreh Nevuchim* and the philosophical sections of *Sefer HaMada* in the *Mishneh Torah*. However, Ramban agreed that public study groups of the *Moreh* should be discouraged for even Rambam had branded such dissemination of what he considered 'the secrets of the Torah' as unworthy and sacrilegious.

Ramban's great respect for Torah scholars of earlier periods led to the writing of *Hasagos HaRamban* in which he defends *Sefer Halachos Gedolos* (Behag), a work of the Geonic era, against the criticisms expressed by Rambam in *Sefer HaMitzvos*. In his popular work *Milchamos HaShem*, Ramban defends the decisions of Rif against the refutations of *Razah in his *Sefer HaMaor*, and in *Sefer HaZechus*, he defends Rif against *Ravad III. Ramban, however, does not blindly accept Rif's rulings. On occasion, when unable to reconcile the rulings laid down by Rif with his own Talmudic interpretation, he adopts his own halachic decision. In most cases, however, Ramban subscribes to Rif's ruling even against the prevalent custom, as in prohibiting the use of wax candles for the Sabbath and insisting only on oil.

Ramban also wrote novellae (*chiddushim*) on most of the Talmud in the style of the Tosafists. His other works include: *Toras HaAdam*, a compendium of laws of mourning, climaxing with *Shaar HaGemul*, a treatise discussing reward and punishment and the resurrection of the dead; *Iggeres HaKodesh*, on the sanctity and significance of marriage; *Iggeres HaMussar*, an ethical epistle addressed to his son; *Sefer HaGeulah* on the coming of the Messiah; a commentary on Job; *Mishpat HaCherem*, on the laws of excommunication, which was printed in *Kol Bo*; *Hilchos Bedikah* on laws governing the examination of the animal's lungs after ritual slaughter (cited by *Rashbatz); *Hilchos Challah* (printed with *Hilchos Bechoros*); and *Hilchos Niddah* (printed with his *chiddushim* to tractate *Niddah*. A kabbalistic treatise *HaEmunah VeHaBitachon* (Venice 5661) is ascribed to him, but this is disputed.

In 1263, Ramban was ordered by King James of Aragon to hold a religious disputation with a Jewish apostate, Pablo Christiani, at Barcelona. The king and his court, including many dignitaries of the church, were present at this dispute. The victorious Ramban was rewarded by James with a gift of three hundred coins. The fanatical Dominicans, however, began spreading the rumor that their side had won the debate. Ramban responded by publishing an exact account of the questions and answers used in the disputation, under the title *Sefer HaVichuach*. The Dominicans presented selected passages from this treatise to the king, charging that they were blasphemies against Christianity. Ramban admitted the charge, but contended that he had only written what he said during the disputation in the presence of the king, who had granted him freedom of speech. Nevertheless, *Sefer HaVichuach* was condemned to be burned and Ramban was expelled from Aragon.

For three years, Ramban sojourned in Castille or Provence, where he began writing his monumental Torah commentary, unique in that it not only interprets the verses, but also analyzes the topics, presenting them in a Torah perspective. Intermingled with aggadic and kabbalistic interpretations are careful examinations of other commentaries, especially Rambam and *Ibn Ezra, whom Ramban severely criticizes for an overrational approach which, in his opinion, deviated from the true Talmudic and kabbalistic interpretations. Ramban also frequently disagrees with *Rashi's rendering, and such later authors as Mizrachi and Maharal wrote rebuttals defending Rashi. The great kabbalist, Arizal, testified to the depth and reliability of the mystical portion of Ramban's commentary, and considered Ramban the last of the ancient Kabbalistic school, who received direct transmission of the mystical secrets that were later concealed. Many supercommentaries were written on the Ramban's Torah commentary, among them, *Meiras Einayim* and *Keser Shem Tov.*

At the age of seventy-two, Ramban decided to settle in *Eretz Yisrael.* Before departing, he gave a dissertation on Ecclesiastes, lauding the Holy Land and the precept of charity. After a difficult journey and much suffering, Ramban arrived in Acco [Acre] in Elul, 1267. He spent Rosh Hashanah in Jerusalem, which was in a deplorable condition as a result of the havoc wrought by the Crusaders. Ramban designated a desolate house as a synagogue, and brought in a Torah scroll from Shechem. In this synagogue he gave a *Drashah* on the laws of *Shofar,* and exhorted the inhabitants of *Eretz Yisrael* to be exceedingly careful that their actions be righteous, for they are like servants in the King's palace. With Ramban's help

the Jewish community in Jerusalem, which had all but ceased to exist, began its revival.

Ramban himself settled in Acco, a Torah center at the time, and gathered about him a circle of pupils. Here he completed the last of his works, the Torah commentary. He kept in close contact with his family in Spain, telling them of conditions in the Holy Land, and admonishing them to ethical behavior and fear of the Almighty.

Various opinions place Ramban's burial site at Hebron, near the cave of Machpelah, Haifa, Acco, or Jerusalem. He was greatly revered by all succeeding generations, and *Rivash writes of him, "All his words are like sparks of fire, and the entire communities of Castille rely upon his halachic ruling as if given directly from the Almighty to Moses."

R' David Bonafil (Bonaped)

ר' דָּוִד (בֶּן רְאוּבֵן) בּוֹנָפִיל (בּוֹנָפֵיד)

Spain, early 13th cent.

Talmudist.

R' David's Talmudic novellae, which have only recently been published on tractates *Sanhedrin* and *Pesachim,* greatly influenced *Ran, who recorded entire portions of it in his commentary. R' David frequently quotes his teacher *Ramban, yet is unique and original in his own approach to Talmudic problems.

R' David HaNaggid

ר' דָּוִד (בֶּן אַבְרָהָם) הַנָּגִיד

b. Cairo, Egypt, 1212 (24 Teves 4973)
d. Cairo, Egypt, 1300 (1 Elul 5060)

Talmudist and Kabbalist.

Like his father *R' Avraham whom he succeeded, and his grandfather *Rambam, R' David was an accomplished Talmudist who earned his livelihood as a physician. R' David delivered lectures at the Academy of Cairo, and was called

Rosh Yeshivah Shel Torah ["Dean of the Torah Academy"], in addition to his title Naggid. He carried on an active correspondence with rabbinical authorities of Spain, Damascus, and Italy.

In 1285, after forty-seven years as Naggid of Egypt, Syria and Eretz Yisrael, R' David was slandered before the Sultan, who replaced him with another Naggid. R' David left with his family for Eretz Yisrael, which was then under Christian rule. Upon his arrival in Acco, where *R' Shlomo Petit was directing a campaign against Rambam's Moreh Nevuchim, R' David launched a counterattack and succeeded in winning over to his side the leaders of Safed, as well as R' Yishai ben Chizkiyah, exilarch of Damascus, and other authorities. When both sides turned to *Rashba for guidance, he tried to arrange a compromise, and also gave R' David financial support. In 1290, R' David returned to Egypt and was reinstated as Naggid.

Three works are attributed to R' David. Most extensive is his Midrash, sometimes referred to as Drashos R' David. Originally written in Arabic, it was read for many generations each Sabbath afternoon in the synagogues of Cairo. Recently a Hebrew edition has appeared (Midrash David, Jerusalem, 1947, 1960). The Drashos contain much material from the Zohar, proving that this kabbalistic work was known among select circles even before it was published by *R' Moshe de Leon.

His commentary to Pirke Avos (Jerusalem, 1944), was also read as part of the synagogue service on the Sabbaths between Passover and Shevuos. A third work, a commentary on the Nevuas HaYeled Nachman, is a mystical treatise.

Advanced in age, R' David shared his authority as Naggid with his son and successor, R' Avraham. R' David was buried in Tiberias.

R' Yitzchak ibn Latif

ר' יִצְחָק (בֶּן אַבְרָהָם) אִבְּן לַטִיף

b. Toledo, Spain, 1220
d. Jerusalem, Eretz Yisrael, c. 1290

Kabbalist.

An expert in Kabbalah as well as philosophy, Ibn Latif tried to reconcile the two by explaining kabbalistic mystery in philosophical terminology. He used a nomenclature for kabbalistic concepts entirely different from the one accepted by his predecessors; for this reason he is often regarded more as a philosopher than as a kabbalist. Unlike most kabbalists of his age, he lauded the philosophical teachings of *Rambam.

Among Ibn Latif's works are: Shaar HaShamayim, Tzuras Olam, Tzror Ha-Mor, Ginzei HaMelech, Iggeres HaTeshuvah, and Rav Pa'alim, all dealing with his unique kabbalistic-philosophic exposition on various topics of the Torah. These compositions have been published (mostly in periodicals). His commentaries to Job and Ecclesiastes are in manuscript.

R' Shem Tov ibn Palquera

ר' שֵׁם טוֹב (בֶּן יוֹסֵף) אִבְּן פַּלְקֵירָא

b. Palquera, Spain, c. 1225
d. Spain, c. 1295

Poet, Philosopher.

Although in his youth he was interested in poetry, R' Shem Tov later turned to philosophy. During the polemic concerning the philosophical works of *Rambam [see Historical Introduction], he zealously sided with Rambam's followers. He composed many works to illustrate the harmony of philosophy and Torah, among them, HaMevakesh (Amsterdam, 1779); Reishis Chochmah; Iggeres HaVikuach (Prague, 1810); Moreh HaMoreh (Pressburg, 1837), a commentary on Rambam's *Moreh Nevuchim;* and *Deios HaPhilosophim.*

R' Shem Tov also authored ethical treatises, including *Sefer HaMaalos, Tzari HaYagon* (Cremona, 1550), and *Iggeres HaMussar,* in verse (Jerusalem, 1936). In addition, he wrote on medicine and history.

R' Shlomo Petit

ר' שְׁלֹמֹה (בֶּן שְׁמוּאֵל) פְּטִיט

Acco (Acre), Eretz Yisrael, late 13th cent.
Talmudist, Kabbalist.

Leader of the second major polemic against the philosophical works of *Rambam, R' Shlomo journeyed to Europe to obtain the consent of the rabbinical authorities there for ordering all copies of Rambam's *Moreh Nevuchim* turned over to him and his disciples for eternal concealment. He was somewhat successful in gaining their support. On his return, however, he encountered the strong opposition of *R' David HaNaggid, Rambam's grandson, who had come to *Eretz Yisrael,* and had won the support of the leaders of Safed, Mosul, Baghdad and Damascus. Both R' Shlomo and R' David turned for guidance and assistance to *Rashba who attempted to effect a compromise and reconciliation.

R' Shlomo's campaign ended in defeat in 1286 when the exilarch of Damascus, R' Yishai ben Chizkiyah, issued a ban against him. Additionally, in 1288 the exilarch of Mosul, R' David ben Daniel, threatened a ban against anyone who persisted in following R' Shlomo in this matter.

Despite the opposition to his stand against Rambam's teachings, R' Shlomo was recognized as an outstanding scholar.

R' Avraham Abulafla

ר' אַבְרָהָם (בֶּן שְׁמוּאֵל) אַבּוּלַעְפְיָא

b. Saragossa, Spain, 1240
d. Greece after 1291
Kabbalist.

Adventurous and bold, R' Avraham began his life of wandering with a journey to *Eretz Yisrael* when he was barely twenty years of age. He wished to proceed to the river *Sambatyon* in search of the ten lost tribes, but was stopped at Acre by the Crusaders. He then set out on a return voyage to Spain. On his way home, he spent some time in Capua, Italy, studying philosophy, particularly *Rambam's *Moreh Nevuchim.* Dissatisfied with this branch of learning, he turned instead to Kabbalah. Returning to Spain in 1271, he settled in Barcelona and applied himself to ardent study of *Sefer Yetzirah* and its commentaries, especially that of *R' Elazar of Worms, whose kabbalistic doctrine he accepted in its entirety. R' Avraham claimed that he was able to rise to the heights of Divine inspiration through the combinations of letters and Divine Names mentioned by R' Elazar. He had numerous disciples, most notable among them, *R' Yosef Gikatilla.

In 1280, he journeyed to Rome with the announced intention of persuading Pope Nicholas III to convert to Judaism. The pope, then vacationing in Suriano, heard of his plans and issued orders to burn the fanatical Jew as soon as he arrived. Although a stake was erected for the purpose, R' Avraham continued on his way. Upon reaching Suriano, however, he learned that the pope had succumbed to a stroke the night before. R' Avraham returned to Rome, where he was thrown into prison but released four weeks later.

He then journeyed to Sicily and settled in Messina, where he surrounded himself with many students and preached of the imminent coming of the Messiah.

His habits and prophecies caused much confusion among the Messina community, and they turned to *Rashba, the generation's foremost Torah authority, for guidance. Rashba condemned Abulafia and his followers in the sharpest terms, and warned the community not to become involved with a false Messianic movement.

Rashba's condemnation compelled Abulafia to seek a new base. He went to Greece, where he composed VeZos LiYehudah and Sheva Nesivos HaTorah defending himself against Rashba's attacks, claiming that Rashba did not know him personally, but judged him from hearsay. Indeed, in a later generation, R' Chaim Vital cites him extensively in Shaarei Kedushah.

In total, R' Avraham authored twenty-six books, plus twenty-two works containing descriptions of his visions. His last known work, Imrei Shefer, a commentary on Genesis, was written in 1291.

One of his works, Moreh HaMoreh, cited by R' Yehudah Chayat, was a kabbalistic commentary on Rambam's Moreh Nevuchim.

R' Aharon HaLevi (Ra'ah)

ר' אַהֲרוֹן (בֶּן יוֹסֵף) הַלֵּוִי (רָא"ה)

b. Gerona, Spain c. 1230
d. Provence, France c. 1300

Talmudist, Halachist.

On his father's side, R' Aharon was a direct descendant of *Razah; on his mother's side he traced his lineage from *R' Asher of Lunel. He studied under his older brother, R' Pinchas HaLevi; his nephew, R' Yitzchak HaLevi; and was an outstanding disciple of *Ramban.

Ra'ah shared the post of rabbi of Barcelona, Spain, with *Rashba. Each rabbi had his own Beis Din, yet they often functioned jointly. They often signed responsa together, and had mutual disciples. Both were officially recognized by King Pedro's government. *Ritva was R' Aharon HaLevi's most noted disciple. R' Crescas Vidal, a scholar whose chidushim to Kesubos are cited in Shitah Mekubetzes, was also his pupil.

When Rashba published his celebrated Toras HaBayis on dietary laws, Ra'ah wrote critical notes on it entitled Bedek HaBayis. Although Bedek HaBayis was very politely and respectfully written, Rashba was chagrined by the critique, and published Mishmeres HaBayis anonymously, in defense of his work.

In 1283, Ra'ah assumed temporary control of the rabbinate of Saragossa in order to resolve the internal strife in that community. He succeeded in establishing many new enactments for communal harmony, and soon returned to Barcelona.

In 1286, he became rabbi of Toledo for a short time, before returning once more to Barcelona. In the last years of his life, he lectured in Montpellier, Provence [France].

Ra'ah's prolific pen produced novellae on the entire Talmud, of which those on tractates Kesubos, Beitzah, Chullin, Berachos, Sukkah, and Taanis have appeared in print. He also wrote responsa and a commentary on *Rif's Sefer HaHalachos. His concise halachic compendium (on the order of Rif's Halachos), Nezer HaKodesh, has not survived. Some ascribe authorship of Sefer HaChinuch to Ra'ah. The basis of this claim is the author's signature — "A Jewish man from the House of Levi, a Barcelonese." This view has been refuted by bibliographers. Ra'ah's halachic decisions regarding wine [Yayin Nesech] appear together with Rashba's Avodas HaKodesh (Venice, 1602), and with Ra'ah's Piskei Niddah.

R' Shlomo Ibn Aderes (Rashba)

ר׳ שְׁלֹמֹה (בֶּן אַבְרָהָם) אִבְּן אַדְרֶת
(רשב״א)

b. Barcelona, Spain, 1235
d. Barcelona, Spain, 1310

Halachist, Talmudist.

Rashba studied under *R' Yonah Gerondi and *Ramban. After spending a few years as a financier, he was called upon by the Barcelona community to serve as their rabbi, a position he held for more than forty years, until his death.

Inquiries were sent to Rashba from *Eretz Yisrael,* Italy, Portugal, France, Germany, North Africa, and of course from all parts of Spain. His responsa, perhaps the most extensive of the early authorities, are concise and to the point. They cover all topics of Judaism, including explanations of difficult passages in Bible, Aggadah and Talmud. These responsa have been frequently cited in later authoritative works, including *Tur* and *Shulchan Aruch,* and weigh heavily in the final halachic decision. They were collected in many different codices; eight different collections of his responsa have been printed. The section known as volume one contains 1255 responsa and was initially printed in Bologna in 1539. The complete collection comprises well over three thousand responsa, but, according to *Ginas Veradim,* this collection itself is only an abridged form of the original. The volume of responsa attributed to Ramban is mostly by Rashba. It should be noted, however, that interspersed among the thousands of responsa in these volumes are decisions written by other sages such as *R' Meir of Rothenburg.

The leader of all Spanish Jewry, Rashba was acknowledged as the foremost halachic authority of his generation by almost all of the world's Jewish communities. His penetrating Talmud commentary, appearing on seventeen tractates, is no doubt a result of the discourses he delivered in the academy he headed. His novellae, which follow the Tosafist method of study, are very popular and a basic text for any serious Talmud student. The novellae to *Kesubos* appearing under his name belong to *Ramban and are so cited in *Shitah Mekubetzes.* Rashba's own novellae to that tractate have been published recently (Jerusalem, 1973) from manuscript. Similarly, *Ritva's novellae to tractate Succah have erroneously been attributed to Rashba. His novellae to *Bava Metzia* and *Bava Basra* and his complete work on Tractate *Niddah* have been published in modern times.

Rashba exerted an overpowering influence on all matters pertaining to the Jewish communities of even far-off lands, and his opinion was sought on all major issues. During the controversy over *Rambam's *Moreh,* Rashba upheld Rambam's honor in response to *R' Shlomo Petit's polemic against it. However, although not an opponent of philosophy itself, Rashba nevertheless feared that preoccupation with the subject would result in neglect of Torah study and might lead some to deviate from the true interpretation of the Aggadah which must conform to the *hashkafah* perspective of the Torah. For this reason he was steadfastly opposed to the philosophic-rationalistic concept of Judaism that then prevailed in some parts of Spain and Provence. In 1305, together with his *beis din* in Barcelona, he pronounced a ban of excommunication over all who studied philosophy and the sciences before reaching the age of twenty-five. The works of Rambam, however, were excluded from the ban, as was the study of medicine for professional purposes.

A special ban was pronounced against

the rationalistic Bible exegetes and those who interpreted Aggadah in a philosophical manner, for example, claiming that the twelve tribes only represented the signs of the zodiac. *R' Yedayah HaPenini wrote an apologetic letter to Rashba, imploring him to lift his ban. The entire series of bans, counter bans, and excommunications revolving around Rambam's works and the study of secular disciplines were subsequently collected and published under the title Minchas Kenaos.

Another problem with which Rashba had to contend with was the rising influence of *R' Avraham Abulafia, who, claiming to be informed through the study of Kabbalah, predicted the imminent coming of the Messiah. The community of Messina, Italy, where Abulafia was preaching, asked Rashba whether to follow him or not. Rashba opposed Abulafia and his followers. A kabbalist himself, Rashba condemned Abulafia's interpretations of kabbalistic doctrine.

Rashba had a good part of Rambam's Mishnah commentary translated into Hebrew from the original Arabic. He also carried on a disputation with a noted Christian scholar, and wrote a refutation of the charges of Raymund Martini, a Dominican monk of Barcelona, who had issued a work misinterpreting passages from the Talmud and Midrash. Rashba also composed a treatise to refute the charges of a Moslem scholar of an earlier generation.

His other works include Toras HaBayis on dietary laws (Venice, 1608), including a synopsis, Toras HaBayis HaKatzer (Cremona, 1566). A previously lost chapter of this work, Sha'ar HaMayim, dealing with the laws of Mikveh was recently published (Budapest, 1933). When *R' Aaron HaLevi composed Bedek HaBayis refuting many of

Rashba's decisions, an anonymous work, Mishmeres HaBayis, appeared defending the original. In one of his responsa, Rashba reveals himself as the author of this volume.

He also composed Avodas HaKodesh concerning the laws of the Sabbath and Festivals (Venice, 1602); Piskei Challah (Constantinople, 1518) on laws pertaining to the separation of dough; and a kabbalistic commentary on Aggadah, quoted frequently by the Kosev in Ein Yaakov, and recently printed (Jerusalem, 1976).

Among his prominent disciples were *Ritva, *R' Shem Tov ibn Gaon, and *R' Bachya ben Asher.

R' Todros Abulafia

ר' טוֹדְרוֹס (בֶּן יוֹסֵף הַלֵּוִי) אַבּוּאַלְעַפְיָא

b. Spain, 1234
d. Seville, Spain, c. 1300

Talmudist, Kabbalist.

R' Todros authored Aliyos Yevamos on tractate Yevamos (not extant), and two works on Kabbalah, Otzar HaKavod (Nowy Dwor, 1808; and Otzar HaKavod HaShalem, (Warsaw, 1879), a mystical interpretation of the Aggadah in the Talmud, and Shaar HaRazim (still in manuscript), describing and defining the ten Sefiros ["Emanations"]. He opposed philosophical explanations of the commandments. In the work Sam HaChaim (Leghorn, 1801), commentaries to tractates Yoma and Megillah attributed to R' Todros are cited (some of these have been published separately with Tosafos R' Asher on tractate Megillah, New York, 1959), but some scholars adduce proofs that these novellae are really a part of Sefer HaMichtam.

A favorite at the Castillian royal court, R' Todros accompanied the Spanish royal party to their meeting with the King of France in Provence. The Provencal Jews welcomed R' Todros warmly and R' Avraham Bedersi composed a poem in his honor.

Although only ten years old at the passing of the *Ramah, his father's uncle, R' Todros nevertheless credited his accomplishments to his uncle's influence. "[I studied with him] when I was a mere ten years old but blessed is the Omnipresent that I was privileged to see his glorious countenance at the time of his advanced age. At that time he placed both his hands on me and blessed me with the threefold blessings. It is this which has stood by me in my youth and into my adulthood and old age."

R' Avraham of Rimon (Granada)

ר' אַבְרָהָם (בֶּן יִצְחָק) מֵרמוֹן

Granada, Spain late 13th early 14th cent.
Kabbalist.

Bris Menuchah (Amsterdam, 1648), R' Avraham's profound kabbalistic work, was acclaimed by R' Moshe Cordevero to be the product of Divine Inspiration, for no one could perceive such hidden secrets by intellect alone. Arizal called it a penetrating and completely reliable kabbalistic source.

In Bris Menuchah, R' Avraham mentions two others works, Megaleh HaTaalumos and Sefer HaGevurah, which have not survived. R' Avraham's Sefer HaBris is quoted by *R' Moshe Botarel in his commentary to Sefer Yetzirah.

R' Moshe de Leon

רַבִּי מֹשֶׁה (בֶּן שֵׁם טוֹב) דִי לֵיאוֹן

b. Leon, Spain, c. 1250
d. Spain, 1305

Kabbalist.

R' Moshe earned his livelihood as a traveling scribe, copying old manuscripts. Thus, he discovered and published the Zohar, the principal book of the Kabbalah, compiled by the Tanna R' Shimon bar Yochai.

R' Moshe himself wrote Sefer HaRimon, which deals with mystical reasons for the commandments (preserved in manuscript). In HaNefesh HaChochmah or Sefer HaMishkal (Basel, 1608), he discusses the Divine nature of the soul and its punishment, and the resurrection of the dead; and he protests against linking Judaism with philosophy. He also authored Shekel HaKodesh (London, 1921) on various kabbalistic topics, and Sefer HaShem (Venice, 1605 with Heichal HaShem; and Zolkiew, 1778), dealing with the ten Sefiros ("Emanations") and the thirteen attributes of mercy (Midos HaRachamim). A work named Mishkan HaEdus, cited in his other books, has not come down to us.

Modern scholars have pointed out that the kabbalistic ideas expressed in R' Moshe's own works do not at all accord with those of the Zohar, making untenable the supposition, first recorded in Yuchasin and echoed by subsequent generations of the Kaballah's opponents, that R' Moshe himself authored the Zohar.

R' Yosef Gikatilla

ר' יוֹסֵף (בֶּן אַבְרָהָם) גִּיקַטְלִיָא

b. Castille, Spain 1248
d. Penafiel, Spain c. 1310

Kabbalist.

R' Yosef, disciple of *R' Avraham Abulafia, was known as a holy man and was often called Baal HaNissim ["master of the miracles"]. Although not a strong opponent of philosophy in his early years, he became quite adverse to that study later on. At the age of twenty-six he composed Ginas Egoz (Hanau, 1615), a kabbalistic treatise dealing with the Names of G-d and the kabbalistic interpretation of the Hebrew vowels (i.e., each vowel corresponding to one of the ten Sefiros ["Emanations"]). In this work he quotes *Rambam, *R' Shlomo ibn Gabirol, *R' Shmuel

HaNaggid, and *R' Avraham ibn Ezra.

His classic in the field of Kabbalah, *Shaarei Orah* (Riva di Trento, 1559), was described by Arizal as "a key to understanding the mystical studies." It discusses the definitions and descriptions of the ten *Sefiros,* mentioning only kabbalistic sources and no philosophical ones, in contrast to his first work. It is frequently quoted in *Yalkut Reuveni,* and has been translated into Latin. R' Mattisyahu Delacrut wrote a commentary to this work.

Among his other works are *Shaarei Zedek* (Riva di Trento, 1561), also on the ten *Sefiros;* a commentary on *Moreh Nevuchim* (Venice, 1574); *Sefer HaNikud* (in *Sheilos R' Shaul HaKohen*), a mystical discussion of the vowels (in *Arzei Levanon,* Venice, 1601); *Sod HaChashmal* or *Shaar HaShamayim* (Warsaw, 1798); *Tzafenas Paaneiach* on the *Haggadah* (1797); and *Sefer HaMeshalim.* His *Otzar HaKavod* on the prayers and his commentary to Song of Songs are still in manuscript. He also composed a halachic treatise titled *Sefer HaMitzvos* which has not been published.

His influence was great among scholars of succeeding generations, who cite his opinions with great reverence. One of his kabbalistic teachings regarding the blessing over the new moon is cited in *Shulchan Aruch* (*Orach Chaim* 426:4).

R' David al-Adeni

ר' דָּוִד (בֶּן עַמְרָם) אֶלְעַדְנִי (הָעַדְנִי)

Aden, 13th or 14th cent.

Author of *Midrash HaGadol.*

R' David's monumental work *Midrash HaGadol* is a compendium of halachic and aggadic material gleaned from tannaitic and amoraitic Midrashim and arranged according to the verses of the Torah. Many of the sources were lost in the course of the centuries, and have come to light only through this work. *Midrash HaGadol,* which is also beneficial in ascertaining the correct Talmudic and Midrashic text, has been discovered and published (in installments) only in this century. Recently the entire series was republished in Jerusalem (1947-76).

R' Yom Tov ibn Asevilli (Ritva)

ר' יוֹם טוֹב (בֶּן אַבְרָהָם) אִבְּן אַשְׁבִּילִי (רִיטְבָּ"א)

Seville, Spain c. 1320

Talmudist, Halachist.

A disciple of *Rashba and *Ra'ah; Ritva was a Talmudist, halachist, kabbalist (see his commentary to *Eruvin* 13b), and philosopher (*Sefer HaZikaron*), who left a vast legacy of writings.

His popular Talmud commentary, which covers most tractates, combines both plain interpretation and Tosafist type analysis. He follows the Talmudic discussion with a synopsis of the interpretations of *Rashi, *Tosafos, *Rif, *Rashba, Ra'ah, and *Ramban, thus making his work a concise, readable compendium of the main Talmudic commentaries.

Ritva wrote novellae on many tractates and mentions a commentary he wrote on *Rif's *Sefer HaHalachos.* Although this work has not been preserved in its entirety, his novellae on tractate *Taanis* are, in reality, a commentary on Rif's work.

Great confusion exists regarding his works. Many originally attributed to Ritva have been proven to be the work of others. Similarly, many of Ritva's novellae have been printed under the names of other authors. A commentary to Ramban's *Hilchos Nedarim* printed in the Vilna edition of the Talmud and attributed to Ritva contains contradictions to comments *R' Yosef Chaviva (in *Nemukei Yosef*) attributes to Ritva.

Some scholars feel that the true author of this work was R' Dan Astruc, a disciple of *R' Aharon HaLevi.

Chukos HaDayanim, (Jerusalem, 1970-4) concerning the laws governing judges and testimony of witnesses, cited by *Nimukei Yosef* and others, was ascribed to Ritva by Chida. However, with the publication of this work it has become clear that the author is actually R' Avraham ben Shlomo Tazarti; another disciple of Rashba.

A commentary to tractate *Pesachim* attributed to Ritva is evidently not his, since he is cited by name in this work. Although some attribute it to R' Yosef Chaviva, recent publication of *Nimukei Yosef* to *Pesachim* (New York, 1960) disproves this view, too.

The novellae on Succah printed as *Chidushei HaRashba* are really by Ritva; those on Shabbos, named *Chidushei HaRitva,* are by Ran, and Ritva's true work on this tractate has been partially printed from a manuscript (New York 5727), while part of it still awaits publication.

His novellae to tractate *Bava Metzia* have been published as *Chidushei HaRitva HaChadashim* (London, 1962); the novellae to that tractate previously attributed to him are probably not his. His novellae on *Bava Basra* were recently published (New York, 1952-4) from manuscript.

Ritva mentions that he composed halachic codes on several subjects but of these only *Hilchos Berachos* have been printed (Leghorn, 1844). A collection of 209 of his responsa, some of which are cited by R' Yosef Karo and others, have been printed (Jerusalem, 1959).

Another work by Ritva is *Sefer HaZikaron,* a refutation of Ramban's criticisms to *Rambam's philosophical views; only fragments of this work remain. Ritva makes it clear that, although his sympathies are with the followers of the kabbalah, his overpowering respect for Rambam induced him to defend his views and make them plausible. A *Haggadah* commentary attributed to Ritva was published in Leghorn in 1838 and in many subsequent *Hagaddos.*

Some see in Ritva's comment to *Bava Basra* 75 (cited by HaKosev in *Ein Yaakov* there) a reference to a commentary on *Sefer Yetzirah* by him but the evidence is inconclusive.

R' Yehoshua HaNaggid

ר׳ יְהוֹשֻׁעַ (בֶּן אַבְרָהָם) הַנָּגִיד

b. Egypt, 1310
d. Egypt, 1355

Halachist.

Son of R' Avraham and grandson of *R' David HaNaggid, R' Yehoshua was the fifth and last of *Rambam's line to bear the title *Naggid,* as his son, R' David, who was to succeed him, moved to Syria for unknown reasons. Like his predecessors, R' Yehoshua was called upon to decide on matters of Halachah and tradition. A volume of inquiries from Yemenite scholars, which contains R' Yehoshua's replies, has been published (Jerusalem, 1941). The responsa, which show extreme clarity and brevity, deal mostly with questions regarding the correct interpretation of Rambam's *Mishneh Torah.*

R' Meir Aldabi

ר׳ מֵאִיר (בֶּן יִצְחָק) אַלְדַבִּי

Toledo, Spain, mid-14th cent.

Scholar, Philosopher.

R' Meir, a grandson of *Rosh, wrote *Shevilei Emunah* (Riva di Trento 1559), a philosophical presentation of Judaism which utilizes science, aggadic exegesis, and some kabbalah. He made use of the works of his predecessors, especially *Shaar HaShamayim* by R' Gershon ben Shlomo.

R' Avraham ben Ismael

ר' אַבְרָהָם בֶּן אִסְמָעֵאל

Spain, c. 1330

Talmudist.

Pupil of *Rashba, he was in turn the teacher of *R' Yerucham, who mentions him in his works. His Talmudic novellae and responsa are mentioned in the writings of his contemporaries, but have not been preserved.

R' Shmuel Motot

ר' שְׁמוּאֵל (בֶּן סְעַדְיָה) מוטוט

Guadalajara, Spain, 14th cent.

Kabbalist, Commentator.

R' Shmuel's best known work is *Megilas Sesarim*, (Venice, 1554) a supercommentary on *R' Avraham ibn Ezra's Torah commentary. R' Shmuel's commentary on *Sefer Yetzirah*, titled *Meshoveiv Nesivos*, is still in manuscript, as are fragments of his kabbalistic Torah interpretation and prayer commentary.

At the request of *Rivash, he translated a philosophical treatise of *Ravad I from Arabic, entitling it *Emunah Nesiah*. However, due to the popularity of R' Shlomo ben Labi's translation, *Emunah Ramah*, the former was never published and remains in manuscript.

R' Yehoshua ibn Shuiv

ר' יְהוֹשֻׁעַ אִבְּן שׁוּעֵיב

Spain, c. 1330

Commentator.

Ibn Shuiv composed a book of sermons on the Torah (Constantinople, 1522). His Midrashic commentary on Psalms and his supercommentary on the kabbalistic points in *Ramban's Torah commentary are still extant in manuscript.

A disciple of *Rashba, he in turn taught *R' Menachem ben Zerach, author of *Tzeidah LaDerech*.

R' Dan Ashkenazi

ר' דָּן אַשְׁכְּנַזִּי

Spain, late 13th-early 14th cent.

Talmudist.

Due to hostile conditions in his native Germany, R' Dan emigrated to Spain where he was acclaimed as a Torah giant. He corresponded with *Rashba and *Rosh. Although he disagreed with *Ritva regarding certain points in halachah, the latter nevertheless lauded R' Dan for his scholarship. Some of his responsa appear in *Teshuvos HaRashba* and *Teshuvos Besamim Rosh*.

After the passing of R' Dan and Ritva, *Ran was asked to decide between their divergent opinions. He replied, "Who am I to decide between these two masters whose little fingers are thicker than my loins!"

Fragments of R' Dan's Torah commentary have been preserved in the collection *Hadras Zekeinim* (Leghorn, 1840). His interpretations are also cited in the Torah commentary of *R' Bachya ben Asher.

R' Nasanel ben Yeshayahu

ר' נְתַנְאֵל בֶּן יְשַׁעְיָהוּ

Yemen, 14th century

Compiler of Midrash.

R' Nasanel compiled the Yemenite Midrash *Or Ha'Afeilah* (Jerusalem, 1957), which draws upon the Talmud, the Midrash, and *Rambam. The work is written in a blend of Hebrew and Arabic.

R' Bachya (Bechaye) ben Asher

ר' בַּחְיֵי בֶּן אָשֵׁר (אִבְּן חָאלָאוָה)

d. Saragossa, Spain, c. 1340

Torah Commentator, Kabbalist.

Although he endured poverty and misfortune, R' Bachya, a pupil of *Rashba, devoted himself to the study of Torah and to writing.

His encyclopedic Torah commentary, *Midrash Rabbeinu Bachya*, is so popular that it has been the subject of at least ten supercommentaries and has been reprinted no less than twenty times (first ed. Naples, 1492). Each Sidrah ["weekly portion"] is preceded by an ethical introduction based on a verse from Proverbs upon which the author expounds, usually according to the writings of *R' Yonah of Gerona. R' Bachya employs four types of interpretations: the plain meaning, usually following *Rashi, *R' Chananel, and *R' Avraham ibn Ezra; Midrashic exegesis; philosophical exegesis demonstrating how the sciences and philosophy are contained in the Torah, and drawing from the works of *R' Bachya ibn Pakudah and *Rambam; and kabbalistic exegesis, drawing mostly from *Ramban and Zohar, which he terms Midrash. A host of supercommentaries have been written on the kabbalistic portions, most notable among them Sefer Naftali, also called Naftulei Elokim.

R' Bachya also wrote Kad HaKemach (Constantinople, 1515) on ethics, the importance of belief and trust in the Creator, and observance of the commandments.

His other works are Sova Semachos, a commentary on Job (Amsterdam 1768); Shulchan Shel Arba, concerning laws applying to meals, and related kabbalistic material; and a commentary on the tractate Avos (Jerusalem 1970). Ohel Moed, which has been lost, is said to have been a commentary on Sefer Yetzirah.

R' Shem Tov ibn Gaon

ר' שֵׁם טוֹב (בֶּן אַבְרָהָם) אִבְּן גָּאוֹן

b. Soria, Spain, 1283
d. c. 1340

Talmudist, Kabbalist.

A disciple of *Rashba, R' Shem Tov studied Kabbalah under R' Yitzchak ben Todros, and spent some time studying in Safed, Eretz Yisrael.

In Migdal Oz, one of the first commentaries on *Rambam's Mishneh Torah, R' Shem Tov defends Rambam against the criticisms of *Ravad III. R' Shem Tov's novellae on several Talmudic tractates are mentioned in Migdal Oz.

His kabbalistic writings include Kesser Shem Tov (Leghorn, 1839), a supercommentary on the mystical sections of *Ramban's Torah commentary; Badei HaAron U'Migdal Chananel; and Sefer HaPe'er, a supercommentary on *Ramah's Ginas Bisan on Genesis.

R' Shem Tov and his brother R' Yehoshua were scribes. Some illuminated scrolls bearing their joint signatures are still extant.

R' Chaim of Tudela

ר' חַיִּים (בֶּן שְׁמוּאֵל) מִטּוּדֵילוֹ

b. Provence, France, c. 1275
d. Spain, c. 1340

Halachist.

Scion of the illustrious Ben-David family of Provence, R' Chaim was related to *Ravad III.

His compendium Tzror HaChayim (Jerusalem, 1966) covers the laws of prayers, Sabbath, and the holidays. In Tzror HaKesef, dealing with monetary law, he draws upon all the early codifiers, but bases his decision, in most cases, on his teachers, *Rashba and *R' Peretz of Corbeil. He also composed dissertations. A commentary on tractate Ta'anis, Shitah L'Ba'al HaTzeroros, (Tel-Aviv, 1969) has been attributed to him.

R' Yitzchak HaYisraeli II

ר' יִצְחָק (בֶּן יוֹסֵף) הַיִּשְׂרְאֵלִי

d. Toledo, Spain, c. 1335

Astronomer.

At the request of his teacher, *Rosh, R' Yitzchak wrote Yesod Olam (Berlin, 1777) on astronomy and calendar calculations, which includes an introduction on geometry and trigonometry. R' Yitzchak devotes one chapter in this book to delineating the chain of traditional scholars listed in *Sefer HaKabbalah* and other historical documents. His other astronomical works, *Shaar HaShamayim* and *Shaar HaMiluim*, are still in manuscript.

R' Yitzchak of Acco

ר' יִצְחָק (בֶּן שְׁמוּאֵל) דְּמִן עַכּוֹ

b. Eretz Yisrael, 1250
d. Toledo, Spain, 1340

Talmudist, Kabbalist.

R' Yitzchak studied under *R' Shlomo Petit in Acco, which was then an important center of learning. In 1291, Acco was captured by Sultan al-Ashraf, of Egypt, and its Jewish and Christian inhabitants were either killed or imprisoned. R' Yitzchak was among those imprisoned. When he was eventually freed, he emigrated to Spain.

His most famous work, *Meiras Einayim,* a supercommentary on the kabbalistic parts of *Ramban's Torah commentary, has recently been published for the first time (Jerusalem, 1975). He also composed a commentary on *Sefer Yetzirah; Leket Shoshanim,* an abridged version of *Meiras Einayim;* and *Sefer HaSodos,* mentioned by R' Yosef Shlomo Delmedigo, all of which have not been published. Additionally, he composed an ethical treatise cited in *Reishis Chochmah.*

His *Sefer HaYamim,* extant in manuscript, describes, among other biographical data, his successful attempt to authenticate the *Zohar.*

Chida mentions that R' Yitzchak's kabbalistic knowledge was very profound and he was an expert in combining Divine Names *(Chochmas HaTziruf)* by which he summoned angels to appear before him and reveal great mysteries of the Torah.

R' Chisdai Crescas I

ר' חִסְדַּאי (בֶּן יְהוּדָה) קְרֶשְׂקַשׂ (הָרִאשׁוֹן)

Spain, c. 1340

Talmudist.

R' Chisdai is cited by his disciple *Rivash in several of the latter's responsa. *Yuchasin* mentions him as the author of Talmudic novellae. His grandson, *R' Chisdai Crescas II, was a noted Talmudist and philosopher.

R' Yerucham

ר' יְרוּחָם (בֶּן מְשׁוּלָּם)

b. Provence, France, c. 1280
d. Toledo, Spain, c. 1350

Halachist.

Exiled from France in the expulsion of 1306, R' Yerucham arrived in Toledo, where he studied under *Rosh. His principal teacher, however, was *R' Avraham ben Ismael.

In 1334 he wrote *Meisharim,* dealing with monetary law. In his introduction, R' Yerucham modestly emphasizes that his work does not contain his own opinions but is rather a compendium of decisions of earlier authorities. A supercommentary to that work, *Nesivos Mishpat,* was written by R' Chaim Algazi (Constantinople,1669).

R' Yerucham's second work, written in 1340, is *Toldos Adam V'Chavah,* a halachic compilation of all the laws affecting an observant Jew. It is divided into two parts: *Toldos Adam,* listing all the laws applicable from birth to marriage, and *Chavah,* on those from marriage until death. It has been printed (Constantinople, 1516), and is cited frequently in *Beis Yosef.*

R' Vidal of Tolosa

ר' וִידָאל דִּי טוֹלוֹשָׁא

Tolosa, Spain, c. 1360

Author of *Maggid Mishneh.*

R' Vidal, a colleague of *Ran, wrote his famous commentary on *Rambam's *Mishneh Torah* to fill what many considered a serious lapse in Rambam's work. *Maggid Mishneh* cites the Talmudic sources for Rambam's halachic decisions, and responds to the objections of *Ravad III. R' Vidal also explains why various decisions precede or follow one another, or are omitted.

Printed in all editions of *Mishneh Torah, Maggid Mishneh* was acclaimed throughout succeeding generations. Most of the later supercommentaries to *Mishneh Torah* respectfully refer to R' Vidal as *HaRav HaMaggid* ["The Rabbi, the *Maggid*"].

*Rivash, who corresponded with R' Vidal's son, R' Yitzchak, on halachic matters, highly praised the author of *Maggid Mishneh,* telling R' Yitzchok that he was a *bnan shel kedoshim* ["son of the holy ones"].

*R' Yosef Karo, in the introduction to his *Kessef Mishneh,* bemoans the fact that he was privileged to see R' Vidal's work on only six of the fourteen books of *Mishneh Torah,* and even these were incomplete in some sections. Even today, only those sections seen by R' Yosef Karo are extant.

It is interesting to note that *Rivash adds the prefix "An" to R' Vidal's name, calling him Anvidal. *Chida notes that this prefix was commonly affixed to names of illustrious people in earlier times. It is a contraction of the word *Adon,* "Master."

R' Peretz HaKohen

ר' פֶּרֶץ (בֶּן יִצְחָק) הַכֹּהֵן

b. Provence, c. 1300
d. Barcelona, Spain, c. 1370

Talmudist.

After the Black Plague of 1348-49, R' Peretz asked his colleague *Ran to secure him a position in Spain. As a result, R' Peretz was elected rabbi of Barcelona, where he directed a Talmudic academy. An acknowledged halachic authority, he was also recognized by the government as the judicial authority of the Jews.

His extensive novellae to *Tractate Nazir* have been published (New York, 1972). Although some ascribe the kabbalistic work *Maareches Elokus* to his authorship, this is doubtful, as his disciple *Rivash (responsa ch. 157) mentions that R' Peretz was not a kabbalist.

R' David Abudraham

ר' דָּוִד (בֶּן יוֹסֵף) אֲבוּדְרָהָם

Seville, Spain late 13th-14th cent.

Halachist.

R' David's major work, a guide and commentary on the prayers, has enjoyed much popularity and was reprinted numerous times (first ed. Lisbon, 1489) under the title *Abudraham.* It contains a clear, insightful commentary on the prayers and blessings, a compendium of rituals and customs, a discussion of the obligation of reciting the *Shema;* the laws of prayer; and the various categories of blessings. He introduces his classic work by saying that he perceived the need for a popularly written work that would acquaint the masses with the meaning and laws of the prayers. He succeeded admirably in achieving his goal. His work remains popular both as a halachic source and as a basic text on the prayer book.

The sources used by R' David include the Babylonian and Jerusalem Talmuds, Geonic writings, and all the codes down to his own time, both Sephardic and Ashkenazic. To these he adds his own comments, sometimes deciding the halachah according to his original explanation. Much of the halachic material of his work is quoted in halachic codes, especially in *Beis Yosef.*

R' David also composed a running commentary on the Temple *Avodah* liturgy recited on Yom Kippur; this was printed as *Tashlum Abudraham (Berlin, 1900).*

R' Yitzchak Abohab I

ר' יִצְחָק אֲבּוֹהָב (הָרִאשׁוֹן)

Spain, 14th cent.

Ethicist.

In the introduction to his ethical classic, R' Yitzchak states that he composed *Menoras HaMaor* to compensate for the neglect of the many beautiful aggadic portions of the Talmud. He therefore grouped this material by topics. The book educated the masses for many generations (first ed. Turkey, 1514), and has been translated into Yiddish, Ladino and German.

Two halachic works which R' Yitzchak mentions in *Menoras HaMaor — Aron HaEidus* and *Shulchan HaPanim —* have been lost.

R' Nissim (Ran)

ר' נִסִים (בֶּן רְאוּבֵן) (ר"ן)

b. Spain, c. 1290
d. Barcelona, Spain, c. 1375

Halachist, Talmudic Commentator.

As rabbi of Barcelona, Ran was for a time imprisoned by the government, together with other communal figures, on false charges, and later released unharmed. The foremost rabbinical authority of his time, R' Nissim received inquiries from France, Italy, Africa, and even *Eretz Yisrael.* However, only seventy-seven of his responsa have been preserved (Rome, 1545). Ran is famous for his extensive commentary on *Rif's Sefer HaHalachos* which is published together with the code on many tractates. An independent thinker, he does not hitate to differ with the earlier authorities.

Among his commentaries on many Talmudic tractates, the one on *Nedarim* appears in the Talmud folio in all of the standard editions. Ran's commentaries to other tractates of the Talmud have appeared in print at various times and have recently been collected and published as *Chidushei HaRan al HaShas.* Some of · these works have however been erroneously identified. The work to tractate *Shabbos* is probably by a disciple of Ran, whereas the commentary known as *Chidushei HaRitva* was really written by Ran. The work on tractate *Megillah* was not by him but is probably by an earlier scholar. R' Elchanan Wasserman maintained that the commentary on *Sanhedrin* is not by Ran.

Ran's commentaries to *Pesachim, Mo'ed Kattan,* and *Bava Basra* have recently surfaced. A commentary to *Kesubos* entitled *Shitah LaRan* has been published, but its authorship by Ran is not certain.

R' Nissim, following in the footsteps of previous generations of Sephardic Talmud scholars (e.g. *Rambam), also left his mark in the field of Jewish thought. His collection of homilies, known as *Derashos HaRan,* is a classic exposition of the fundamentals of the Jewish religion. It has been conclusively proven (see preface to *Derashos HaRan,* Jerusalem, 5634) that Ran is the true author of this work, and not a disciple of *Ramban with the same name, as was once supposed. Though these homilies are presented as commentaries to specific passages of the Torah, their main purpose is to explain and illuminate the tenets of the faith. Here Ran synthesizes the approaches of Rambam, Ramban, *Ralbag and other great thinkers. In many instances he offers his original approach to profound questions. Many giants of Jewish thought after Ran, such as *R' Chisdai Crescas, *R' Yosef Albo, R' Yitzchak Abarbanel, and *R' Yitzchak Arama, used his *Derashos* as the basis for their own philosophical systems.

Ran refrained from involvement in the study of Kabbalah, and even disapproved of Ramban's preoccupation with the mystical lore, which he described as "excessive."

At an advanced age, Ran began writing his Torah commentary, which presents a rational explanation combining the plain meaning with Talmudic elaboration. Unfortunately, he died before completing the work. The part he did write has recently been published (Jerusalem, 5728). He also composed liturgical hymns.

Ran studied under his father, and possibly under *Rashba. He was a colleague of *R' Vidal of Tolosa and *R' Peretz HaKohen. Among his notable disciples were *Rivash, *R' Yosef of Saragossa, *R' Chisdai Crescas II, R' Vidal Ephraim Gerondi, and *R' Yoseph Chaviva, author of Nimukei Yosef. Ran had two sons who were scholars, R' Chisdai and R' Reuven. About the latter, Rivash wrote, "Fruit of the righteous, the wise son, R' Reuven."

R' Menachem ben Zerach

ר' מְנַחֵם (בֶּן אַהֲרֹן) בֶּן זֶרַח

b. France c. 1310
d. Spain, 1385 (10 Av 5145)

Halachist.

R' Menachem's father was a native of France. When Philip IV (the Fair) expelled all the Jews from his realm in 1306, he settled in Estella, in the kingdom of Navarre. In an anti-Semitic outbreak in 1328, the Jewish population of Estella was massacred, and R' Menachem's parents and four younger brothers were among the martyrs. He, too, was seriously wounded and lay among the dead, unable to move. A knight, who was a friend of his father, found him, brought him to his home, and nursed him back to health. After regaining his strength, R' Menachem moved to Toledo and dedicated himself to Torah study. In this Torah center he studied under *R' Yehoshua ibn Shuiv and *R' Yehudah ben Asher.

R' Menachem served as rabbi in Alcala de Henarez (near Toledo) from 1350-68. In the civil war which broke out in 1369, he lost all his belongings along with his position and was left destitute.

Don Shmuel Abarbanel secured the positions of rabbi of Toledo and dean of its Talmud academy for ' Menachem. Because his service to the king did not permit Don Shmuel much time for Talmudic and halachic studies, R' Menachem wrote a halachic compendium, Tzeidah LaDerech, for him. This work is interspersed with remarks on ethics and philosophy.

R' Yosef Tuv Elem (Bonfils) II

ר' יוֹסֵף (בֶּן אֱלִיעֶזֶר) טוּב עֶלֶם (הַשֵּׁנִי)

b. Toledo, Spain, c. 1320
d. Jerusalem, Eretz Yisrael, c. 1390

Bible Commentator.

R' Yosef journeyed from Spain to Candia (Crete), and from there to Egypt. Eventually he made his way to Jerusalem, where he began to plan his work on *R' Avraham ibn Ezra's Torah commentary, feeling that due to its brevity, this work had been misunderstood by most students. R' Yosef's supercommentary, Zofnas Paneach, would explain the terse remarks of Ibn Ezra by drawing on other works where Ibn Ezra had discussed the topic more fully. However personal circumstances forced R' Yosef to spend some time in Damascus, and his project was delayed until R' David ben *R' Yehoshua HaNaggid, a direct descendant of *Rambam, encouraged R' Yosef to return to Jerusalem and begin his work.

First published in an abridged and error-filled edition (Amsterdam, 1722) under the name Ohel Yosef, Zofnas Paneach was later published in a two volume corrected edition (vol. 1,

Cracow, 1912; vol. 2, Berlin, 1930). R' Yosef's *Tikkun Shearim,* concerning astronomy and the fixing of the calendar, is still in manuscript.

R' Yisrael al-Nakavah (Ankavah)
ר' יִשְׂרָאֵל (בֶּן יוֹסֵף) אַלְנַקָאוָה

d. Toledo, Spain, 139

Ethician.

His ethical treatise, *Menoras HaMaor* (New York, 1929-32), which covers almost every aspect of proper behavior, both religious and social, greatly influenced *R' Yitzchak Abohab I in his work of the same name.

During the massacres of 1391 (see Historical Introduction), R' Yisrael was killed. His son *R' Ephraim, escaped to Africa.

R' Moshe Botarel
ר' מֹשֶׁה בּוֹטַרִיל

Spain, late 14th-early 15th cent.

Kabbalist.

A disciple of R' Yaakov Sephardi, R' Moshe composed a commentary on *Sefer Yetzirah* (Mantua, 1562), which became quite popular and was published in most editions of the book. He attended the disputation at Tortosa (1413-14, see Historical Introduction) and is said to have written a polemic against Geronimo de Santa Fe, who represented the Church. *R' Chisdai Crescas II held R' Moshe in high esteem.

R' Yitzchak ben Sheshes Perfet (Rivash)
ר' יִצְחָק בֶּן שֵׁשֶׁת פֶּרְפֶט (ריב"ש)

b. Barcelona, Spain, 1326
d. Algiers, N. Africa, 1407

Halachist.

R' Yitzchak studied under *R' Peretz HaKohen, *Ran and *R' Chisdai Crescas I. Although he was recognized for his scholarship at a young age and actively participated in community affairs, R'

Yitzchak earned his livelihood as a merchant.

In 1367 he was arrested and imprisoned on false charges along with his brother; his teacher, Ran; and his colleague, *R' Chisdai Crescas II.

After his release, he accepted the position of rabbi of Saragossa; however, due to a rift within the community he decided to leave Saragossa in favor of a position in the less important city of Calatayud. When the communal leaders of Saragossa sought his pardon and begged him to stay, he consented, only to become frustrated by further community strife. Finally, he moved to Valencia, where he directed a Talmudic academy.

During the widespread massacres of 1391 (see Historical Introduction) Rivash fled to Algiers, in North Africa, where he was appointed rabbi. Even there, however, his peace was disturbed. Another Spanish refugee, who had settled in Algiers before Rivash's arrival, aspired to become the leader of the community. He harassed Rivash by issuing opposing halachic decisions. Although the community implored him time after time to place the insolent man under ban, the humble and unassuming rabbi refused. However, when a ship arrived from Majorca with forty-five Marranos, Rivash's enemy asked the governor of Algiers to forbid the ship to dock or to block entrance to further refugees. In the face of the threat to his brethren, Rivash could no longer remain silent and excommunicated the troublemaker. In order to secure for Rivash adequate protection and the power to enforce his edict, R' Shaul HaKohen Astruk persuaded the government to officially confirm Rivash's appointment as rabbi of Algiers. However, this act aroused the opposition of *Rashbatz, a member of Rivash's *beis din* and his eventual successor, who disapproved of any government intervention in rabbinical affairs.

Recognized as the leading rabbinical authority of his era, Rivash's opinion, as found in his responsa, weighs heavily in halachic decisions. From these responsa, it is evident that Rivash was also well acquainted with philosophy, even though he strongly opposed Aristotle's approach. He also opposed the study of Kabbalah.

Rivash also authored a Torah commentary, and novellae on several Talmudic tractates; some of these are cited in Shitah Mekubetzes to Kesubos. His memory was long revered by Algerian Jewry, who made annual pilgrimages to his tomb on his Yahrzeit.

R' Chisdai Crescas II

ר' חִסְדַאי (בֶּן אַבְרָהָם) קְרֶשְׂקָשׂ (הַשֵּׁנִי)

b. Barcelona, Spain, c. 1340
d. Barcelona, Spain, c. 1415

Halachist, Talmudist.

Although influential in royal circles, this grandson and namesake of *R' Chisdai Crescas I was imprisoned on false charges for a short time, together with his teacher *Ran, and his colleague *Rivash in 1367. During the massacres of 1391 he lost his only son, aged twenty, and endured other sufferings. Nevertheless, he did not leave Spain, and two years later received government permission to rebuild the communities of Barcelona and Valencia.

R' Chisdai lectured on Talmud, and corresponded with Rivash on halachic matters. He took an active part in all affairs affecting the Jewish communities of Spain, and his influence was great. It is reported that rain fell once in immediate response to his prayer (Tzror HaMor, Bechukosai).

R' Chisdai is known for his religio-philosophical work, Or Hashem (Ferrara, 1556), which defends Orthodox belief from the influence of Aristotelian philosophy, by attacking Aristotle's principles and criticizing *Rambam for his use of the Greek philosophy. Or Hashem met with opposition from such sworn adherents of Rambam's philosophy as *R' Shem Tov ibn Shem Tov, but its influence is felt in the classic Ikkarim, written by R' Chisdai's disciple, *R' Yosef Albo.

Or Hashem was to be the first part of an extensive compendium of halachic application, which was to be called Ner Hashem (or Ner Mitzvah), but the latter work was never written.

Although R' Chisdai's work did not gain much popularity, it nevertheless had a profound impact upon thinkers and it anticipated, or perhaps even influenced, subsequent patterns of thought. Previously, Aristotle had been the ultimate and perfect model for philosophical speculation. Where Rambam had disagreed with the Greek philosopher in only some basics — e.g., the Aristotelian belief in a world without beginning [olam kadmon] which negates the fundamental belief in creation ex nihilo — subsequent generations of Jewish thinkers, specifically *Ralbag, had attempted to interpret Scripture in a way agreeable to this Aristotelian tenet. True, normative Jewish thought had previously rejected these slavish attempts to conform the Torah to Aristotelianism, but only on the basis that this was contrary to tradition and to the apparent meaning of the Bible. But R' Chisdai met the philosophers on their own ground, refuting (in the first section of Or Hashem) many of the fundamentals upon which rested the edifice of Aristotelianism. In this he anticipated later philosophers who repudiated Aristotles's system in many points. He asserted that ultimate truth must rest, not on philosophical speculation, but on faith and revelation.

*R' Shimon Duran, a fervent follower of Rambam, devoted an entire treatise, Or HaChaim (not extant), to the refutations of R' Chisdai's views.

R' Chisdai wrote a refutation of Christianity in Spanish, which was translated into Hebrew by *R' Yosef ibn Shem Tov under the title Bitul Ikrei HaNotzrim.

R' Profiat Yitzchak Duran

ר' פְּרוֹפַיְיט (יִצְחָק בֶּן מֹשֶׁה הַלֵוִי) דּוּרָאן (הָאֵפוֹדִי)

Spain, late 14th-early 15th cent.
Philosopher, Polemicist, Grammarian.

In his youth, R' Profiat studied Torah in Germany and also acquired a knowledge of philosophy, grammar, and science. Later in Spain, he served as a tutor in the home of *R' Chisdai Crescas II. During the massacres of 1391 (see Historical Introduction), he was forcibly baptized. At the first opportunity, he left Spain in order to return to Judaism, and went to Provence. There he awaited the arrival of his friend David Bonet Bongoron, a victim of the same fate, with whom he hoped to journey to Eretz Yisrael. Instead, R' Profiat received a letter from David saying that after hearing the persuasions of an eminent bishop, he decided to remain a Christian. To this, Duran replied with his famous epistle, Al Tehi KeAvosecha, a satire on Christianity, so ingeniously written that at first the Christians did not recognize that its barbs were directed against them. *R' Yosef ben Shem Tov wrote a commentary on it (first ed. Constantinople, 1554).

The thrust of R' Profiat's comments is to demonstrate that the tenets of Judaism accord with and are based upon the fundamentals of rational philosophy, whereas the fundamental dogma of Christianity contradicts the basic processes of thought, forcing it to negate the intellect and demand the blind faith of its adherents.

At the request of R' Chisdai Crescas II, R' Profiat also wrote a criticism of Christian dogma titled Kelimas HaGoyim (Budapest, 1913-14; Otzar Vikuchim).

In addition, R' Profiat composed a commentary on *Rambam's Moreh Nevuchim, published in many editions of the Moreh and called Ephodi; and Maaseh Ephod, a treatise on Hebrew grammar (Vienna, 1865). He used the word ephod in the titles of his works, because it is an acronym of אני פרופייט דוראן ["I am Profiat Duran"]. His unpublished works are Cheishev HaEphod on astronomy and calendar fixing; and Zichron HaShmaddos, a historical chronicle of Jewish martyrdom since the destruction of the Second Temple, quoted by R' Yitzchak Abarbanel in Yeshuos Meshicho.

R' Yosef Chaviva

ר' יוֹסֵף חֲבִיבָא

Spain, late 14th-early 15th cent.
Halachic Commentator.

R' Yosef's commentary Nimukei Yosef on *Rif's Sefer HaHalachos, published together with that halachic code on seven tractates, quotes Talmudists of the preceding generations, including *Rosh, *Ritva, *Ran and Maggid Mishneh. According to *Chida, R' Yosef wrote on the entire Sefer HaHalachos, but his work was originally printed only where the publishers did not have Ran's commentary to Rif.

R' Moshe ibn Chaviv, author of Get Pashut, was a descendant of R' Yosef.

R' Yosef of Saragossa

ר' יוֹסֵף (בֶּן דָּוִד) מִסַּרְגּוֹסָה

b. Spain c. 1340
d. Constantine, Algeria, 1420
Torah Commentator.

A disciple of *Ran; R' Yosef served as

dayan of Saragossa jointly with his younger colleague *Rivash. Although the two were friends, Rivash disputed many of R' Yosef's lenient halachic decisions and his upholding of certain customs which Rivash maintained were contrary to halachah.

None of R' Yosef's responsa have been preserved. His Torah commentary, which was recently published (Jerusalem, 1973), is unique in that it interposes halachic analysis into the Scriptural interpretation. R' Yosef evidently left Spain, after the massacres of 1391 (see Historical Introduction), and spent the latter part of his life in North Africa. In Constantine, he was appointed dayan, and differed with the elderly R' Yitzchak Bon Astruk concerning the validity of certain types of mikvaos and Torah scrolls.

R' Shem Tov ibn Shem Tov I

ר' שֵׁם טוֹב אִבְּן שֵׁם טוֹב הָרִאשׁוֹן

d. Spain c. 1430

Kabbalist.

In Sefer HaEmunos (Ferrara, 1556), R' Shem Tov attacked the pursuit of philosophy, as being foreign to Judaism, and criticized *Rambam, *Ibn Ezra and *Ralbag for their philosophic writings. He maintained that Judaism is based on pure faith and Talmudic and kabbalistic knowledge. He argued that many of his generation were unable to withstand persecution and left their faith under threat of death because philosophy had weakened their religious convictions, whereas previous generations who had not been exposed to philosophy chose martyrdom, and sanctified G–d's Name.

R' Shem Tov also wrote kabbalistic works, some of which are in manuscript.

R' Moshe al-Askar in his responsa dedicated a long essay to the refutation of R' Shem Tov's attacks on Rambam's views.

R' Ephraim al-Nakavah (Ankavah)

ר' אֶפְרַיִם (בֶּן יִשְׂרָאֵל) אַנְקָאוָה

b. Toledo, Spain
d. Tlemcen, Algeria, 1442

Rabbi.

During the massacres of 1391 in Spain (see Historical Introduction), R' Ephraim, son of *R' Yisrael al-Nakavah, escaped to North Africa, living at first in Morocco, and later in Algiers.

Chida refers to R' Ephraim as a miracle worker, and relates that he was an excellent physician. After all other physicians had failed, he succeeded in curing the only daughter of the king of Tlemcen. Refusing the rewards of gold and silver offered by the king, R' Ephraim requested instead that the Jews in the Tlemcen vicinity be granted the right to live in the city, where they had formerly been forbidden entrance. The request was granted, and the Tlemcen Jewish community was formed. R' Ephraim erected a great synagogue there. He became known throughout North Africa as "the Rav."

To his son R' Yisrael, R' Ephraim addressed Shaar Kevod Hashem containing answers to *Ramban's criticisms of *Rambam's Moreh Nevuchim. R' Ephraim corresponded with *Rivash.

R' Shimon Duran (Rashbatz)

ר' שִׁמְעוֹן (בֶּן צֶמַח) דּוּרָאן (רשב"ץ)

b. Palma, Majorca, Spain, 1361
d. Algiers, N. Africa, 1444

Halachist, Bible exegete.

A scion of an old Provencal family, R' Shimon was a descendant of *Ramban and a relative of *Ralbag. From R' Vidal Ephraim, a disciple of *Ran, Rashbatz received not only Talmudic instruction, but also knowledge of the sciences and mathematics, and he became proficient in astronomy and philosophy. He earned his livelihood as a physician, and became the son-in-law of R' Yonah de Maistre.

During the massacres of 1391 (see Historical Introduction), Rashbatz fled with his entire family to Algiers, where he was warmly received by *Rivash, the spiritual leader of the community, himself a Spanish refugee. Upon the death of Rivash, Rashbatz was chosen as his successor, but he accepted the appointment on the condition that the government would not be asked to confirm him. In this matter, Rashbatz was consistent with his opposition to Rivash's desire to have government backing. Where Rivash felt that the rabbinate needed this prop to its authority, Rashbatz held that Judaism did not require the imprimatur of non-Jewish rulers.

Rashbatz was a prolific writer and, by his own reckoning, wrote fourteen works, some of which are collections of several smaller treatises. He continued to write almost until his death, writing his work on the laws of chametz and a commentary on the Haggadah in his eightieth year. His most famous work is the collection of his responsa Tashbatz (an acronym for Teshuvos **Sh**imon **B**en **Tz**emach) in three volumes, containing approximately 800 responsa. In these correspondences, R' Shimon discusses all facets of Judaism, from Halachah (which is the major topic) to Aggadah, philosophy and astronomy. This work sheds much light on the condition of the Jewish communities in Spain and North Africa of that time. Rashbatz disputed *Rambam's halachic decision that a rabbi is forbidden to accept a salary from his congregants. Rashbatz permitted this practice so that a rabbi would be able to devote his undivided attention to the interests of his community, and he himself accepted a salary from the community of Algiers on those grounds. He reiterates this opinion in his commentary to Avos.

Rashbatz composed commentaries to various Talmudic tractates (Rosh Hashanah, Eduyos, Kinnim, Niddah), and a commentary on *Rif's Sefer HaHalachos, tractate Berachos.

In Zohar HaRakiya, a commentary to the Azharos (*Ibn Gabirol's liturgical poem enumerating the 613 precepts), Rashbatz discusses which precepts are to be included in the 613 and follows the view of Rambam, defending him against Ramban's critique. Rashbatz composed liturgical hymns, and also wrote commentaries to ancient liturgical poems.

Rashbatz also composed Yavin Shmuah, a guide to kosher slaughter; Maamar Chametz, dealing with the laws of Passover; and Afikoman, a commentary on the Haggadah.

His Magen Avos is a philosophical discussion of the ideological fundamentals of Judaism, e.g., the nature of the Deity, prophecy, the Torah and its eternal nature, the coming of the Messiah and the resuscitation of the dead, and finally a commentary on tractate Avos. This work also refuted the claims of other regions. The censors excised the refutation from the regular editions of this book, but it was later printed separately as Keshes U'Magen.

His contributions to Bible exegesis are Ohev Mishpat, a commentary on Job, with a religious philosophical introduction, and Livyas Chen, which contains a critique of the Torah commentary by *Ralbag and of the philosophical views of *R' Chisdai Crescas II. Rashbatz also wrote a controversial treatise, Or HaChayim, against R' Chisdai Crescas II's Or Hashem. Most of Rashbatz's works were later printed.

He was succeeded by his son, *R' Shlomo (Rashbash).

R' Yosef Albo

ר' יוֹסֵף אַלְבּוֹ

b. Spain, c. 1380
d. Spain, c. 1444

Religious Philosopher.

A disciple of *R' Chisdai Crescas II, R' Yosef served as rabbi of Daroka, a suburb of Saragossa, and afterwards journeyed to Castille. In 1413, he was one of the principal Jewish participants in the religious debate held at Tortosa (see Historical Introduction), where he valiantly defended the Talmud against the attacks of the apostate Joshua Halurki.

R' Yosef was proficient in medicine, mathematics, and philosophy, and he is famous for his religio-philosophical work, Sefer HaIkkarim ["Book of Principles"], in which he discusses the principles of faith. In this work he divides religious belief into three categories: principles [ikkarim], roots [shorashim] and branches [anafim]. The "principles" are the ideas which are essential to any faith, and whose denial would negate it. They are three in number: (a) The existence of G-d; (b) A Divinely revealed code of laws and beliefs (Torah min HaShamayim); and (c) Divine reward and retribution. The "roots" are corollaries — derivative principles — based on the logical conclusions drawn from the fundamentals. Thus one who denies the corollary can be regarded as denying the fundamental serving as its basis. The roots issuing from the first fundamental are: (a) G-d's unity; (b) His incorporeality; (c) His independence of time; and (d) His perfection. The second fundamental predicates the belief in: (a) Divine omniscience; (b) prophecy; and (c) the possibility of verifying a prophet. The third fundamental leads us to conclude that G-d takes an active interest in the actions of His creations (Hashgachah). The principles and roots

are so essential to Judaism that whoever disregards them is a heretic.

R' Yosef's third category consists of what he calls "branches;" beliefs that are required, but that are of a lower order, in a sense, than the principles and roots. Those who do not accept the "branches" are sinners, but they are still classified as believers. Among these "branches" are some dogmas that *Rambam lists as principles of Judaism. A popular work, Ikkarim, was republished many times (first ed. Soncino, 1485). Two commentaries, Ohel Yaakov and Etz Shasul, were written on the book, which has been translated into Latin, German, and English.

R' Shlomo Duran (Rashbash)

ר' שְׁלֹמֹה (בֶּן שִׁמְעוֹן) דּוּרָאן (רשב"ש)

b. Algiers, Africa, c. 1400
d. Algiers, Africa, 1467

Halachist.

The son of *Rashbatz, R' Shlomo succeeded his father as rabbi of Algiers, and, like his father, wrote many responsa. His defense of the Talmud, written in 1437 to refute the attacks of the apostate Geronimo de Santa Fe, appeared under the title Milchemes Chovah Santa.

He was succeeded by his son, R' Shimon, who, together with his brother R' Tzemach, wrote the responsa Yachin U'Boaz. The Algerian rabbinate remained in the hands of the Duran family for many generations.

R' Yosef ibn Shem Tov

ר' יוֹסֵף (בֶּן שֵׁם טוֹב) אִבְּן שֵׁם טוֹב

b. Castille, Spain, c. 1400
d. Spain, c. 1460

Religious Philosopher.

The son of *R' Shem Tov ibn Shem Tov, R' Yosef did not share his father's opinion regarding the study of philosophy. In Kevod Elokim (Ferrara,

1556), he quoted extensively from Aristotle. R' Yosef maintained that philosophy could be a help to understanding the true principles of religion rather than a contradiction to it, and he lauded *Rambam's philosophical works. He did, however, point out that there is no basis to consider philosophical pursuit identical with the study of religion, as many mistake it to be, for there are major differences between the two regarding Divine prophecy and miracles. Furthermore, the true reasons for the commandments of the Torah can only be discovered through the study of Kabbalah. In his works, R' Yosef stressed that the Jew, being in possession of Divine revelation, could dispense with the study of "Greek wisdom" (i.e., philosophy and sciences); although such knowledge is helpful in perfecting someone, it is not indispensable. Its study should be delayed to age 25 or 30, in accordance with *Rashba's decree. In short, R' Yosef took a position midway between the adherents of philosophy and its opponents, not negating its study entirely, but also not elevating it.

His influence at the royal court brought R' Yosef into contact with Christian scholars, and led him into public disputations with them regarding religion. These contacts probably prompted him to write a commentary on *R' Profiat Duran's Igeres Al Tehi KeAvosecha (Constantinople, c. 1577) and Daas Elyon, both refutations of Christianity, and to translate the work of *R' Chisdai Crescas II, Bitul Ikrei

HaNotzrim, from Spanish into Hebrew.

R' Yosef composed a commentary on Lamentations, and some interpretations of Torah, which have not been published. He also wrote an unpublished commentary on *R' Yedayah HaPenini's Bechinos Olam.

In addition, he wrote a book of sermons, Ein HaKoreh; Sefeikos Belkkarim al Maaseh Yeshu HaNotzri, a critical examination of many Christian dogmas; and Hanhagas HaBayis on economics according to Aristotle's views. These and many philosophical treatises remain extant in manuscript.

According to some scholars, R' Yosef died a martyr's death. His son, R' Shem Tov ben Yosef, authored the commentary Shem Tov printed with most editions of Moreh Nevuchim.

R' Yitzchak Kanpanton

ר' יִצְחָק (בֶּן יַעֲקֹב) קַנְפַּנְטוֹן

b. Spain, 1360
d. Penafiel, Spain, 1463

Halachist and teacher.

Known as the Gaon of Castille, R' Yitzchak headed a Talmudic academy which produced many great scholars, including R' Yitzchak de Leon, R' Yitzchak Aboab II, and R' Shmuel of Valencia. After the departure of *Rivash from Spain and the death of *R' Chisdai Crescas II, R' Yitzchak remained the outstanding authority of the illustrious Spanish rabbinate which had flourished for centuries.

He wrote Darkei HaGemara, which gives rules for studying the Talmud and defines Talmudic terminology.

France and Germany

France and Germany

R' Amnon

ר' אַמְנוֹן

Mainz, Germany, c. 1000

Author of *Unesaneh Tokef*, the stirring liturgical composition for the *Mussaf* services of Rosh Hashanah and Yom Kippur.

According to tradition, the bishop of Mainz insisted that his friend and advisor, R' Amnon, convert to Christianity. In order to buy time, R' Amnon asked for three days grace to meditate on the question. Upon returning home he was distraught at having given the impression that he considered betraying his G—d.

R' Amnon spent the three days in solitude, fasting and praying to be forgiven for his sin. At the end of the allotted time, the bishop demanded an answer. R' Amnon replied that his tongue, which had sinned by saying he would consider the matter, should be cut out. Furious, the bishop ordered his hands and feet cut off, and R' Amnon was transported home.

When Rosh Hashanah arrived a few days later, R' Amnon asked to be carried to the Ark. Before the congregation recited Kedushah, R' Amnon asked to be allowed to hallow G—d's name. He recited *Unesaneh Tokef* and then died.

Three days later, R' Amnon appeared in a dream to *R' Klonimos ben Meshullam and taught him the text of the prayer, instructing him to send it to all parts of Jewry to be entered in their liturgy. R' Amnon's wish was carried out, and the prayer became an integral part of the Rosh Hashanah and Yom Kippur services.

R' Yehudah Leontin (the elder)

ר' יְהוּדָה (בֶּן מֵאִיר) הַכֹּהֵן (הַזָּקֵן) לִיאוֹנְטִין

France-Germany, c. 1000

Talmudist.

R' Leontin was one of the founders of Talmudic scholarship in France and Germany. *R' Gershom Meor HaGolah wrote of him, "My teacher of blessed memory, who instructed me in the entire Talmud ... was an outstanding sage, and his halachic decisions are not to be neglected."

R' Shimon HaGadol (the Great)

ר' שִׁמְעוֹן (בֶּן יִצְחָק) הַגָּדוֹל

b. Mainz, Germany, c. 950
d. Mainz, Germany, c. 1020

Talmudist and Paytan.

R' Shimon is best known for his liturgical compositions, *selichos* ["supplications"] and *krovos* [prayers recited during the *chazan's* repetition of the *Amidah*] (collected and published under the title *Piyutei R' Shimon ben Yitzchak*, Berlin-Jerusalem, 1938). More than a dozen of his *piyutim* have entered the Rosh Hashanah, Yom Kippur, and Festivals *machzorim*. The popular composition *Baruch Hashem, Yom Yom,* traditionally recited at the Sabbath morning meal, was composed by him.

R' Shimon is reported to have mastered the kabbalistic secrets pertaining to the prayers and to have transmitted them to his cousin and disciple *R' Eliezer HaGadol.

He served on the *beis din* of Mainz together with *R' Gershom Meor HaGolah. Because of his great wisdom and impressive appearance, R' Shimon was often sent by the community to persuade monarchs and clergymen to abolish harsh decrees proposed against the Jews, and in many cases he succeeded. In a responsum, *R' *Tam* describes him as, "R' Shimon ben Yitzchok HaGadol, with whom miracles were common."

According to a popular story, R' Shimon had two sons, Yitzchak and Elchanan. Elchanan was kidnapped by the family's trusted gentile maid, who handed him over to a monastery where he was raised in the Christian faith. His keen mind absorbed so much knowledge that he was continually raised in rank, until he eventually became pope. Some time after his election, R' Shimon journeyed to Rome in order to gain an audience with the new pope and plead with him to nullify a cruel edict against the Jews. During this visit the pope invited his guest to play a game of chess. R' Shimon, a master of chess who had never before been defeated, was stunned when the pope checkmated him. R' Shimon, who had taught chess to his sons, suspected that the pope might have acquired his chess training from him. When he questioned the pope concerning his skills, the truth surfaced, and father and son embraced.

After issuing many decrees in favor of the Jews, Elchanan disappeared with his father, and became an outstanding scholar.

Some identify R' Shimon *HaGadol* with *R' Shimon HaZaken, *Rashi's uncle.

Rabbeinu Gershom Meor HaGolah

ר' גֵּרְשׁוֹם (בֶּן יְהוּדָה) מְאוֹר הַגּוֹלָה

b. Metz, France, c. 960
d. Mainz, Germany, 1040
Talmudist, Halachist, Teacher.

Rabbeinu Gershom was a disciple of *R' Yehudah Leontin. One of the first great scholars of Ashkenazic Jewry, R' Gershom's Talmudic academy at Mainz, which attracted numerous pupils from various countries, including Provence and Spain, laid the foundation for advanced Talmudic study and halachic decision in the Ashkenazic countries. It was the most prestigious center of Talmudic learning of the day, eclipsing even the ancient Babylonian academies of Sura and Pumpedisa. Among its disciples were *Rashi's teachers, *R' Yaakov ben Yakar; *R' Yitzchak HaLevi; and *R' Yitzchak ben Yehudah, and *R' Eliezer HaGadol (the Great).

R' Gershom corrected the text of the Talmud from reliable manuscripts, thereby clarifying many obscure passages [Rashi had access to a Talmud text written in R' Gershom's hand], and composed a commentary on various tractates. *Tzeidah LaDerech* mentions that R' Gershom wrote a lengthy commentary on the entire Talmud, but it is not extant. He also wrote *Hilchos Treifos* on dietary laws, a work which is mentioned in *Tosafos,* and *Sefer Rokeach,* responsa, and is cited in the works of his students. The appellation Meor HaGolah ["The Light of the Diaspora"] appended to R' Gershom's name is indicative of the great esteem in which he was held. In a responsum, Rashi gives the following estimation of R' Gershom's greatness: 'R' Gershom, may the remembrance of the righteous and holy be for a blessing, illuminated the Diaspora and all of us "live from his mouth" (i.e., our lives are governed by his rulings); the entire diaspora in Germany ... are disciples of his disciples.'

R' Gershom's best-known contributions are the enactments adopted by rabbinic synods at his behest, and accepted as law throughout Ashkenazic

Jewry, and in some instances by the entire Diaspora. A partial list of these enactments appears at the end of *Teshuvos Maharam Lublin* (ed. Prague) and in *Kol Bo* (116). Two of these enactments have had a profound effect upon Jewish family life: His bans against polygamy, and against divorce without the wife's consent. He also prohibited the shaming of those who renounced Judaism under duress, once they had returned to the Jewish fold.

This last enactment was necessitated by the common Christian tactic of forcibly converting Jews by threatening them with death or expulsion. The Halachah requires Jews to submit to death rather than renounce their faith. Indeed, entire Jewish communities in Germany and France gave up their lives to sanctify G—d's Name, but some individuals were unable to withstand the test. R' Gershom's only son was compelled to convert to Christianity, and when he died soon after without having had the chance to return to his faith, R' Gershom observed a two week period of mourning — one week for the loss of his life, and another for the loss of his soul.

The terrible suffering of his people in those times is depicted in R' Gershom's *selichos* ["supplications"]. One of his liturgical pieces, *Z'chor Bris Avraham,* is recited during the *Ne'ilah* service of Yom Kippur.

R' Gershom had a brother *R' Machir whose works are also quoted by Rashi.

R' Yosef Tuv Elem I

ר׳ יוֹסֵף (בֶּן שְׁמוּאֵל) טוֹב עֶלֶם הָרִאשׁוֹן

d. France, c. 1040

Commentator, Halachist, Liturgist.

Although a native of Narbonne, in Provence, R' Yosef, a contemporary of *R' Gershom Meor HaGolah's disciples, became a spiritual leader in the northern French community of Limoges and the province of Anjou.

R' Yosef was an excellent and punctilious scribe and the texts of his copies of such geonic works as the *Halachos Gedolos,* or *Halachos Pesukos, Seder Tannaim VaAmoraim,* and geonic responsa are cited by the early commentators as authoritative. He also edited a collection of geonic responsa which has been identified by some scholars with the *Teshuvos Geonim Kadmonim.* His *Hilchos Tikun Shtaros* (on the laws regarding the text of legal documents) and his Torah and Talmud commentaries are mentioned in the early authorities but have not survived. Some of his responsa have been incorporated in collections of other responsa (see *Teshuvos Maharam 950-1,* ed. Prague; the caption *'Hilchos Mas'* there is a misnomer which has led some scholars to ascribe the authorship to someone else). R' Yosef was a prolific *paytan;* more than seventy compositions by him are recorded. Of special importance is his *yotzer* for Shabbos HaGadol (in the liturgy of eastern European communities); the segment of this liturgy which describes in detail the laws pertaining to the removal of chametz, baking of matzos, the Pesach Seder, and the reasons for these laws is quoted extensively by Tosafos. An extensive commentary to it was composed by the eminent Tosafist R' Shmuel of Falaise. The concluding stanza to the segment pertaining to the laws — *Chasal Siddur Pesach* — has been incorporated into the Ashkenazic version of the Hagaddah.

R' Yosef ben Shmuel Tuv Elem I should not be confused with a later scholar (early 13th century) by the same name who is mentioned in the Cremona edition of *Teshuvos Maharam,* though the latter may have been a descendant of the former. Yet another

*R' Yosef Tuv Elem (R' Yosef ben Eliezer) is the Sephardic author of the supercommentary *Ohel Yosef* (or *Zafnas Pa'aneach*) on Ibn Ezra's commentary to Torah (b. 1320).

R' Machir ben Yehudah

ר' מָכִיר בֶּן יְהוּדָה

d. Mainz, Germany, c. 1040

Talmudist, Grammarian.

R' Machir's lexicon of difficult Talmudic words and phrases, entitled *Alfa-Beisa de R' Machir,* is quoted by *Rashi in both his Bible and Talmud commentaries, but has not survived.

R' Machir was the brother of *R' Gershom Meor HaGolah. His two sons *R' Menachem and R' Nassan compiled *Maaseh HaMachiri,* a halachic work used extensively in such works as *Sefer HaPardes* and *Sefer HaOrah.*

R' Shimon HaZaken (the Elder)

ר' שִׁמְעוֹן הַזָּקֵן

Germany, c. 1050

Talmudist.

This disciple of *R' Gershom Meor HaGolah was the brother of *Rashi's mother. He is quoted in Rashi's Talmud commentary *(Shabbos* 85b), but it is doubtful whether the two scholars ever studied together. Some identify R' Shimon HaZaken (the Elder) with *R' Shimon HaGadol (the Great).

R' Yehudah HaKohen

ר' יְהוּדָה (בֶּן מֵאִיר) הַכֹּהֵן

Mainz, Germany c. 1050

Halachist.

R' Yehudah was a disciple of R' Gershom Meor HaGolah. His halachic treatise, *Sefer HaDinim,* is quoted in the works of the early codifiers.

His most noted disciple was *R' Eliezer HaGadol (the Great), who reputedly received kabbalistic as well as Talmudic instruction from R' Yehudah.

R' Eliezer HaGadol (the Great)

ר' אֱלִיעֶזֶר (בֶּן יִצְחָק) הַגָּדוֹל

b. Worms, France
d. Mainz, Germany, c. 1055

Teacher.

When R' Eliezer was orphaned as a child, he left his birthplace, Worms, and repaired to the home of his relative *R' Shimon HaGadol in Mainz, where he studied under R' Shimon, *R' Gershom Meor HaGolah and *R' Yehudah HaKohen.

Among R' Eliezer's many disciples were *R' Yitzchak ben Yehudah, a teacher of *Rashi, and *R' Meshullam ben Moshe. There is also evidence that Rashi himself studied under R' Eliezer.

R' Menachem de Lanzano ascribes the ethical code *Orchos Chaim* to R' Eliezer HaGadol; however, R' Gershon Henach Leiner of Radzin attributes the work to the Tanna R' Eliezer ben Hyrkanos.

R' Eliezer's scrupulous ethical conduct set the example for his descendant *R' Yehudah HaChassid.

R' Yaakov ben Yakar

ר' יַעֲקֹב בֶּן יָקָר

d. Worms, France, 1064

Talmudist, Teacher.

This disciple of *R' Gershom Meor HaGolah headed the Talmudic academy of Mainz, where *Rashi came to study. Whenever Rashi uses the term "my teacher," the reference is to R' Yaakov.

R' Yaakov was known for his extreme humility. Concerning an innovation introduced by *R' Yitzchak HaLevi in the Rosh Hashanah service, Rashi wrote that this did not contradict the opinion of R' Yaakov, explaining that R' Yaakov refrained from making the innovation himself only because of his extreme modesty. "I know he was the greatest of all, yet he considered himself as lowly as a doorstep which is tread upon, and he therefore did not wish to institute new enactments in order to avoid giving himself credit, authority, and too much renown" (Machzor Vitri p. 358).

R' Yitzchak HaLevi

ר' יִצְחָק הַלֵוִי

d. Worms, Germany, 1070
Talmudist, Teacher.

R' Yitzchak studied under *R' Gershom Meor HaGolah and later became the head of the Talmudic academy of Worms. Among his many students was *Rashi, who lauds his master's ability and acumen, and mentions him in his Talmud commentary, calling him Leviah ["the Levite"].

R' Yitzchak ben Yehudah

ר' יִצְחָק בֶּן יְהוּדָה

d. Mainz, Germany, 1064
Talmudist, Teacher.

R' Yitzchak left his native Lorraine, in France, to study under *R' Gershom Meor HaGolah. There is some evidence that he also knew R' Hai Gaon and received instruction from him; however, the evidence is less than conclusive. Eventually he himself became the head of the Talmudic academy of Mainz, where he taught *Rashi, who refers to him as Mori Zedek ["my righteous teacher"]. His responsa are scattered in Sefer HaPardes, and in the works of other codifiers. His commentary on tractate Bava Kamma is cited by Rashi.

R' Yitzchak's son, Yehudah, and grandson, Yitzchak, were both martyred during the Crusades of 1096.

R' Meir ben Yitzchak

ר' מֵאִיר בֶּן יִצְחָק (שְׁלִיחַ צִיבּוּר)

Germany, mid-11th cent.
Talmudist, Liturgist.

R' Meir was a great Torah scholar, often quoted by *Rashi. He is cited extensively in Siddur Rashi, Responsa of Rashi, Machzor Vitry, and Shibolei HaLeket, as well as in the Tosafos to Rosh Hashanah. It is known that he was the composer of forty-nine liturgical poems, forty in Hebrew, and nine in Aramaic, but only about fifteen of them are still known to exist. He was also the author of a book on synagogue liturgy and customs which is no longer extant.

Of his hymns which have come down to us, the most celebrated is Akdamus, an awesome exultation of the Torah, G—d, and the Jewish nation, recited on Shavuos.

Legend records that R' Meir's hymns were so beautiful and inspiring that the angels would sing them before G—d in their own name.

R' Menachem ben Machir

ר' מְנַחֵם בֶּן מָכִיר

Germany, late 11th-early 12th cent.
Halachist.

R' Menachem and his brother R' Nassan were sons of *R' Machir ben Yehudah and nephews of *R' Gershom Meor HaGolah. Together, the brothers compiled a halachic work entitled Maaseh HaMachiri.

R' Menachem corresponded with his brother and *R' Yitzchak ben Yehudah (to whom he was related) on questions of halachah, and some of this correspondence has been preserved in the collections Sefer HaOrach and Sefer HaPardes.

R' Menachem commemorated the massacres of 1096 (see Historical Introduction) in liturgical compositions of which the kinnah, Eivel A'oreir, is recited on Tishah B'Av.

He is also credited with Adam Bekum, recited on the Fast of Esther; Kehoshata Adam, recited on the Sabbath which falls during Succos; and the lengthy reshus ("permission") by which the chasan Torah ["groom of the Torah," the person called on Simchas Torah to read the final portion of the Pentateuch, as its annual synagogue reading is completed] is called to his *aliyah*.

R' Shlomo Yitzchaki (Rashi)

ר׳ שְׁלמה (בֶּן יִצְחָק) יִצְחָקִי (רשׁ״י)

b. Troyes, France, 1040
d. Troyes, France, 1105
[29 Tammuz 4865]

The Father of Commentators.

The words of the greatest commentator continue to teach his people throughout the world to this day. Rashi's father, R' Yitzchak, was a Talmudic scholar, descended from an illustrious rabbinical family tracing its ancestry back through the tanna R' Yochanan HaSandler to King David. The story is told that a diamond of fantastic value once came into R' Yitzchak's possession. The local priests sought to purchase the precious stone for use in church vestments, and offered R' Yitzchak a huge sum. Because of the purpose the gem would serve, R' Yitzchak refused to sell. Finally the priests hired a ship, enticed R' Yitzchak aboard under false pretenses, and set sail. When they were away from land, the priests demanded that R' Yitzchak sell them the jewel immediately. Instead, R' Yitzchak flung the diamond into the sea. According to another version, he pretended to give them the stone and then "lost his balance," dropping the gem into the water. A heavenly voice then decreed, "You, who sacrificed a brilliant diamond for the glory of G–d, will be blessed with a son who will illuminate the eyes of the entire Jewish people." Soon after, Rashi was born.

His mother, also of illustrious lineage, was the sister of *R' Shimon HaZaken. Rashi received his early Talmudic training in his native Troyes, which had had a thriving Jewish population with many scholars since the close of the

tenth century. After absorbing all there was to learn in Troyes, Rashi traveled to Mainz and Worms to study under the disciples of *R' Gershom Meor HaGolah, who headed academies there. *R' Yaakov ben Yakar, whom Rashi terms "my elder teacher," was his main teacher and source of inspiration, but he also studied under *R' Yitzchak HaLevi and *R' Yitzchak ben Yehudah. Even after his return to his native Troyes to be married, Rashi continued to travel abroad in quest of additional knowledge at the cost of great personal deprivation.

By the time Rashi returned to Troyes at the age of twenty-five, he was considered one of the leading Talmudists of his day. He gained the respect of all who knew him, and his teacher R' Yitzchak HaLevi wrote to him: "The generation which possesses you is not orphaned; may many like yourself multiply in Israel."

An extremely humble man, Rashi refused to accept a rabbinic position. He taught and wrote while earning his livelihood as a wine merchant.

Rashi spent almost his entire life working on his Talmud commentary. Brief, concise, and enlightening, his comments are matchless in their clarity. Without them the Talmud would have remained a closed book to the masses who would be unable to spend the necessary years absorbing the oral interpretation of the Talmud from masters. Indeed, every student knows that Talmud and Rashi are inseparable.

Until his times, a student would record his teacher's comments in his own private diary. Rashi did likewise, incorporating also the interpretations of *R' Gershom Meor HaGolah, to whose notes he had access during his stay in Mainz. Rashi synthesized these and various other notebooks into a lucid commentary that explains the Talmudic phrase by phrase, rather than summarizing and interpreting the broad themes. These notebooks eventually developed into the famous Rashi commentary, which succeeding generations simply termed *kuntres* ["notebook"]. Because of the great popularity and authority his commentary enjoyed, most of the emendations suggested by Rashi were eventually incorporated into the text itself, making other versions obsolete. From time to time, he redacted his Talmud commentary, and we possess the third edition. No other commentary has had the impact of Rashi's.

Equally famous is Rashi's Torah commentary, the fundamental tool in Bible interpretation to both the young student and the advanced scholar. Rashi's commentary gives the simple meaning of the verse as well as the aggadic interpretation of the Talmud and Midrash. Although it is the very model of conciseness and clarity, Rashi's commentary also demonstrates his encyclopedic grasp of the full range of Talmudic and Midrashic interpretation; from that massive body of wisdom, Rashi chose only what he regarded as essential to an understanding of the text. Accepted as the standard Torah commentary, it is printed together with virtually every edition. Rashi composed a similar, although less comprehensive, commentary on the Prophets and Writings.

Perhaps the greatest indication of the commentary's greatness is the fact that about 200 *seforim* have been written on it. Among the authors are such major figures as Mizrachi, Maharal, Bertinoro, *Taz, Levush,* and *Sifsei Chachamim* to name just a few. Additionally, the famed commentaries of *Ramban and *R' Bachya use Rashi's commentary as their starting point.

Although acclaimed as a commentator, Rashi was also involved in halachic

discourse and carried on a vast correspondence. His decisions were very popular among the earlier authorities, including the Tosafists, *Ravan, *Ravyah, *Mordechai, *Ittur,* *Maharam Rothenburg, *Rosh, *Manhig, Shibolei HaLeket, Or Zarua, Tashbatz,* and *Tur.* Unfortunately, however, most of the original collection was lost. Only 360 of his responsa, dealing mainly with dietary laws, holidays, marriage, and money matters are extant. Questions concerning mourning and the benedictions and prayers also appear, and occasionally even interpretations of a difficult Bible verse, and rules of grammar.

Although he always quotes the opinions of his masters with the utmost respect, Rashi does not hesitate to disagree with their views and render his independent ruling. Rashi strove to be lenient in his decisions, especially where monetary loss, albeit minor, was at stake, and he admonished authorities who chose to be stringent wherever the law was doubtful to them. Concerning customs, however, Rashi was quite strict, ruling that they should be upheld without the slightest deviation. He was stern with questioners who wondered whether certain customs need be observed meticulously.

Many statements regarding ethical behavior are found in Rashi's responsa. He stresses that the actions of a Jew should reflect higher moral standards than those of a Gentile. He expresses concern for the weak and the oppressed and a great respect for family life. He lauds peace as the loftiest goal, for it brings harmony and bliss to all.

Among the most popular works heavily influenced by Rashi's halachic opinions are *Sefer HaPardes* and *Machzor Vitri.* Another halachic work, *Sefer HaOrah,* mentioned by the early authorities was subsequently lost but has resurfaced this century and been published (Lvov, 5664). A new collection of Rashi's responsa, entitled *Teshuvos Rashi,* has also appeared (New York, 1943).

In addition to being a halachist, Rashi was also a kabbalist, as seen from his commentaries *(Sukkah* 45a).

Rashi, who had no sons, chose the best of his disciples, *R' Yehudah ben Nasan and *R' Meir ben Shmuel, as sons-in-law; his grandsons were the famous Tosafists *Rashbam and *Rabbeinu Tam*; *R' Yitzchak of Dampierre (Ri) was his great-grandson. His other disciples include *R' Simchah of Vitry, and *R' Shemayah.

Rashi's later years were marred by the excruciating suffering of the Jews during the first crusade in 1096, when many important Jewish communities were destroyed (see Historical Introduction). In memorial, Rashi composed *selichos* ["supplications"] to plead the case of his suffering people before G—d.

Rashi has remained the supreme educator of the Jewish nation to this day.

R' Shemayah

ר' שְׁמַעְיָה

France, late 11th-early 12th cent.

Talmudist.

R' Shemayah, a disciple of *Rashi, assisted his teacher in redacting his notes for the final draft of his commentary on the Bible and Talmud. As Rashi's secretary, R' Shemayah recorded his master's halachic views and replies, and many of R' Shemayah's notes concerning Rashi's customs are incorporated in *R' Simchah's *Machzor Vitry. Sefer HaOrah,* containing Rashi's legal decisions, was probably compiled by R' Shemayah's son, R' Moshe, under his father's direction. The ties between teacher and disciple were further cemented by the marriage of R'

Shemayah's daughter to Rashi's grandson, *Rashbam.

So high was Rashi's regard for his disciple's scholarship that in a responsum regarding a difficulty in Rashi's commentary to Ezekiel, the master writes that he consulted "our brother Shemayah" in working out an emendation.

In his own right, R' Shemayah composed original commentaries, cited by the Tosafists, to tractates *Berachos, Eruvin, Sukkah, Gittin, Kiddushin, Avodah Zarah,* and *Chullin.* On the tractates *Tamid* and *Middos,* there is a commentary of R' Shemayah 'written in the presence of Rashi.' R' Shemayah's comments on the Mishnaic tractates of *Zeraim* are cited by *R' Yitzchak of Simponto.

R' Simchah of Vitry

ר' שִׂמְחָה (בֶּן שְׁמוּאֵל) מִוִּיטְרִי

d. Vitry, France, 1105

Halachist.

In *Machzor Vitry* (Berlin, 1889-97), R' Simchah, an outstanding disciple of *Rashi, records many of the halachic decisions and rules which he heard either directly from Rashi or through his close colleague *R' Shemayah in their teacher's name. He also cites R' Amram Gaon, R' Hai Gaon, *R' Gershom Meor HaGolah, and *Rif.

Machzor Vitry begins with the laws of prayer and benediction followed by a discussion of the text of the daily prayers. The next section, devoted to the Sabbath liturgy, also discusses the laws governing work forbidden on the Sabbath and defines the thirty-nine categories of creative work. The laws and prayers of the various holidays follow. A special section (by a different author) is devoted to expounding tractate *Avos,* customarily recited following the Sabbath afternoon service during the summer. Halachic data concerning dietary law, family purity, *tefillin, mezuzah,* and ethics are included. Many aggadic quotes and citations from the Jerusalem Talmud cited in *Machzor Vitry* have been preserved in that work alone.

Machzor Vitry became a popular classic among the early halachic authorities, and is cited by *Mordechai, Abudraham, Hagahos Maimoniyos, Agudah, Sefer HaTerumah,* and others. In the course of time, certain additions were made to the original work, especially by R' Yitzchak ben Durbalo and *R' Avraham HaYarchi.

R' Simchah's son, R' Shmuel, married Rashi's grand-daughter Miriam (daughter of *R' Meir ben Shmuel and Rashi's daughter Yocheved), and their son was the Tosafist *R' Yitzchak of Dampierre, better known as Ri.

R' Menachem ben Chelbo

ר' מְנַחֵם בֶּן חֶלְבּוּ

France, late 11th cent.
Bible Commentator.

For a time he lived in Provence, where he studied under R' Yehudah, son of *R' Moshe HaDarshan, who had been a disciple of *R' Gershom Meor HaGolah.

In his Biblical interpretations called *Pisronim,* which earned him the appellation *HaKara* (from *Mikra* ["Scripture"]), R' Menachem stressed the plain meaning of the text above all other forms of explanation. His nephew and most ardent disciple, *R' Yosef Kara, would often quote R' Menachem's comments to *Rashi, who received them warmly, and incorporated several of them in his own commentary, especially on the Book of Ezekiel. Except for those mentioned by Rashi and R' Yosef Kara in their commentaries, few of R' Menachem's *Pisronim* have survived.

R' Menachem's commentaries to the

Scriptures have been collected as *Pisronei R' Menachem ben Chelbo* (Warsaw, 1904). This collection contains a comment on R' Elazar HaKalir's Rosh Hashanah liturgy, indicating that R' Menachem occupied himself with the elucidation of the *piyutim* as well.

R' Yosef Kara

ר' יוֹסֵף (בֶּן שִׁמְעוֹן) קָרָא

Troyes, France, late 11th-early 12th cent.
Bible Commentator.

Like his uncle and teacher, *R' Menachem ben Chelbo, R' Yosef acquired the name *Kara* (from *Mikra* ["Scripture"]) for his work in Biblical commentary. Like R' Menachem, whose comments he conveyed to *Rashi, R' Yosef considered the plain meaning to be the objective of the text, and the homiletic explanations an added attraction. Of R' Yosef's own running commentary, covering most of the Bible, some is printed together with the Scriptures in *Nach Lublin* (Lublin, 1897), and some separately.

Rashi admired and praised R' Yosef, and incorporated some of his suggestions into his commentary on the Scriptures. Some of R' Yosef's comments, originally written as glosses in the margin of Rashi, subsequently found their way into the extant version of the commentary.

R' Yehudah ben Nassan (Rivan)

ר' יְהוּדָה בֶּן נָתָן (ריב"ן)

France, late 11th-early 12th cent.
Talmudist.

A disciple and son-in-law of *Rashi, Rivan followed the method of study of the French school, whose main object was comprehensive and lucid Talmud interpretation. His own Talmud commentary, covering most tractates, is quoted by the Tosafists.

Parts of this commentary, most notably that on the last sections of tractate *Makos* [which were left without Rashi's interpretation when Rashi passed away before completing his work], has been printed in the Talmud to serve as a substitute for Rashi's commentary.

He also authored a Bible commentary which stresses the plain meaning of the text even more so than Rashi's.

Rivan's son was the Tosafist, *R' Yom Tov of Falaise. Rivan's daughter, Alvina, transmitted some of Rashi's customs, which she had been taught by her mother Miriam (Rashi's daughter) to her cousin *R' Yitzchak of Dampierre.

R' Meir ben Shmuel

ר' מֵאִיר בֶּן שְׁמוּאֵל

b. Lorraine, France, c. 1060
d. Ramerupt, France, c. 1130

Talmudist.

After studying with the sages of Lorraine, R' Meir became a disciple of *Rashi, who gave him his daughter Yocheved in marriage. After his marriage, R' Meir repaired to Worms, Germany, where he studied under *R' Yitzchak HaLevi, who had been one of Rashi's masters. Upon his return from Germany, R' Meir took up residence in Ramerupt, where he headed an academy and attracted many disciples. R' Meir is frequently quoted by the Tosafists, and his commentaries to various Talmudic tractates are cited by his son, *R' Yaakov Tam in *Sefer HaYashar,* and by Tosafos.

R' Meir was termed *Avi HaRabbanim* ["father of the rabbis"], as his three sons, *Rashbam, *Rivam, and R' Yaakov Tam, were eminent Talmudic scholars and the most prominent of the Tosafists. According to some he had a fourth son, R' Shlomo, who was a grammarian.

R' Shmuel ben Meir (Rashbam)

ר' שְׁמוּאֵל בֶּן מֵאִיר (רשב"ם)

b. Ramerupt, France, c. 1085
d. France, 1174

Talmudist, Bible Commentator.

Son of *R' Meir ben Shmuel and *Rashi's daughter, Yocheved, Rashbam studied under both his father and his illustrious grandfather. At a young age he became a recognized Torah authority. He disputed Rashi concerning Biblical interpretation and Halachah; and Rashi conceded to his arguments many times. After Rashi's demise, Rashbam left Troyes and settled in Ramerupt, where his father headed a flourishing academy. He is known to have at least visited Caen and Paris. He earned his livelihood as a merchant of wine and wool, and he owned his own vineyards and flocks of sheep.

Although a halachist in every sense of the word, where Biblical clarity is demanded, Rashbam strictly adheres to the principle that the interpretation of Torah must always be approached on more than one level. There is a responsibility to interpret a verse in its plain, literal sense whenever possible. Simultaneously, however, one must not forget that the *essence* of Torah learning — its laws and precepts — must be elicited by the various hermeneutic rules from allusions in the text. He writes that "the early ones, because of their piety, leaned toward the primary task of Talmudic interpretation which, as the Sages taught, is the most laudable pursuit. Therefore they did not accustom themselves to pursue the depth of the *literal* interpretation of Scripture." Nevertheless, he maintains, that not to be overlooked is the Rabbinic dictum, "A Scriptural text [though it is subject to *midrashic interpretation*] is never deprived of its literal meaning." Rashbam states that Rashi, his grandfather, had conceded to him that if he had the time he would have composed another commentary dealing only with the literal interpretations of the verses.

In his monumental Torah commentary, Rashbam stresses the plain meaning of the text more than any of his predecessors, and ingeniously combines the literal translation with a clear, plain explanation, avoiding any extraneous matter. In his striving for the true interpretation, he is most critical of the Biblical commentators who preceded him, accusing them of stretching the literal sense too far, and even his grandfather, Rashi, does not escape this scrutiny. Nevertheless, R' Shmuel spares no words in praising Rashi's commentary. "Whoever would set his heart to the word of our Creator should not stir from the explanations of my grandfather, R' Shlomo, for almost all the Halachos and interpretations found in them are based upon the literal meaning of the verses."

There is evidence that Rashbam wrote interpretations of all the books of the the Bible, but only his commentary on the Pentateuch has been preserved in its entirety.

Several of Rashbam's Talmud commentaries have also been preserved, and his commentary to tractate Bava Basra and the last chapter of Pesachim have been incorporated into the standard Talmud edition.

Rashbam's Talmud commentary is lengthier than that of Rashi and that of his uncle, *Rivan. He uses concise analysis, quotes earlier commentators, and redacts the text of the Talmud itself. His deletion of entire phrases was frowned upon by his colleagues, especially his brother, *Rabbeinu Tam.

Rashbam appears to be the first French scholar to make extensive use of *Rif's halachic code. He incorporated many of his own comments in Sefer HaHalachos, adding much material from the French and German schools.

He was renowned for his extreme piety, intense search for the truth, and great love of peace.

R' Yitzchak ben Meir (Rivam)

ר' יִצְחָק בֶּן מֵאִיר (רִיבַ"ם)

b. Ramerupt, France, c. 1090
d. France, c. 1130

Tosafist.

The brother of *Rashbam and *Rabbeinu Tam, he died during the lifetime of his father, *R' Meir ben Shmuel, and left seven orphans. His widow later married his cousin, R' Yehudah ben Yom Tov, grandson of *Rivan.

Rabbeinu Tam described his brother as a keen scholar able to analyze the most difficult topic with utmost clarity. His novellae are quoted often in Tosafos.

R' Yaakov ben Meir (Rabbeinu Tam)

ר' יַעֲקֹב בֶּן מֵאִיר (רַבֵּינוּ תָּם)

b. Ramerupt, France, 1100
d. Troyes, France, 1171
[4 Tammuz 4931]

Tosafist, Halachist, Teacher.

The most famous of *R' Meir ben Shmuel's sons was Rabbeinu Yaakov Tam, so called after the verse, but Yaakov was a tam ["wholesome man"] abiding in tents [of Torah] (Genesis 25:27).

As a wine merchant and financier he became quite wealthy and employed a large staff of Jewish and non-Jewish servants. His business loans brought him into contact with the nobility but did not allow him sufficient time to reply to halachic inquiries at great length, as he reported in his responsa.

Rabbeinu Tam studied under his father, *R' Meir ben Shmuel, and his older brother, *Rashbam, and was acclaimed as a prodigy. Scholars of renown flocked to his academy in Ramerupt, where he delivered his Talmudic discourses with lengthy elaborations, dissecting the topic and clarifying all its implications and applications. He compared the various Talmudic discussions on one subject in order to uncover the basic principles they share, as well as the differences between them. These lectures served as the basis for the famous running Talmud commentary called *Tosafos,* meaning *additions* to the basic commentary (i.e., *Rashi*) on the Talmud, which include critical examination of Rashi's interpretation as well as comparisons to parallel texts and the resolution of contradictory passages. At one time, Rabbeinu Tam's academy had an enrollment of eighty of the most prominent Tosafists, including *R' Chaim Cohen, *R' Eliezer of Metz, and *R' Shimshon of Sens (Shantz).

Considered the greatest Talmudist of his generation, Rabbeinu Tam was referred to as *the light of the world.* In the words of *Rivash, "No one excelled in such intricate Talmudic analysis since the days of the Amoraim." Rabbeinu Tam's methods of acquiring new insights in Talmudic learning was universally accepted by the Ashkenazic Tosafist school for centuries.

As the leading halachist of his day, Rabbeinu Tam was called upon to decide most halachic problems of Ashkenazic Jewry. Some of his responsa were collected in *Sefer HaYashar* (Vienna, 1811), Rabbeinu Tam's original work on Talmudic topics. Its style is similar to that of the *Tosafos* in its penetrating analysis of texts; comparisons of variations in superficially parallel passages, and the elucidation of the subtle differences that were alluded to in the differing texts; and in seeking the logical underpinnings of Talmudic

dicta. Rabbeinu Tam was dedicated to explaining and preserving the transmitted versions of the Talmudic text and he devoted himself to justifying apparently difficult textual readings. In this he differed from his brother, Rashbam, who often emended texts as a means of resolving difficulties, a policy that Rabbeinu Tam criticized strongly.

In halachah, Rabbeinu Tam was an original thinker with a strong personality, and a leader keenly aware of the state of affairs of his era. He was known for his strong advocacy of his views, not wavering from his sometimes controversial lenient opinions where a stringent ruling would cause great financial hardship; although on occasion he would rule with the commonly held opinion even if it contradicted what he held in theory. He towered as the giant of his age in all aspects of Torah and in all matters governing communal life.

Rabbeinu Tam was well acquainted with the rules of Hebrew grammar and usage and authored a treatise titled *Hachra'os* in which he defends the famed grammarian *R' Menachem ben Saruk, against the attacks of *R' Donash ben Lavrat. In some isolated cases, though, he subscribes to the latter's view, and in some instances, discards both opinions and offers his own observation.

Rabbeinu Tam composed many liturgical hymns in the spirit of his Ashkenazic predecessors, but on occasion he attempted to emulate the Sefardic method, scrupulously adhering to certain rhythm. He approved of introducing *piyutim* ["hymns"] into the liturgy and did not view them as an interruption of the service.

Rabbeinu Tam did not escape the turmoil of the era. During *Shavuos* of 1146, Crusaders entered Ramerupt, and pillaged his home, took all of his possessions, desecrated a Torah scroll, and inflicted five knife wounds in his head. Miraculously, a nobleman who recognized the sage saved him by promising the angry mob that he would convert the rabbi to Christianity. On 20 Sivan 1171, a blood libel in Blois led to the burning of the city's entire congregation and Rabbeinu Tam decreed this day as a public fast day for all generations.

Rabbeinu Tam corresponded with *R' Avraham ibn Ezra, whom he greatly admired and respected, and received most cordially when the latter visited France.

R' Yitzchak ben Asher (Riva)

ר' יִצְחָק בֶּן אָשֵׁר (רִיב"א)

d. Speyer, Germany, c. 1130
Tosafist, Teacher.

In his youth, Riva studied under *R' Yitzchak ben Yehudah in Mainz, and thereafter became a pupil of *Rashi. After spending a few years as a merchant, which sometimes involved business trips as far as Russia, he repaired to Speyer, where he gathered many disciples who later became the leaders of German Jewry.

His Tosafos, the earliest known, are quoted by later Tosafists, and by such halachic authorities as *Or Zarua*, *Ravan, and *Shibolei HaLeket*. *Rabbeinu Tam, in *Sefer HaYashar*, however, warns that the Tosafos ascribed to Riva were not actually written by him, but by his disciples, and are not always accurate. His Tosafos on tractate *Sanhedrin* have recently been published (Jerusalem, 1974).

R' Eliyahu of Paris

ר' אֵלִיָּהוּ (בֶּן יְהוּדָה) מִפָּארִיש

Paris, France, c. 1150
Tosafist, Halachist.

R' Eliyahu's decisions are recorded in Tosafos and practically all of the early codes. He disagreed with his contem-

porary, *Rabbeinu Tam, concerning *tefillin,* maintaining that the knot of the hand *tefillin* was to be undone and retied each day.

R' Eliyahu also composed liturgical hymns, of which only two — *Ometz Yom HaBikurim* and *Berov Am Azuzecha* for Shavuos — are known.

R' Eliezer ben Nassan (Ravan)

ר' אֱלִיעֶזֶר בֶּן נָתָן (רַאב"ן)

b. Mainz, Germany, c. 1090
d. Germany, c. 1170
Tosafist, Halachist.

Also known as R' Eliezer HaZaken ["the elder"], Ravan studied under *Riva and maintained an active correspondence with the French school, including *Rashbam and *Rabbeinu Tam, who regarded him highly. Ravan was a prominent figure in the conclave of 150 rabbis held in Troyes in 1150 (see Historical Introduction) where several important enactments were issued, such as the excommunication of those who took their legal disputes before a non-Jewish tribunal, and the prohibition of attaining a rabbinical position through intercession of the government. Ravan was one of the signers of these enactments.

His halachic decisions were eagerly sought, and he recorded his halachic analysis in *Even HaEzer* (Prague, 1610) which is also known as *Tzafnas Paaneach*. Generally he was inclined to strict views. He preferred to interpret the words of his predecessors rather than to raise new arguments in disagreement with their view. The work contains personal experiences as well as important data on customs followed in many Jewish communities. *Even HaEzer* is divided into three parts: responsa; halachic analysis of the topics in tractates *Berachos, Chullin, Avodah Zarah,* and *Niddah;* and similar analyses of other halachic sections of the Talmud.

[The word Even (אֶבֶן) in the title of this work forms the initials of his name, אֱלִיעֶזֶר בֶּן נָתָן.

He also wrote Even HaRoshah, mentioned by Chida to be a compendium of its author's halachic decisions; a commentary to Tractate Avos, mentioned in Minchah Chadashah; and Kovetz Minhagim, a compilation of customs mentioned in Sefer Rokeach. His commentaries to the prayers are mentioned in Teshuvos Beis Ephraim, whose author had it in manuscript. Only fragments of it were printed (Ostrog, 1817; Slavita, 1823).

Ravan composed liturgical hymns some of which have found their way into the various machzorim. He also authored a descriptive history (Leipzig, 1854) of the terrible persecutions suffered by the Jewish communities along the Rhine during the first crusade in 1096 (see Historical Introduction).

The four daughters of Ravan married prominent scholars — *R' Shmuel ben Natronai, R' Yoel HaLevi, father of *Ravyah, R' Uri, and R' Eliakim ben Yosef, grandfather of *Rosh.

R' Shmuel HaChassid

ר' שְׁמוּאֵל (בֶּן קְלוֹנִימוֹס) הֶחָסִיד

b. Speyer, Germany, c. 1120
d. Speyer, Germany, c. 1175
Kabbalist, Talmudist.

R' Abun the Great, one of the earliest known scholars in Germany (see Historical Introduction), was an eminent kabbalist. Secret interpretations of the liturgy were handed down in his family from father to son. Before R' Klonimos, a descendant of R' Abun, died in 1126, he entrusted his young son Shmuel to the care of R' Eliezer ben Meshullam Chazan, to whom he also entrusted the manuscripts containing the mystical instruction he had received from his ancestors and which were to be given to

R' Shmuel when he came of age.

R' Shmuel absorbed the esoteric knowledge, and became a pillar of righteousness who dedicated his life wholly to God's service. He was the forerunner of a German movement which stressed ethical, pious behavior and Divine service according to the secrets of the Kabbalah and thereby acquired the appellation HaChassid ["the pious one"]. This school, whose followers were known as Chassidei Ashkenaz ["the pious ones of Ashkenaz"], stressed strong and simple faith, which sustained the Jews of Germany in all their horrible ordeals (see Historical Introduction).

Additionally, R' Shmuel was sometimes called HaNavi ["the prophet"] and owing to his asceticism, HaKadosh ["the holy one"].

R' Shmuel was also a Talmudist and is sometimes cited in Tosafos. His commentary on tractate Tamid is mentioned in the commentary to that tractate attributed to Ravad. He also wrote Sefer Shakod, a kabbalistic treatise of which fragments remain; a commentary on Mechilta and Sifra, and interpretations derived by the method of gematria [numerical value of letters]. Some also attribute to his authorship Shir HaYichud, and Kihoshata Av Hamon, a hymn of the Hoshana liturgy, recited on the Sabbath of Succos in Ashkenazic commmunities.

R' Avraham of Speyer, a halachist mentioned with great reverence by *Ravan, and *R' Yehudah HaChassid were his sons.

R' Meshullam of Melun

ר' מְשׁוּלָם (בֶּן נָתָן) מִמֶּלוּן

b. Narbonne, Provence, c. 1120
d. Melun, France, c. 1180
Tosafist, Halachist.

In Provence, R' Meshullam was a

member of the *beis din* of *Ravad II. In about 1150, R' Meshullam settled at Melun in Northern France, where he attained considerable recognition for his great erudition. However, *Rabbeinu Tam sharply opposed many of R' Meshullam's decisions, which he regarded as innovations, and a polemic correspondence ensued between the two scholars. From the fragments of this correspondence that have been preserved, it seems that R' Meshullam, not being of the northern French school, disregarded many customs observed in this vicinity. Rabbeinu Tam who traced many of these traditions directly back to the Geonim, forbade any deviation from their strict observance.

R' Eliezer of Metz

ר' אֱלִיעֶזֶר (בֶּן שְׁמוּאֵל) מִמֵּיץ

Metz, France, c. 1175

Tosafist.

Since his residence in Metz, France, was situated near the German border, R' Eliezer served as an intermediary between the German and French scholars, conveying the interpretations and decisions of his teacher, *Rabbeinu Tam of France, to the German region. Among his disciples were the important German scholars, *Ravyah and *R' Elazar Rokeach of Worms.

Sefer Yereim (Vilna, 1892) is R' Eliezer's halachic compendium, arranged according to the 613 commandments, and containing some dissertations on ethics as well. The work gained immediate popularity and, already in 1179, was frequently quoted in *Ittur*. *R' Binyamin HaRofei's abridgment of *Sefer Yereim* was first printed at Venice (1565) and reprinted thereafter many times before the work, in its original form, was printed with the commentary *Toafos Re'eim* by R' Avraham Schiff (Vilna, 1892).

R' Eliezer's *Tosafos* to several tractates are cited by various halachists but have not come down to us.

He had no sons, and his personal life was marred by the loss of his daughters.

R' Pesachyah of Regensburg

ר' פְּתַחְיָה (בֶּן יַעֲקֹב) מֵרֶגֶינְשְׁבּוּרג

b. Prague, Bohemia (Czechoslovakia), c. 1120
d. Regensburg, Germany, c. 1190

Traveler.

The brother of *R' Yitzchak HaLavan, R' Pesachyah traveled extensively throughout Poland, Russia, Armenia, Persia, Babylon, and Syria. Reaching Eretz Yisrael at last, he toured the land extensively in order to view all the holy places. A description of these travels (which took place in the period between 1170 and 1185), including the customs prevalent among the Jewish communities that he visited, was recorded as *Sivuv* ["Journey of"] *R' Pesachyah* (Prague, 1595).

R' Ephraim of Bonn

ר' אֶפְרַיִם (בֶּן יַעֲקֹב) מִבּוֹנָא

b. Bonn, Germany, 1133
d. Germany, c. 1198

Talmudist, Paytan.

R' Ephraim served as chief judge of the *beis din* of Bonn, while *Ravyah was an associate member. In *Sefer Zechirah* he gives a detailed account of the persecutions of the Jews in Germany, France, and England between 1146 and 1196. Much of this chronicle is eyewitness testimony, as he himself saw most of these events and narrowly escaped several massacres. His liturgical compositions lament the suffering of the Jews at that time and express hope for a speedy redemption.

R' Yosef HaMekane Official

ר' יוֹסֵף (בֶּן נָתָן) הַמְקַנֵּא אוֹפִצִיאַל

Sens, France, early 13th century

Author of *Teshuvos HaMinim*, a

rebuttal of Christianic interpretations of Scripture.

R' Yosef succeeded his father R' Nassan to a high position at the palace of the bishop of Sens. This post, from which R' Nassan and his sons received the surname Official, gave R' Yosef occasion to dispute with the Christian members of the court, who tried to prove from Scripture that their religion was the true one. He successfully refuted all their arguments, and collected his rebuttals in *Teshuvos HaMinim*, also known as *Yosef HaMekane*, of which only one part was published. The book is said to have influenced *R' Yom Tov Lipman Milhausen in his *Sefer HaNitzachon*.

R' Yehudah ben Klonimos (Ribak)

ר' יְהוּדָה בֶּן קְלוֹנִימוֹס (בֶּן מֵאִיר) (ריב"ק)

d. Speyer, Germany, c. 1200

Tosafist.

*R' Yehudah's unique treatise *Yichusei Tannaim V'Amoraim* lists the Talmudic sages in alphabetical order and gives historical data, scholarly analysis, and interpretations of numerous statements of each scholar. Unfortunately only a small part of this enormous work has been preserved and published (Lyck, 1874; Jerusalem, 1963). He also composed *Agron*, which seems to have been a Talmudic dictionary; a treatise on the laws of benedictions, cited in *Sefer Rokeach;* and *Tosafos* to tractates *Beitzah* and *Sotah.*

Ribak's cousins, R' Avraham of Speyer and *R' Yehudah HaChassid, sons of *R' Shmuel HaChassid, were also his teachers, and *R' Elazar Rokeach was his disciple.

R' Yaakov of Marvege

ר'. יַעֲקֹב (הַלֵּוִי) מִמַּרְוִיש

Marvege, France, c. 1200

Halachist.

R' Yaakov's halachic work *Shaalos U'Teshuvos Min HaShamayim* ["Questions and Answers from Heaven"] (Tel Aviv, 1957) contains answers to questions he addressed to the Heavenly Court through a kabbalistic *sh'eilas chalom* ["inquiry through dreams"]. The work is cited by halachists, such as *Shibbolei HaLeket* and Radvaz as authoritative.

R' Yitzchak of Dampierre (Ri)

ר' יִצְחָק (בֶּן שְׁמוּאֵל) מִדַּנְפִּיר (ר"י)

b. Ramerupt, France, c. 1120
d. Dampierre, France, c. 1200

Tosafist.

Ri's paternal grandfather was *R' Simchah of Vitry; his maternal grandfather was *Rashi's son-in-law *R' Meir ben Shmuel; and he was a nephew and a disciple of both *Rashbam and *Rabbeinu Tam.

Among all the Tosafists, only the name of Rabbeinu Tam appears more often then does Ri's in our edition of *Tosafos*. After Rabbeinu Tam moved to Troyes, Ri directed the Talmudic academy at Ramerupt and later settled at Dampierre, where he founded a flourishing yeshivah. *R' Menachem ben Zerach tells us that Ri had sixty erudite pupils, each of whom knew an entire tractate by heart, so that during the lectures virtually the entire Talmudic literature on each subject could be scrutinized intensely. Under Ri's tenure, the Tosafist method of Talmudical analysis reached its fullest expression. His name is mentioned on most pages of the *Tosafos,* and even many of the insights given anonymously are attributed to him in other sources. Among those who attended Ri's academy were *R' Shimshon of Sens, the famous redactor of *Tosafos,* who recorded his mentor's views and made them the nucleus of his writings, R' Baruch ben Yitzchak, *R' Yehudah of Paris, Ri's own son *R' Elchanan, and *R' Yitzchak ben Avraham (to distinguish between Ri and his pupil R' Yitzchak, the teacher was referred to as R' Yitzchak, or Ri HaZaken ["the elder"], while the latter was called R' Yitzchak HaBachur ["the younger"]).

In spite of his great stature as a Talmudic scholar, Ri, out of reverence and awe for the erudition of his uncle and mentor *Rabbeinu Tam, would usually follow the latter's halachic decisions completely, even if he was of another opinion. Some of Ri's responsa appear in the works of the codifiers. His decisions are extensively quoted in both Or Zarua and Hagahos Maimonios, by *Maharam Rothenburg in his responsa, and by *Mordechai. *Rosh cites a commentary on *Ri's Sefer HaHalachos. A kabbalist, Ri prayed at great length, and lived an ascetic life, constantly fasting, and even observing Yom Kippur for two days. Ri's disciples often style their master as HaKadosh, ["the saint"]. R' Elchanan Yitzchak ben Yakar in his commentary to Sefer Yetzirah reports that he received instruction in this esoteric work from a scholar "who learned it from our teacher R' Yitzchak HaZaken."

Ri is reputed to have composed Biblical commentaries entitled Yalkut Midrash, cited in Minchas Yehudah.

R' Yitzchak ben Avraham (Ritzba)

ר' יִצְחָק בֶּן אַבְרָהָם (רִיצְבָּ"א)

d. Dampierre, France c. 1210

Tosafist.

Ritzba was a grandson of R' Shimshon HaZaken of Falaise. A pupil of *Rabbeinu Tam in his early years, he later studied under *Ri in Dampierre, and eventually succeeded him. Among his pupils was *R' Nassan ben Meir of Trinquetaille, one of the teachers of *Ramban, *R' Yehudah ben Yakar, and probably *R' Shmuel ben Shneur of Evreux. *R' Shimshon of Sens was

Ritzba's younger brother.

Ritzba composed Tosafos, and is mentioned in our editions. His Yesod Leil Pesach, a guide to the rituals of the Seder, and his comments on the Hagadah is quoted by later authors. R' Yitzchak was skilled in rendering practical decisions on difficult matters, as indicated by the great number of responsa quoted by contemporary and later authors. His opinion was sought by scholars who resided far from France: *R' Meir HaLevi Abulafia of Toledo; *R' Yehonasan of Lunel; and *R' Yitzchak of Vienna. Ritzba's aquaintance with *Rambam's code was probably a result of his correspondence with these scholars. R' Yehonasan was a fervid admirer of Rambam and corresponded extensively with him. The questions R' Meir HaLevi addressed to Ritzba were directly concerned with views expressed in Rambam's code. Ritzba is known to have been prompt in answering religious questions even when it was difficult for him to do so because of poor health.

Ritzba is sometimes referred to as R' Yitzchak HaBachur, ["the younger"] to distinguish him from his teacher *R' Yitzchak of Dampierre.

R' Yehudah HaChassid

ר' יְהוּדָה (בֶּן שְׁמוּאֵל) הֶחָסִיד

b. Speyer, Germany, c. 1150
d. Regensburg, Germany, 1217
[13 Adar 4977]

Ethician, Tosafist.

*R' Shmuel HaChassid transmitted to his son, R' Yehudah, the vast kabbalistic knowledge inherited from his forefathers. Like his father, R' Yehudah was an extremely pious man of solid faith, who laid great emphasis on the underlying mystical intent of the prayers and strict adherence to custom. It was his custom to fast nearly every day, eating only at night. He was known to fast even on the Sabbath, for, after having fasted the entire week, the change of practice would have caused him suffering, and therefore his Sabbath enjoyment was fasting rather than eating.

His popular *Sefer Chassidim* (Bologna, 1538) is one of the most colorful works to come down to us from this age. It covers the entire scope of Jewish life. Here, alongside the most lofty ethical instruction, inspiration to the worship of God through prayer, thoughts on the themes of reward and punishment, and sin and penitence, one also finds detailed practical guidance on halachic questions pertaining to the laws of the Sabbath, eating and other matters. R' Yehudah's method of teaching ethics, by citing specific examples from life experiences rather than by formulating abstract principles, endeared this classic work to scholar and layman alike throughout the ages. Interspersed throughout this sefer and his so called "testament" (appended to most editions of *Sefer Chassidim*) are instructions based on Kabbalah rather than Halachah. These have, out of great reverence for the author's erudition and saintliness, been widely accepted in the Jewish community, and have been endorsed by many later halachic greats. An example of this is the widely held custom to refrain from marrying a woman with the same name as one's mother.

The kabbalistic works of R' Yehudah HaChassid, known either from the quotations of other authors or from manuscripts, are *Sefer Gematrios, Taamei HaMitzvos, Sod HaYichud, Sod Aleinu, Shem Ayin-Beis, Sefer HaOrach* and *Sefer HaKavod*. A commentary to *Sefer Yetzirah* has been attributed to R' Yehudah HaChassid; as well as *Gan Bosem*, a halachic compendium, and *Sefer HaChochmah* on the laws of writing Torah scrolls and *tefillin*. R' Yehudah also wrote liturgical poetry; the famous composition *Shir HaKavod*, also called *An'im Zemiros*, which closes the Sabbath morning service, is attributed to him.

Among his many disciples in Regensburg were *R' Elazar Rokeach; *R' Yitzchak, author of *Or Zarua;* and *R' Yehudah ben Klonimos. He is mentioned in *Tosafos*, and his influence was very great, both in his time and in succeeding generations. Jews and Gentiles alike esteemed him as a holy man who performed miracles. Christian officials, such as the Duke of Regensburg, sought his counsel.

On *Shabbos Zachor* of 4977, R' Yehudah took ill, and passed away four days later on the Fast of Esther.

R' Eliezer ben R' Yoel HaLevi (Ravyah)

ר' אֱלִיעֶזֶר בֶּן ר' יוֹאֵל הַלֵּוִי (ראבי"ה)

b. Mainz, Germany, c. 1140
d. probably Wurzburg, Germany, c. 1225
Tosafist, Halachist, Liturgist.

As a child R' Eliezer studied under his great-grandfather R' Eliakim ben Yosef. Later he studied under his grandfather *Ravan, his father R' Yoel HaLevi, *R' Yehudah HaChassid, R' Yitzchak ben Asher II, *R' Yehudah ben Klonimos, and *R' Eliezer of Metz. These studies took him through most of Germany and France.

Not wanting to use his Talmudic training as a means of livelihood, he refused to accept a rabbinical position, and, being from a wealthy family, he was able to spend much of his time studying, teaching, and corresponding with the great authorities of the day. However, when his father passed away in 1200, R' Eliezer consented to succeed him as rabbi of Cologne, where he also directed a Talmudic academy. Among his disciples were *R' Yitzchak of

Vienna, and *R' Avraham ben Azriel.

Inquiries were sent to Ravyah from near and far, and part of the accumulated responsa is recorded in his own writings and in that of his disciple, Or Zarua. Ravyah's extensive halachic compendium, Avi HaEzri, although cited often by such early authors as *Rosh, *Mordechai, and *R' Yaakov Baal HaTurim, was subsequently lost and became unknown to scholars. In recent times, manuscript editions have come to light and most of it has been published in installments (Cracow, 1882; Berlin, 1913, 1926; Jerusalem, 1935, 1965, 1976). This work contains essays and responsa on diverse Talmudic topics in the method of the Tosafists, arranged according to the tractates of the Talmud (specifically Berachos, Seder Moed, Chullin and some miscellaneous halachos), but restricted to matters pertaining to practical halachah. No doubt this work served as a model for later similar codes (e.g., Or Zarua, Rosh, Mordechai) whose authors made liberal use of Ravyah's opus. Another sefer, Aviassaf, similar to Avi HaEzri in style, on the Talmudic Sedarim Nashim and Nezikin, is mentioned by R' Eliezer himself and cited by later authors. Ch da reports that he saw it in manuscript, but no extant text is known. Ravyah's impact upon the halachah, as evidenced by the many times he is cited by other scholars, especially Tur, was profound. His Tosafos to several tractates are referred to (and sometimes reproduced) in Avi HaEzri and in writings of other authors. Many of his homiletic comments to the Chumash are scattered through the various codices containing the thoughts of the Tosafists (Minchas Yehudah, Da'as Zekeinim, Moshav Zekeinim, etc.). The titles Avi HaEzer and Aviassaf allude to Ravyah's name (the initial letters of Eliezer ben Yoel form the acronym אבי, Avi). He was sometimes referred to as R'

Avi HaEzri and as R' Aviassaf.

A revealing episode from R' Eliezer's life is told by *R' Meir of Rothenburg, a disciple of Ravyah's disciple. During his sojourn at Cologne, the position of chazzan ["cantor"] became available. Probably out of desire to earn his livelihood from a source other than the rabbinate, Ravyah applied for the position. A well meaning but poorly informed Jew, intending to honor the eminent scholar, arranged that the local bishop formally invest R' Eliezer in his new post. The bishop called for Ravyah, removed his own mitre and placed it on the rabbi's head saying, "Here you have the post of chazzan."

Furious at this development, R' Eliezer retorted, "My lord, it is not fitting that I receive from you the worship of our Creator!" Because he felt that being installed by the bishop would imply that Christianity was superior to Judaism, Ravyah refused the position he had previously agreed to accept.

Some of R' Eliezer's liturgical compositions have survived, including a lamentation over the First Crusade in 1096.

R' Yehudah of Paris (Sir Leon)
ר' יְהוּדָה (בֶּן יִצְחָק) מִפַּארִיש (שִׁיר לֵיאון)

b. Paris, France, 1166
d. Paris, France, 1224

Teacher, Tosafist.

After the departure of *R' Shimshon of Sens for the Holy Land, R' Yehudah's academy in Paris became the center of the Tosafist movement. R' Yehudah was a direct descendant of *R' Yehudah ben Nassan, Rashi's son-in-law, and a disciple of his uncle, *Ri (his paternal aunt married Ri). His own pupils included *R' Yechiel of Paris, *R' Yitzchak ben Moshe*, and *R' Moshe of Coucy.

R' Yehudah composed Tosafos based

on the lectures and manuscripts of earlier masters. In his *Tosafos* to *Berachos* (Warsaw, 1863), he makes extensive use of the Jerusalem Talmud, and mentions his *Tosafos* on twelve other tractates, which were still extant two centuries later. Some of his responsa appear in the codices of his disciples, *Or Zarua* and *Semag*.

R' Shimshon of Sens (Rash)

ר' שִׁמְשׁוֹן (בֶּן אַבְרָהָם) מִשַׁאנְץ (ר"ש)

b. France, c. 1150
d. Eretz Yisrael, c. 1230

Teacher, Tosafist, Halachist.

R' Shimshon was a grandson of R' Shimshon HaZaken of Falaise.

Like his older brother, *Ritzba, R' Shimshon [sometimes called Rashba, but not to be confused with *R' Shlomo ibn Aderes who was also called by the acronym Rashba] studied in his early youth under *Rabbeinu Tam, but his principal teacher was *Ri.

R' Shimshon established his academy in the French city of Sens, which was already a Torah center. He disseminated the teachings of his master, Ri, with elaboration and emendation, making extensive use of the Jerusalem Talmud. His lectures were later recorded and came to be known as *Tosefos Shantz* (Sens), and they have come down to us on many Talmudic tractates. *Rosh considered R' Shimshon one of the most eminent of the Tosafists, and classified him as the most important figure in the development of *Tosafos* after *Rabbeinu Tam and *Ri. Our editions of *Tosafos* are basically those of R' Shimshon, edited and shortened by later Tosafists, with additional comments from Tosafists of later generations.

All Talmudic editions of the orders *Zeraim* and *Taharos,* upon which no Babylonian Talmud exists, incorporate R' Shimshon's comprehensive Mishnah commentary [usually called Rash]. As in *Rashi's commentary, each phrase is individually interpreted, but R' Shimshon utilizes the Tosafist manner of analysis to explain details at great length. A facet unique to R' Shimshon's commentaries is his extensive use of the Jerusalem Talmud and Tosefta. A commentary to Sifra, the halachic Midrash on Leviticus (Warsaw 1866), is attributed to R' Shimshon but serious doubts have been cast upon this by scholars. He was frequently consulted on questions of Jewish law, and some of these responsa were preserved in the works of the codifiers. In many instances these were in opposition to the views of *Rambam.

R' Shimshon played a pivotal role in the controversy concerning Rambam's code. *R' Meir HaLevi Abulafia took exception to Rambam's statement (*Hilchos Teshuvah* 8:2): "In the World to Come there is no body or corporeality; there is but the disembodied souls of the righteous similar to the ministering angels ..." Ramah maintained that this view contradicted the opinion of the Talmudic sages and Jewish tradition. He hastened to point out numerous other passages in the code which could not be reconciled with the Talmud. When R' Aharon ben Meshullam, one of the outstanding scholars of Lunel (Provence), refuted R' Meir's arguments, admonishing him for his intemperate language, Ramah turned to the sages of northern France, among them R' Shimshon, to render their opinion on this matter. Although he agreed with Ramah in most of his objections, and pointed out additional difficult passages in the code, he did not hide his admiration for Rambam, who had previously been unknown to him; and said, "Those [of my disciples who possess parts of the code and are] able to read the handwriting [it seems that the script in which the code was written was unfamiliar to most French scholars] read before me ... and I understood from the topics discussed that ... he discerned wonders in G−d's Torah ..."

R' Shimshon also reports, "I have heard that the gates of wisdom have been revealed to him." However, he counseled against intensive study of the code because Rambam did not name his sources. Concerning the matter of corporeality in the World to Come, Rash asserts that in general we must take the words of the Sages literally, and adduces proof to this tenet from the Talmud. Rambam's son, *R' Avraham, heard that R' Shimshon disagreed with his father (presumably on matters basic to Judaism, e.g., G−d's incorporeality) but refused to credit the report.

Due to hostilities against the Jews in France and England (see Historical Introduction), R' Shimshon, together with three hundred scholars from those lands and their families, emigrated to the Holy Land in 1211. This pilgrimage gained R' Shimshon the title *Ish Yerushalayim* ["the Jerusalemite"]. He lies buried in Acre, at the foot of Mount Carmel. Among his disciples were R' Moshe ben Shneur and his brother, R' Shmuel of Evreux.

R' Elazar Rokeach of Worms
ר' אֶלְעָזָר (בֶּן יְהוּדָה) רֹקֵחַ מִגֶּרְמַיְיזָא

b. Mainz, Germany, c. 1160
d. Worms, Germany, c. 1238
Halachist, Kabbalist.

A descendant of the distinguished Klonimos line (see Historical Introduction), R' Elazar studied under his father R' Yehudah ben Klonimos of Mainz, *R' Yehudah ben Klonimos of Speyer, *R' Moshe ben Shlomo, and *R' Eliezer of Metz.

R' Elazar is best known for *Sefer HaRokeach* (Fano, 1505), a guide to ethics and Halachah, with an introduction entitled *Hilchos Chassidim*. The title

HaRokeach ["the Perfumer"] alludes to its author's name, since the numerical value of the word *Rokeach* is the equivalent of Elazar.

Other works of R' Elazar include the halachic compendium *Maaseh Rokeach* (Sanuk, 1912); a commentary on tractate *Shekalim* of the Jerusalem Talmud (not extant); *Sefer HaKaparos* or *Moreh Chataim* (Venice, 1543) on the regulations of repentance for each particular sin; *Tosafos* to tractate *Bava Kamma* (mentioned in *Shitah Mekubetzes);* a commentary on the Torah, and *Yayin HaRekach,* a commentary on the five *Megillos,* of which only the sections on Song of Songs and Ruth have been published (Lublin, 1608).

*R' Yehudah HaChassid and R' Elazar's father, who instructed R' Elazar in Kabbalah, transmitted to him the mystical meanings and correct text of the prayers which, according to their traditions, dated back to the Tannaim. R' Elazar wrote a commentary on *Sefer Yetzirah* published in most editions; a kabbalistic commentary on the prayers, in manuscript; *Sode Razya* (Bilgorai, 1936); *Shaarei Binah; Sefer HaShem;* and many other unpublished treatises on Kabbalah.

In 1197, crusaders murdered R' Elazar's wife and two daughters before his very eyes, and then wounded him and his young son; however, he survived this tragic incident and memorialized it in a touching elegy.

R' Moshe of Coucy
ר' מֹשֶׁה (בֶּן יַעֲקֹב) מִקּוֹצִי

Coucy, France; early 13th cent.
Tosafist, Halachist.

A gifted orator, R' Moshe traveled through Provence and Spain in 1236, rebuking the masses for their neglect in the fulfillment of the precepts, especially *tefillin.* In Spain, he was forced to preach concerning a sin even more grievous — for the Jews of that land were intermarrying with Christians and Moslems. His sermons were successful, and many divorced their Gentile wives. In 1240, after returning to northern France, R' Moshe served on the Jewish delegation, headed by *R' Yechiel of Paris, which disputed the charges of the apostate Nicholas Donin that the Talmud contained blasphemies against Christianity.

R' Moshe's greatest accomplishment was Sefer Mitzvos Gadol, abbreviated Semag (Soncino, 1489), which carefully defined the 613 commandments and explained their halachic implications. This book, which drew on the works of predecessors and followed the decisions of the Tosafists, is an authoritative halachic source and became the subject of supercommentaries by R' Eliyahu Mizrachi, *R' Isaac Stein, Maharshal, Maharik and Bris Moshe. In the era preceding the publication of the Shulchan Aruch, Semag was the principal halachic code studied in Ashkenazic academies, especially in Italy. This is why Ayn Mishpat (the reference work by the Italian scholar R' Yehoshua Boaz printed on the margin of all standard editions of Talmud) gives references to Semag alongside those to Tur and *Rambam's Yad.

R' Moshe was the first scholar of the French-German school to make extensive use of Rambam's code; indeed it is a major source in Semag. His praise of this Sephardic Torah giant is unstinting: "He was an extraordinary scholar — we have not heard of anyone his equal in recent generations."

R' Moshe wrote a commentary on the Chumash (cited extensively in Minchas Yehudah and in other treatises of this genre), and Tosafos to the Talmud. He was the author of Tosafos Yeshanim on tractate Yoma.

R' Moshe's maternal grandfather was R' Chaim HaKohen. He was the brother-in-law of *R' Shimshon of Sens, and a disciple of *R' Yehudah of Paris.

R' Avraham ben Azriel

ר' אַבְרָהָם בֶּן עֲזְרִיאֵל

Bohemia (Czechoslovakia), c. 1235
Liturgical Commentator.

In addition to studying under R' Eliezer ben Yitzchak of Prague, he also traveled to the great academies of Germany and France. He was particularly influenced by *R' Yehudah HaChassid and *Rokeach.

In Arugas HaBosem (Jerusalem, 1939-63), a unique commentary on the liturgical hymns, he cites the sources of each stanza, the views of other authorities, and kabbalistic interpretations. Among his disciples was *R' Yitzchak of Vienna (who mentions R' Avraham's decisions in Or Zarua).

R' Yechiel of Paris

ר' יְחִיאֵל (בֶּן יוֹסֵף) מְפַּארִיש

b. Meaux, France, c. 1190
d. Eretz Yisrael, c. 1268
Tosafist.

*R' Yehudah of Paris was succeeded by his disciple R' Yechiel as dean of the Tosafist academy of Paris in 1224. Three hundred pupils came to hear R' Yechiel's lectures, including the Tosafists *R' Yitzchak of Corbeil, who was also his son-in-law; R' Peretz of Corbeil; and *Maharam of Rothenburg.

Our Tosafos editions mention R' Yechiel of Paris, and the early codifiers quote his Tosafos on many Talmudic tractates. Many of his halachic decisions are recorded in Orchos Chaim and Kol Bo.

In 1240 the French government ordered R' Yechiel to debate the apostate Nicholas Donin, who had denounced the Talmud to the pope as containing blasphemies against Christianity. Together with R' Yechiel, three other Tosafists participated in the debate, *R' Moshe of Coucy, R' Shmuel ben Shlomo of Falaise, and R' Yehudah ben David of Melun. Although R' Yechiel and his colleagues displayed great courage and dignity, the official verdict against them was a foregone conclusion. The outcome of the disputation was that on a Friday morning in 1242, twenty-four cartloads of Talmud volumes were burned in the streets of Paris. That Friday (Parshas Chukas) was observed as a day of mourning and fasting for many generations (Shibolei HaLeket ch. 263), and Maharam of Rothenburg composed the lamentation Shaali Serufah BaEish (in the kinos service for Tisha B'Av) in commemoration of the horrible incident.

With the conditions of the Jews in France steadily worsening, R' Yechiel emigrated to Eretz Yisrael in 1260 together with his son, R' Yosef, and other scholars. He settled in Acre, where he established the Talmudic academy Medrash HaGadol d'Paris.

R' Yitzchak of Vienna

ר' יִצְחָק (בֶּן מֹשֶׁה) מִוִּינָא

b. Bohemia (Czechoslovakia), late 12th cent.
d. Vienna, Austria, mid-13th cent.
Halachist.

After studying under *R' Avraham ben Azriel in his native Bohemia, R' Yitzchak journeyed to the great yeshivos of Germany and northern France, especially to the academy of *R' Yehudah of Paris. He also studied under *R' Shimshon of Coucy, R' Simchah of Speyer, *Ravyah, R' Yonasan of Wurzburg, *R' Elazar Rokeach of Worms and R' Yitzchak ben Mordechai. *R' Yehudah HaChassid instructed R' Yitzchak in Kabbalah.

R' Yitzchak was the author of Or Zarua, a halachic guide popular among Ashkenazic Jewry. The compendium, arranged according to the Talmudic tractates, includes many Tosafos and responsa from R' Yitzchak's predecessors and contemporaries. The entire work is quite extensive. Two parts were published in Zhitomir (1862), and two in Jerusalem (1887).

*Rid referred to R' Yitzchak as Mofes HaDor ["wonder of the age"].

*Maharam of Rothenburg was one of R' Yitzchak's pupils.

R' Yitzchak of Corbeil

ר' יִצְחָק (בֶּן יוֹסֵף) מִקּוֹרְבֵּיל

d. Corbeil, France, 1280
[28 Iyar 5040]
Tosafist, Halachist.

Also known as R' Yitzchak Baal HaChotem, he was a pupil and son-in-law of *R' Yechiel of Paris, and studied at the Tosafist academy of Evreux.

Because R' Yitzchak's halachic compendium Amudei HaGolah is much briefer than *R' Moshe of Coucy's comprehensive Semag [Sefer Mitzvos Gadol — "The large Book of Mitzvos"], this work became known as Semak [Sefer Mitzvos Kattan (Or Katzar — "The Small (Abridged) Book of Mitzvos"]. This compendium lists all the mitzvos applicable in the post-Temple era, gives a short synopsis of the mitzvah and, occasionally, some of the most pertinent halachic details. Because of its pertinence to Jewish living, it was divided into seven parts, corresponding to the days of the week, so that it could be reviewed constantly. Semak at once became a popular code and was accepted as an authoritative halachic source cited by all codifiers, including Tur. R' Yitzchak sent copies to various communities at his own expense and asked them in turn to make more copies available for public use. It was first published in Constantinople (1510) and thereafter reprinted many times.

*R' Peretz of Corbeil (R' Yitzchak's disciple) added glosses to this treatise;

these were later printed in all the editions.

R' Yitzchak also wrote *Tosafos* and responsa. He emphasized ethical behavior and stringent religious principles.

R' Yaakov Chazan

ר' יַעֲקֹב (בֶּן יְהוּדָה) חַזָן

London, England, c. 1285

Halachist.

Etz Chayim (Jerusalem, 1967), R' Yaakov's halachic compendium, draws strongly on *Mishneh Torah, Semag,* and *Semak.* The work is divided into two parts: *Sefer HaTorah,* on the laws between man and G—d, and *Sefer HaMishpat,* dealing with jurisprudence. Strangely enough, while in the first portion he constantly records the decisions of the English sages, in the second part not even one of their names is mentioned. *Etz Chayim* is cited in *Yam Shel Shlomo* and *Shiltei HaGibborim.*

R' Meir of Rothenburg (Maharam)

ר' מֵאִיר (בֶּן בָּרוּךְ) מֵרוֹטֶנְבּוּרְג (מהר"ם)

b. Worms, Germany, c. 1215
d. Ensisheim, Alsace, France, 1293
[19 Iyar 5053]

Talmudist, Halachist, Teacher.

After studying under *R' Yitzchak of Vienna and R' Shmuel of Wurzburg, R' Meir traveled to the French Tosafist academies to study under *R' Yechiel of Paris, R' Shmuel of Falaise, and R' Shmuel of Evreux. When Maharam returned to Germany, he was considered the greatest authority in the country, and his decisions and decrees were considered binding throughout Germany.

Maharam lived and served as rabbi in the communitites of Worms and Rothenburg. In the latter city he established a Talmudic academy which attracted numerous disciples, and it was from there that he sent most of his responsa.

Among the many pupils who flocked to him were *Rosh, *R' Mordechai ben Hillel, *R' Shimshon ben Tzaddok, *R' Meir ben Yekusiel, *R' Chaim Or Zarua, and *R' Yitzchak of Duren, R' Avraham of Sinaheim who authored *Tikkun Tefillin,* and R' Moshe Parnes of Rothenburg, who recorded his teacher's customs in *Sefer HaParnes.* Some scholars assume that the author of the halachic compendium *Al HaKol* (Berditchev, 1908) was a disciple of Maharam, but serious objections to this assumption have been raised.

Because the condition of the Jews in Germany deteriorated from day to day with new taxes, harsh decrees, and massacres, Maharam decided to leave the country and seek refuge in another land. When he arrived with his family in Lombardy, he was recognized by the apostate Kneppe, who informed the bishop of Basel (who was passing by) of Maharam's identity. The bishop forthwith notified the local lord who arrested R' Meir (4 Tamuz 1286) and turned him over to the Emperor. Emperor Rudolph I subsequently imprisoned the sage in order to extort a huge ransom from the Jewish community. Although the exorbitant sum of thirty thousand marks was raised, Maharam, following the Mishnaic ruling *(Gittin* 4:6), would not permit it to be paid, for fear that it would encourage the government to imprison other community leaders.

During his seven years in prison, Maharam learned, taught, and continued to reply in writing to all questions of Jewish law. R' Shimshon ben Tzaddok, who received permission from the authorities to visit his teacher frequently, recorded his regulations and customs in a work that later became known as *Tashbetz* (not to be confused with a work of the same name by R' Shimon ben Tzemach). Maharam also maintained a voluminous correspondence with the rest of his disciples, who were not granted permission to see him.

Even after Maharam died in prison, the government, rebuffed in its attempt to extort the ransom, would not free his body for burial. It remained in the prison for an additional fourteen years. Finally, in 1307 [4 Adar 5067], R' Alexander ben Shlomo Wimpen spent most of his wealth to bring Maharam's remains to a Jewish burial. In return, he asked only to be buried next to the great sage, a request that was granted.

Maharam left a great legacy of writings. He composed commentaries to sedarim Zeraim and Taharos, Tosafos to various tractates, and the Tosafos in our edition of tractate Yoma. Various parts of his extensive responsa have appeared (Cremona 1557, Prague 1608, Lemberg 1860, Berlin 1891); these responsa have recently been reprinted (Jerusalem, 1968-9). Additional responsa have been incorporated into Shaalos U'Teshuvos R' Yitzchak Or Zorua (Jerusalem, 1943). He also wrote Birchos Maharam concerning laws of benedictions (Riva di Trento, 1558); Hilchos Shechitah, (in manuscript) on laws of ritual slaughter; Hilchos Semachos, on laws of mourning (Jerusalem 1966; also incompletely, Salonika, 1795 and Leghorn 1819-28); Halachos Pesukos, halachic decisions on various subjects; novellae to many Talmudic and Mishnaic tractates, of which Chida had a copy; Piskei Eruvin, on the laws of the eruv; and many other works.

Twenty of Maharam's liturgical hymns are known, the most famous being his lamentation Shaali Serufah BaEish on the burning of the Talmud in Paris in 1242, which is recited in the kinnos of Tisha B'Av.

Maharshal wrote of him, "modest and pure, there were none in the latter generations to liken unto him."

R' Yitzchak of Duren

ר' יִצְחָק (בֶּן מֵאִיר) מִדּוּרָא

Duren, Germany, late 13th-early 14th cent.
Halachist.

Shearim Beissur VeHeter, popularly known as Shaarei Dura (Cracow, 1534), was the standard code of dietary laws for Ashkenazic Jews until the Shulchan Aruch came into widespread use some three hundred years later. It has left an indelible mark upon these halachos as a major source for the decisions of Rama and the later authorities. A host of supercommentaries were written on Shaarei Dura, including notes by *R' Yisrael Isserlin, Maharshal, and Rama, and Mevo Shearim, all of which were published.

R' Yitzchak was a disciple of *Maharam of Rothenburg.

R' Shimshon ben Tzaddok

ר' שִׁמְשׁוֹן בֶּן צָדוֹק

Germany, c. 1285
Halachist.

During the seven years that *Maharam of Rothenburg was in prison, his disciple, R' Shimshon, served as his attendant. In the halachic compilation Tashbetz [not to be confused with the work of R' Shimon ben Tzemach] (Cremona, 1556) he recorded all the customs, rituals, and halachic utterances of his master during this period. *R' Peretz of Corbeil, under whom R' Shimshon studied, added glosses, citing the prevalent practice when it was contrary to Maharam's ruling.

R' Mordechai ben Hillel

ר' מָרְדְּכַי בֶּן הֵלֵל

b. Germany, c. 1240
d. Nuremberg, Germany, 1298 [22 Av 5058]
Halachist.

R' Mordechai, a descendant of

*Ravyah, was a principal disciple of *Maharam of Rothenburg, and also studied under *R' Peretz of Corbeil.

His great halachic compendium, known simply as *Mordechai* after its author, quotes the views of the French and German masters, many of which have not been preserved otherwise and are known to us only through this work. It also gives the halachic opinion of the Tosafists without the entire Tosafist discussion. *Mordechai* is arranged according to the Talmudic tractates and is printed as an appendix to Rif's *Sefer HaHalachos* in our Talmud editions.

There are two different editions of *Mordechai* — the Rhenish and Austrian versions — each of which contains material not found in the other. The Austrian version seems to have been longer and was already rare in the times of *R' Yisrael Isserlein. The Rhenish edition contains only a third of the material found in the Austrian. Citations from the authorities also differ, as many quotations from the Rhenish and French scholars, which appear in the Rhenish edition, are replaced by quotations from the Austrian authorities, especially *Or Zarua*, in the Austrian version. Our copies of the Talmud contain the Rhenish edition.

Several commentaries were written on this popular compilation: *Hagahos Mordechai*, by R' Shmuel ben Aaron of Schlettstadt, which contains material from the Austrian version, and commentaries by *Shalah* and by R' Mordechai Benet, all printed in our Talmud editions. *Mordechai* is cited as an authoritative halachic code, and is often quoted by Rama, who lectured on *Mordechai* in his Talmudic academy at Cracow.

R' Mordechai also composed a treatise on dietary laws entitled *Hilchos Shechitah U'Bedikah VeIssur VeHeter* (Venice, 1550).

He and his entire family perished as martyrs during the Rindfleish massacres (see Historical Introduction).

R' Meir ben Yekusiel

ר' מֵאִיר בֶּן יְקוּתִיאֵל (הַכֹּהֵן)

d. Germany, 1298

Halachist.

R' Meir was a disciple of *Maharam of Rothenburg and *R' Peretz of Corbeil.

Hagahos Maimoniyos, R' Meir's glosses on *Rambam's *Mishneh Torah*, stresses the views of the Tosafists and Ashkenazic scholars. It is a popular work, printed in most editions of Rambam.

R' Meir and his entire family perished during the Rindfleish massacres (see Historical Introduction).

R' Asher ben Yechiel (Rosh)

ר' אָשֵׁר בֶּן יְחִיאֵל (רא"ש)

b. Germany, c. 1250
d. Toledo, Spain, 1327
[15 MarCheshvan 5088]

Halachist, Talmudist.

R' Asher, who studied under his older brother R' Chaim and subsequently became the most important disciple of *Maharam Rothenburg, was a member of a prominent rabbinical family which traced its ancestry to *R' Gershom Meor HaGolah and *Ravan. R' Asher succeeded Maharam Rothenburg as spiritual leader and halachic authority of German Jewry. Following the Rindfleish massacres [see Historical Introduction], Rosh convened a synod to determine the distribution of the property of the victims who left no heirs, and he also introduced new enactments. When his fame spread, Rosh began to fear that he, too, would be imprisoned and held for ransom as his teacher had been, and he therefore left Germany in 1303.

Via Provence, Rosh journeyed to Spain where he arrived in 1306. In Barcelona, he was warmly received at the home of *Rashba, with whom he had been corresponding for years. Rashba announced the arrival of the eminent German scholar throughout Spain, and soon a call was received from the community of Toledo inviting Rosh to serve as their rabbi.

In Toledo, Rosh assumed full charge of the beis din, which was empowered by the government with full jurisdiction over all Jewish affairs, with the power to enforce its decrees and inflict punishments — even the death penalty.

The halachic decisions of Rosh were eagerly sought by Jews in Germany, Provence, and North Africa. After Rashba's death, inquiries came from all of Spain as well, for Rosh was recognized as his successor. His responsa, collected in Teshuvos HaRosh (Venice, 1552), are an authoritative halachic source.

All full editions of the Talmud contain his monumental halachic compilation. Rosh's code follows the Talmudic tractates, giving the Talmudic sources of all decisions to facilitate their study, application, and comparison. In this he differed with *Rambam, who formulated a new system of classification, not based on the order of the Talmud, and who summarized the laws without giving sources. Rosh also considered it necessary to list all main opinions with their respective reasonings in order to show how the final decision is arrived at. He therefore generally begins the presentation of the topic with a verbatim quote from *Rif's Halachos and then adds those portions of the Tosafos discussions with direct halachic implications. This code became the authoritative legal codex in many regions of Spain and later in other Sephardic communities of North Africa until R' Yosef Karo's Shulchan Aruch supplanted it.

Even when he dwelled in Spain, Rosh carefully preserved his Ashkenazic customs because he regarded them as more authoritative, having been transmitted from generation to generation since the destruction of the Temple. He opposed excessive philosophical speculation, because he maintained that the future of Judaism was based on strong faith and solid Torah knowledge.

His pupils included *R' Yerucham, *R' Eshtori HaParchi, and his own eight sons, the most famous of whom were R' Yechiel, whose halachic decisions are often cited in Tur; *R' Yaakov Baal HaTurim; and *R' Yehudah who succeeded his father as Rabbi of Toledo.

Rosh was instrumental in disseminating in Spain the teachings of the Tosafists and their methods. He compiled his own Tosafos (Tosefos HaRosh) containing mainly the teachings of the Tosafists preceding him with some of his own novellae. These Tosafos are distinctive in their style, because of Rosh's conciseness and clarity of expression. Most of his Tosafos to Talmud have been reprinted recently. R' Asher also contributed to the field of Talmudic commentary. He composed commentaries to the Mishnah of orders Zeraim (found in most editions of the Talmud) and Taharos. His commentaries to the tractates Nedarim, Nazir, and Tamid, and the Mishnah tractates Midos and Kinim, are found in the Vilna editions of the Talmud. His running commentary to Shekalim (which served as the basis for R' Ovadyah Bertinoro's commentary on that tractate) was published in modern times (Jerusalem, 1943).

Rosh composed the short ethical treatise Orchos Chaim. A work on dietary laws by him is quoted by Radbaz, and a commentary to Torah (printed with Hadar Zekeinim, Leghorn, 1840) is attributed to him.

R' Shimshon of Chinon

ר' שִׁמְשׁוֹן (בֶּן יִצְחָק) מְקִינוֹן

b. Chinon, France, c. 1260
d. Marseilles (?), France, c. 1330

Halachist.

R' Shimshon left his native Northern France in 1306 during the general expulsion of Jews (see Historical Introduction) and settled in Marseilles.

In *Sefer Kerisus* (Constantinople, 1515), a work on the methodology of the Talmud, R' Shimshon explains the application of the thirteen hermeneutic principles of R' Yishmael, and the thirty-two rules of R' Eliezer ben Yose HaGelili. He also gives rules for determining the correct halachah in controversies between Tannaim or Amoraim, and general rules for the understanding of the Talmud.

*Maharik quotes some of R' Shimshon's responsa. His *Kuntres*, a commentary on tractates *Eruvin* and *Avodah Zarah*, mentioned in *Sefer Kerisus*, and his *Biyur HaGet*, on the laws of divorce, have not been published.

*Rashba corresponded with R' Shimshon. *R' Peretz HaKohen considered him the greatest rabbi of the generation.

R' Yaakov Baal HaTurim

ר' יַעֲקֹב (בֶּן אָשֵׁר) בַּעַל הַטוּרִים

b. Germany, c. 1275
d. Toledo, Spain, c. 1340

Halachist, Torah Commentator.

R' Yaakov, third son of *Rosh, studied under his father and under his older brother R' Yechiel. When Rosh fled Germany (1303) with his entire household, R' Yaakov lived at first with his brother, R' Yechiel in Barcelona, and thereafter moved to Toledo, where his father was rabbi. In 1329, R' Yaakov wrote regarding Germany: "It is forbidden for a person to even traverse a place of mortal danger, let alone to live in the land of blood ... anyone who succeeds in bringing a person out from there [Germany] is considered as having saved a Jewish soul."

R' Yaakov's younger brother, *R' Yehudah — who was to marry R' Yaakov's daughter — succeeded Rosh as rabbi of Toledo, while R' Yaakov accepted a position on the Toledo Beis Din. R' Yaakov preferred learning and writing to serving as a rabbi. He condensed his father's Talmud commentary, giving only the halachic decisions while omitting the discussions and arguments. *Kitzur Piskei HaRosh,* or *Rimzei HaRosh,* as the abridgment is called, is printed in all full Talmud editions.

In his Torah commentary, R' Yaakov drew upon *Ramban, *Rashbam, and *Rosh. Each section is prefaced with an abridged commentary based on *gematria* and Masoretic interpretations. These prefaces are printed in most editions of the Pentateuch under the title *Baal HaTurim.* The extensive exegetical part of the commentary is known as *Peirush HaTur Ha'Aruch* (Zolkiev,1806).

R' Yaakov's magnum opus was his halachic compendium *Arba'ah Turim* ["Four Rows"] (1st ed. Pieve de Sachi, 1475), which remains the standard source-text for *Halachah* to this day. R' Yosef Karo wrote his monumental work *Beis Yosef* — the basis for his decisions in *Shulchan Aruch* — as a commentary to *Arba'ah Turim* and patterned his *Shulchan Aruch* on R' Yaakov's system of classifying *halachos.* Similarly Rama's *Darkei Moshe* on Tur (as *Arba'ah Turim* is known colloquially) contains the bases of his rulings in his notes on the *Shulchan Aruch.* Numerous other greats commented on the *Tur,* among them R' Yoel Sirkis *(Beis Chadash),* R' Yoshua Falik HaKohen *(Derishah UPerishah),* Maharal of Prague and others. Chida comments that, without a proper study of *Tur* and its commentaries, one cannot begin to determine Halachah.

R' Yaakov begins each discussion with the relevant Talmudic quotations and continues with the various interpretations of each Talmudic statement and their respective halachic implications. Thereby he provides a clear picture of the differences of opinion among the decisors. R' Yaakov went further than his father, Rosh, in citing opinions of earlier codifiers. Virtually all opinions available to him — from the Geonim through the Sephardic and Ashkenazic authorities — are mentioned, and a wealth of customs are also incorporated in the work. He concludes with a halachic decision, based on whichever opinion he considers most correct and on the prevalent customs. Unlike Rosh, who arranged his code according to Talmudic tractates, R' Yaakov ordered his by topic, as did *Rambam but in a different order. His arrangement is designed to provide the reader with a clear understanding of each subject in its entirety, and to enable him to find the desired decision quickly and easily.

Unlike Rambam, R' Yaakov wrote his code for the exile period, and therefore omitted any of the laws relating to service in the Holy Temple or ritual purity.

The Four *Turim* are *Orach Chaim* ["Path of Life"], on daily, Sabbath, and holiday practices; *Yoreh Deah* ["Teacher of Wisdom"], on dietary laws, oaths, usury, *niddah, mikveh* and mourning; *Even HaEzer* ["The Rock of Assistance"], on marriage and divorce; and *Choshen Mishpat* ["Breastplate of Judgment"], on business, disputes, and compensation for injury and damage.

R' Yaakov's last testament to his children (see *Tzava'os Gedolei Yisrael*) is a gem of ethical instruction and a testament to its author's loftiness and pureness of soul.

*R' David Abudraham is thought to have been R' Yaakov's disciple; however in his frequent quotes from *Tur,* Abudraham does not indicate that its author was his teacher.

R' Chaim Paltiel

רַבִּי חַיִּים פַּלְטִיאֵל

Falaise, France c. 1300

Tosafist and Bible commentator.

Descendant of R' Shmuel of Falaise and R' Yaakov of Provence, R' Chaim Paltiel carried on halachic correspondence with *Maharam Rothenburg and is cited in his responsa. He also composed a treatise on customs, which served as a foundation for *R' Avraham Klausner's work on that subject.

R' Chaim Paltiel's greatest contribution is his Torah commentary which remained in manuscript for close to seven centuries and was published only recently (Jerusalem, 1981). Covering the entire Pentateuch, it is a collection of comments from *Rashi, *Rashbam, *R' Yosef Bechor Shor, *R' Yosef Kara, *R' Yehudah HaChassid and *R' Elazar Rokeach. Original comments also appear, especially concerning Halachah.

The book was edited by R' Chaim Paltiel's son, and its style and content greatly resemble *Paneach Raza,* which some attribute to an otherwise unknown *rishon,* R' Yitzchak ben Yehudah HaLevi.

R' Chaim Or Zarua

ר' חַיִּים (אֱלִיעֶזֶר בֶּן יִצְחָק מְווֹינָא) אוֹר זָרוּעַ

Vienna, Austria, 14th century

Halachist.

R' Chaim composed an abridgment of *Or Zarua,* the halachic work of his father, *R' Yitzchak of Vienna, in order to make the book more accessible to the masses by presenting only the decisions without the preceding analyses. The section of this work pertaining to tractate Yevamos is printed in the Vilna edition of the Talmud as Or Zorua HaKatzer. R' Chaim himself wrote a halachic compendium on the holidays titled Drashos which is cited by *Maharil, and responsa (Leipzig, 1860). In these responsa, R' Chaim, who was practically unknown prior to their publication, reveals himself as an independent thinker in Talmudical interpretation. He presents solutions that are startling in their boldness and originality. Many of the Torah giants of recent generations — especially the famous halachic authority Maharsham of Brezan — valued R' Chaim's ideas, and utilized them in their works.

Another of R' Chaim's works, Derashos or Piskei R' Chaim Or Zorua, a collection of homilies on the weekly Torah portion was published recently (Jerusalem, 1973). These sermons are short halachic decisions that are connected to the Torah portion. Etz Chaim, a treatise on monetary law (in Chamishah Kuntreisim, Vienna, 1864), has been attributed to R' Chaim by some scholars.

R' Chaim was a student of *Maharam Rothenburg, and served as rabbi of Wiener Neustadt, Vienna, and Cologne.

Although his father named him Chaim, he sometimes signed his name Chaim Eliezer. This second name was probably added during a serious illness, in keeping with the custom of altering a person's name in times of overwhelming distress.

R' Alexander Zuslein HaKohen
ר' אֲלֶכְּסַנְדֶּר זוּסְלֵין הַכֹּהֵן
d. Frankfurt, Germany, 1348

Talmudist, Halachist.

R' Alexander, disciple of *R' Yitzchak of Duren, served as rabbi of Cologne,

Worms, and finally Frankfurt. He is best known as author of Agudah (Cracow, 1571), a halachic compendium which cites rabbinical decisions that cover most of Talmudic law. This popular and authorative code is cited by *R' Yaakov Weil, *Maharil, and Rama. An abridged version was also published under the title Chiddushei Agudah in Teshuvos R' Yaakov Weil (Hanau, 1610, and later editions). Maharil and R' Yaakov Weil greatly valued R' Alexander's opinions noting that he lived yet prior to the persecutions (gezeiros) (see Historical Introduction), which caused a great decline in the level of scholarship in Germany.

Some are of the opinion that R' Alexander perished in his hometown, Erfurt, during the massacres following the Black Death (see Historical Introduction).

R' Yehudah ben Asher
ר' יְהוּדָה בֶּן אָשֵׁר
b. Germany, c. 1280
d. Toledo, Spain, 1349

Rabbi.

Before *Rosh left Germany, he sent his son R' Yehudah to Spain to arrange for the family's settlement there. Upon his father's death in 1328, R' Yehudah succeeded him as rabbi of Toledo.

When the leading members of the Toledo community wished to have all cases judged according to the view of *Rambam, except where *Rosh disagreed, R' Yehudah objected. He explained the proper method of reaching halachic decisions, whatever the case, required a thorough examination of all Talmudic and halachic literature related to the subject. Then an objective, logical evaluation of the diverse views must be used to reach the true decision. Probably because of this disagreement with the community, R' Yehudah made plans to move to Seville.

However, the community of Toledo accepted his arguments, urged him to remain, and increased his salary considerably.

Inquiries were sent to R' Yehudah from most of the Spanish communities, and some of his responsa have been published under the title *Zichron Yehudah* (Berlin, 1846). He is also quoted in *Nimukei Yosef*. R' Yehudah maintained halachic correspondence with *R' Chisdai Crescas I and *R' Avraham ben Ishmael. *R' Menachem ben Zerach was one of R' Yehudah's pupils.

R' Yehudah married the daughter of his eldest brother, R' Yechiel, and she bore him five sons, whom he advised to return to Germany, where the dedication to Torah and tradition were stronger. In his last testament to his children, known as *Iggeres Tochachas*, R' Yehudah admonished them to pursue zealously the study of the Torah, particularly Halachah, and make themselves worthy of their great ancestors. His second wife was the daughter of his brother *R' Yaakov Baal HaTurim.

R' Shimshon ben Eliezer

ר׳ שִׁמְשׁוֹן בֶּן אֱלִיעֶזֶר

b. Saxony, Germany
d. Eretz Yisrael, c. 1360

Halachist, Scribe.

As a young child, R' Shimshon journeyed with his parents to Prague. When he was orphaned at the age of eight, he was adopted by R' Yisachar, a learned scribe who taught him his skill. R' Shimshon developed into an expert scribe, and was referred to as "the head of all scribes" by Maharshal.

R' Shimshon compiled *Baruch Sheamar* (Shklov, 1804), composed of *Tikun Tefillin*, a treatise by R' Avraham of Sonsheim (a pupil of *Maharam Rothenburg), with R' Shimshon's glosses, gleaned from the most authoritative halachic sources. *Baruch Sheamar* was accepted as an authoritative halachic work on the laws pertaining to the writing of Torah scrolls, *mezuzos* and *Tefillin* and is quoted by *Beis Yosef* and others.

R' Yisrael of Krems

ר׳ יִשְׂרָאֵל מִקְרֵימְז

Krems, Austria, c. 1375

Halachist.

R' Yisrael's notes and additions to *Rosh's Halachic compilation are called *Hagahos Ashri* and are printed in all Talmud editions. They are a rich lode of quotes from otherwise unknown decisions by the Tosafists, and until modern times were the primary source for the views of *R' Yitzchak Or Zarua.

The author of *Terumas HaDeshen*, who was R' Yisrael's great-grandson, quotes R' Yisrael in his commentary on *Rashi.

*R' Shalom of Neustadt may have been R' Yisrael's disciple.

R' Moshe of Zurich

ר׳ מֹשֶׁה (בֶּן זוּסְמַאן) מְצוּרִיךְ

Switzerland, 14th century

Halachist.

R' Moshe is the author of *Semak-MiZurich* (Jerusalem, 1973), important glosses on the *Semak*, *R' Yitzchak of Corbeil's abridged halachic compendium. These glosses, three times as long as *Semak*, are gleaned from the views of the early authorities, especially the Tosafists.

R' Moshe served as rabbi of Zurich until the destruction of the Jewish community in 1349. Some scholars assume that R' Moshe perished during these persecutions, while others maintain that he moved to the neighboring city of Bern (Switzerland). Some scholars identify him with R' Moshe HaKohen Neumark of Berne, who was the father of *Maharil's first wife. However, this is unlikely since Maharil in his references to Semak Zurich never alludes to the author's relationship to him.

R' Matisyahu Treves

ר' מַתִּתְיָהוּ (בֶּן יוֹסֵף) טְרֵיוִיש

b. Paris, France, c. 1325
d. Paris, France, c. 1387

Rabbi, Teacher.

R' Matisyahu Treves studied under *Ran and *R' Peretz HaKohen. He resided in Spain until 1361, and then returned to France, where he founded a Talmudic academy in Paris for the few remaining French scholars. An observation of his on the methodology of the Talmud has been preserved in She'eiris Yosef of R' Yosef ibn Verga (Nesiv HaMishnah, Klal 5). In 1363, King Charles V appointed him chief rabbi of Paris, a post he held until his death. His son *R' Yochanan Treves succeeded him as chief rabbi.

R' Meir ben Baruch HaLevi

ר' מֵאִיר בֶּן בָּרוּךְ הַלֵּוִי

b. Fulda, Germany, c. 1320
d. Vienna, Austria, 1390

Talmudist and Halachist.

Rabbi of Vienna from 1360 until his death, R' Meir's erudition and authority were acknowledged not only throughout Ashkenazic communities, but even by Spanish rabbis.

Due to persecutions in Germany, the number of competent rabbis had decreased and unqualified persons began assuming rabbinical roles. R' Meir, therefore, issued an order that a Talmudic student could not officiate as a rabbi unless a properly ordained rabbi had conferred the title Moreinu upon him. This practice of ordaining rabbis was followed by Ashkenazic communities in all succeeding generations down to this day.

R' Meir wished to introduce this system into France also, and ordained the French scholar, R' Yeshayahu ben Abba Mari, as chief rabbi of France with sole authority to ordain other rabbis in the French empire. This evoked strong opposition from the incumbent chief rabbi, *R' Yochanan Treves, with whom the Spanish rabbis sided. The controversy ended when the Jews were expelled from France in 1394.

R' Avraham Klausner

ר' אַבְרָהָם קְלוֹיזְנֶער

Vienna, Austria, 14th century

Talmudist, Halachist.

R' Avraham shared the rabbinate of Vienna with *R' Meir ben Baruch HaLevi. R' Aharon Blumlein and *R' Shalom of Neustadt were his contemporaries; and *Maharil and *R' Isaac Tirna his disciples. R' Avraham's collection of customs and notes was published under the title Minhagei R' Avraham Klausner (Riva di Trento, 1559). He is quoted in Terumas HaDeshen and by Rama and other later authorities.

R' Shalom of Neustadt

ר' שָׁלוֹם (בֶּן יִצְחָק זְקֵיל) מנוּישטאט

Austria, 14th cent.

Talmudist, Halachist.

A native of Vienna, R' Shalom was a disciple of his father, *R' Yisrael of Krems, and two otherwise unknown scholars, R' Ozer of Schweidnitz (Swidniza in Silesia, Poland) and R' Mushel Muzneim. R' Shalom later lived at Wiener Neustadt and was greatly revered; his disciples referred to him as HaSar ("The Prince") R' Shalom of Austria, an allusion to the verse in Isaiah (9:5) where the word Shalom appears in conjunction with the word Sar (Sar Shalom — "Prince of Peace"). Maharil, the acknowledged halachic authority of Germany in his day, was a devoted disciple of R' Shalom, and quoted him often in his works. He conducted himself mostly according to the customs of his mentor, as attested to by the author of *Minhagei Maharil;* indeed a section containing some of R' Shalom's decisions appears in this work. R' Aharon Blumlein of Vienna, was also a disciple of the 'Prince.' A collection of R' Shalom's manuscripts was in possession of Maharshal.

R' Shalom's most prominent disciple, *Maharil, considered his customs and decisions binding, and quoted them often. R' Shalom is also cited by *R' Yisrael Brunna. Recently a collection of his decisions was printed as *Hilchos UMinhagei R' Shalom* (Jerusalem 5737).

R' Yom Tov Lipman Milhausen

ר' יוֹם טוֹב לִיפְמַן (בֶּן שְׁלֹמֹה) מִילְהוֹיזֶן

Prague, Bohemia (Czechoslovakia), late 14th-early 15th cent.

Halachist, Kabbalist.

In *Sefer HaNitzachon,* a refutation of Scriptural proofs offered in support of Christianity, R' Yom Tov demonstrates their errors and makes them appear utterly absurd. For fear of reprisals from the Church, the book was kept in manuscript and handed down from generation to generation to be used for disputations. The Church leaders, aware that such a book existed, endeavored to trace it. Finally a monk seized it from the rabbi of Schneittach, translated it and published it with his notes (Altdorf, 1644). For generations thereafter, Christians attempted to refute R' Yom Tov's arguments in many works published in Latin. The Church's fear of this work can be seen in the fact that a papal edict forbade Jews to keep R' Yom Tov's book in their possession.

In 1399, R' Yom Tov and many other Jews were thrown into prison at the instigation of the apostate Peter, who accused them of insulting Christianity in their writings. Asked to justify themselves, R' Yom Tov brilliantly refuted Peter's accusations. Nevertheless, as a result of the charges eighty Jews were martyred and only R' Yom Tov escaped death.

R' Yom Tov served as *Dayan* of Prague. His halachic decisions are cited by *R' Yisrael Isserlein. His kabbalistic works include *Alfa Beisa* on the form of the letters of the Hebrew alphabet, printed in *Baruch Sheamar* (Shklov, 5564); *Sefer HaEshkol* (New York 1927) on mystical concepts; and *Kavanos HaTefillah* (New York 1927), an interpretation of the prayers; and a commentary on the liturgical poem *Shir HaYichud.*

R' Isaac Tirna

ר' אַייזִיק טִירְנָא

Tirnau (Czechoslovakia), late 14th-early 15th cent.

Halachist.

R' Isaac's *Minhagim LeChol HaShanah,* an authoritative compendium of customs and practices observed in various Ashkenazic communities of Eastern Europe (Venice, 1616), became a popular code for Ashkenazic Jewry and is cited very often by *Magen Avraham, Levush,* and other codifiers.

R' Isaac was a disciple of *R' Avraham Klausner.

A popular legend relates that R' Isaac's daughter was kidnapped by a duke who subsequently became a sincere convert to Judaism.

R' Yaakov Moelin (Maharil)

ר' יַעֲקֹב (בֶּן מֹשֶׁה הַלֵּוִי) מוֹלִין (מהרי"ל)

b. Mainz, Germany, c. 1365
d. Worms, Germany, 1427
[21 Elul 5187]

Halachist.

The Ashkenazic Jews in his generation regarded Maharil [an acronym for *Moreinu HaRav Yaakov, Levi*] as their leading halachic authority, especially in regard to customs and synagogue ritual. His decisions usually followed the opinion of *R' Alexander Zusslein HaKohen's *Agudah* and *R' Shalom of Neustadt. Maharil demanded complete adherence to Ashkenazic tradition, even with regard to the melodies of the High Holiday service.

Minhagei Maharil (Sabbionetta, 1556), describing his customs, was written by his pupil R' Zalman of St. Goar. This authoritative halachic code is quoted frequently in Rama's notes on *Shulchan Aruch*. Part of Maharil's extensive responsa was also published (Venice, 1549). An additional volume of his responsa has recently been published (Jerusalem, 1977). Another work, *Biurei Yoreh Deah*, is in manuscript.

Maharil lived during trying times. In 1420 he witnessed the mass slaughter of the Jews of Austria (see Historical Introduction), which he then referred to as "the land of blood" in his responsa. One year later the Hussite wars broke out, bringing misery and suffering to the Jews of Bavaria and the Rhine. When they appealed to Maharil to intercede with G—d, he proclaimed a three day fast, and soon afterward the armies which had threatened the Jews dispersed and came to beg bread from them.

A principal disciple of *R' Shalom of Neustadt, Maharil himself attracted many students, including *R' Yaakov Weil. He was the son-in-law of R' Moshe HaKohen Neumark of Bern, whom some scholars identify with *R' Moshe of Zurich.

R' Menachem of Merseburg

ר׳ מְנַחֵם (בֶּן פְּנְחָס) מִמֶּירְזְבּוּרְק

Merseburg, Germany, c. 1430

Halachist.

R' Menachem's halachic decisions were acknowledged throughout Sax-

ony. His best known enactment was the abolition of *miyun*. [According to Torah law, a father may marry off his daughter without her consent before she reaches puberty. If her father is not living, her mother and adult brothers are granted the same right by Rabbinic decree. In this case, however, the girl may unilaterally dissolve the union — before she reaches puberty — by declaring her unwillingness ["*miyun*"] to continue the marriage. A formal writ of divorce ["*get*"] is not required when the law of *miyun* is invoked. R' Menachem discontinued the law of *miyun* and forbade its use; thenceforth, a formal *get* was required. Although his edict was generally accepted, R' Yaakov Pollack utilized *miyun* in one instance a generation later.

Fragments of R' Menachem's halachic compilation appear at the end of *R' Yaakov Weil's responsa, under the heading *Nimukei R' Menachem Merseburg*. R' Menachem was also known as R'Menachem Me'il Tzedek; some scholars think that the surname *Me'il Tzedek* comes from a work of that name composed by R' Menachem.

R' Yochanan Treves

ר׳ יוֹחָנָן (בֶּן מַתִּתְיָהוּ) טְרֵיוִיש

d. Italy, 1439

When *R' Matisyahu Treves died, his son and disciple, R' Yochanan, was appointed his successor as chief rabbi of France by the community and King Charles VI. However, another of his father's disciples, R' Yeshayahu ben Abba Mari, received an approbation from *R' Meir ben Baruch of Vienna (*Maharam Levi*) designating him as the chief rabbi. This caused great confusion in the community, and R' Yochanan put the problem before *Rivash and *R' Chisdai Crescas II, both of whom decided in R' Yochanan's favor. The controversy, however, raged on until the expulsion of the Jews from France in 1394, whereupon R' Yochanan relocated to Italy.

R' Avigdor Kara

ר' אֲבִיגְדוֹר (בֶּן יִצְחָק) קָרָא

d. Prague, Bohemia (Czechoslovakia), 1439
[9 Iyar 5199]

Talmudist, Kabbalist, Liturgist.

King Wenceslaus of Bohemia enjoyed conversing with R' Avigdor on religious matters. He served as a cantor and composed liturgical poems, including: *Echad Yachid Umiyuchad* (the beginning of this *piyut* is sung in many communities while a bridegroom is pelted with nuts and candies at the conclusion of his *aliyah* to the Torah on the Sabbath preceding his marriage); *Boker Tishma Koli; HaShem Keil Emes;* and *Es Kol HaTela'ah,* a penitential hymn on the persecution and slaughter of Jews in Prague in 1389. The last three are found in various rare *machzorim.*

His commentary on the Torah; responsa on matters of faith; and *Kodesh Hillulim,* a kabbalistic treatise, are all unpublished. Some ascribe to R' Avigdor the authorship of the kabbalistic treatises *Sefer HaKanah* (Poryek, 1786) concerning the meaning of the *mitzvos,* and *Sefer HaPliah,* sometimes also known as *Sefer HaKanah* (Koretz, 1784), a commentary on the portion *Bereishis.*

R' Yaakov Weil (Mahariv)

ר' יַעֲקֹב (בֶּן יְהוּדָה) וֵייל (מהרי"ו)

d. Germany, c. 1455

Halachist.

R' Yaakov, one of *Maharil's principal disciples served as rabbi of Augsburg and Erfurt. Previously, he had been offered the rabbinate at Nuremberg, but declined the position to avoid offending a scholar who resided in that town and had served in the capacity of

rabbi until then. In a parallel situation, however, R' Yaakov himself ruled *(Sheilos U'Teshuvos Mahariv:* 157) that halachically it was permissible to accept a position under such circumstances. He was recognized as the leading halachic authority of Germany in his generation. Inquiries from all German communities were addressed to him, even from such scholars as *R' Yisrael Isserlein.

Some additional responsa appear in the work of his disciple *R' Yisrael Brunna and his younger contemporary *R' Yosef Colon.

R' Yaakov's book of responsa, known as *Shaalos VeTeshuvos Mahariv* (Venice, 1523), includes an appendix titled *Shechitos U'Bedikos* on the laws of ritual slaughter and examination of the carcass after slaughter (in the Venice 1549 and later editions). This was considered authoritative by Maharshal and other later authorities. It was reprinted many times and used as a text for ritual slaughterers. Maharshal and other scholars composed notes to this work, which went through more than seventy editions.

R' Yisrael Isserlein

ר' יִשְׂרָאֵל (בֶּן פְּתַחְיָה) אִיסֶרְלִין

b. Regensburg, Germany, c. 1390
d. Wiener Neustadt, Austria, 1460

Halachist.

R' Yisrael, great-grandson of *R' Yisrael of Krems, studied under his uncle, R' Aharon Blumlein of Wiener-Neustadt. After the massacre at Neustadt in 1421, in which R' Yisrael's mother and his teacher were killed, R' Yisrael fled to Italy. From there he proceeded to Marburg, Styria (Austria), where he remained for a considerable time. In 1445, he returned to Wiener-Neustadt, where he founded a Talmudic academy and attracted many students.

R' Yisrael was a humble, peaceable person who readily replied to all halachic queries. His responsa appear in *Leket Yosher,* and responsa of *R' Yisrael Brunna; in the responsa of *R' Yaakov Weil; as well as in his own *Terumas HaDeshen* (Venice, 1519). This work is considered a very authoritative halachic source, and its decisions are frequently cited by later authorities, particularly Maharshal. The work consists of three hundred and fifty-four [the numerical equivalent of *"deshen"*] halachic essays presented in the form of responsa. Although both questions and answers were written by the author, there is evidence that many of these decisions were originally composed in response to actual inquiries but were later rewritten and recast to fit the format of the *Terumas HaDeshen.* Some of R' Isserlein's actual responsa were published in *Pesakim U'Kesavim* (Venice, 1519).

R' Yisrael's dietary manual, *Shearim BeDinei Issur VeHeter,* published in modern times (Jerusalem, 5700) was the source for his notes on *Sha'arei Dura* (published with that work). He also wrote *Seder HaGet* on divorce (New York, 5703), previously known only through its mention in other works; a few liturgical and poetic hymns for the Passover Seder; and a supercommentary on *Rashi's Torah commentary (Venice, 1519).

R' Yisrael Brunna

ר' יִשְׂרָאֵל (בֶּן חַיִּים) בְּרוּנָא

b. Germany, c. 1400
d. Prague, Bohemia (Czechoslovakia), c. 1480
Halachist.

In his youth R' Yisrael seems to have traveled extensively in keeping with the dictum *(Avos* 4), "Emigrate to a place of Torah," and seems to have had a multitude of teachers. He studied under the two greatest authorities in Germany, *R' Yaakov Weil and *R' Yisrael Isserlein,

both of whom mention him in their works. He also received instruction from lesser known scholars, such as, R' David Schweidnitz, under whom he learned in his early youth, R' Meir (whom he titles, 'My teacher and master, the Gaon R' Meir'), R' Meir Kohen (otherwise unknown), and R' Zalman Katz of Nuremberg (known as *Maharzach*).

R' Yisrael served as rabbi in Brunna, Moravia (Czechoslovakia), until the Jews were expelled from that city in 1451. He then settled in Regensburg, where he taught disciples, and thereby antagonized R' Anshel, who headed an academy there and considered R' Yisrael to be encroaching. However, *R' Yaakov Weil and *R' Yisrael Isserlein upheld R' Yisrael's halachic right to teach, and reproved those who harassed him.

At a later date, Frederick III imprisoned R' Yisrael for refusing to issue a ban of excommunication against his coreligionists who would not hand over one third of their wealth to the royal treasury. After a short prison term, R' Yisrael was released.

In 1474, he was again imprisoned, this time on a ritual murder charge. After he was sentenced to die, the true murderer, a Christian, confessed and was executed in his stead. Following this incident R' Yisrael left Germany, and spent his remaining years in peace in Prague.

Shaalos U'Teshuvos Mahari Brunna (Salonica, 1798), his collection of responsa, is an authoritative halachic source, frequently cited by Rama and other authorities.

R' Asher Enshkin

ר' אָשֵׁר (בֶּן יְשַׁעְיָהוּ) עֶנְשְׁקִין

b. Germany, c. 1415
d. Italy, c. 1485
Talmudist and Halachist.

In his later years, R' Asher, a disciple of *R' Yaakov Weil, emigrated to Italy, where *Maharik welcomed him warmly and lauded him for his erudition and piety. R' Asher served as collector for funds for the needy of Jerusalem. Among his disciples was R' Yehudah Mintz of Padua, who was also his relative.

R' Moshe Mintz (Maharam Mintz)
ר' מֹשֶׁה (בֶּן יִצְחָק) מִינְץ (מהר"ס מִינְץ)

b. Mainz, Germany, c. 1415
d. Posen, Poland, c. 1485

Halachist.

A disciple of *R' Yaakov Weil, R' Moshe served as rabbi of Mainz, Landau, and Bamberg, and corresponded with the leading halachic authorities of Germany and Italy, including *R' Yisrael Isserlein. During the persecutions at Mainz in 1462, most of R' Moshe's manuscripts were destroyed, and due to the steadily deteriorating conditions in Germany, he moved to Posen in Poland. He is one of the first known Torah personalities in Poland and the first known to have officiated as Rav of a city in that country. Although he left Germany without his books, he continued writing responsa citing previous authorities from memory. A part of his responsa has been preserved and published under the title of *Shaalos U'Teshuvos Maharam Mintz* (Cracow, 1617). He was a cousin of R' Yehudah Mintz of Padua.

R' Yaakov Landau
ר' יַעֲקֹב (בֶּן יְהוּדָה) לַנְדָּא

d. Italy, c. 1487

Halachist.

R' Yaakov's father R' Yehudah was a well known scholar who was related to *R' Yaakov Weil and corresponded with *Maharil, *R' Yisrael Isserlein, and

*Maharik. His son R' Yaakov reports that he had thousands of disciples.

From his native Germany, R' Yaakov moved to Italy, residing in Naples and Pavia. In 1480 he wrote *Agur* (Naples, 1487), in which he compiled halachic material and customs gleaned from the entire range of halachic literature until his day. This work is cited by Rama in his notes on *Shulchan Aruch*.

At the end of the book, R' Yaakov added *Sefer Chazon*, a book of halachic riddles.

R' Yosef ben Moshe
ר' יוֹסֵף בֶּן מֹשֶׁה

b. Hochstadt, Bavaria (Germany), c. 1420
d. Bavaria, c. 1490

Halachist.

R' Yosef, a devoted and principal disciple of *R' Yisrael Isserlein, began to commit his master's teachings and customs to writing in 1463. This work was published in Berlin (1903-04) under the name *Leket Yosher*. In this remarkable chronicle, we catch a brief glimpse into the most intimate facets of the life of one of the Torah giants of half a millennium ago. The book, arranged in the order of the *Turim*, is a valuable halachic work which also sheds much light on the conditions of the Talmudic academies and their rabbinic heads.

R' Isaac Stein
ר' אַייזִיק שְׁטֵיין

b. Nuremberg, Germany, c. 1420
d. Regensburg, Germany, 1495
[Rosh HaShanah 5256]

Talmudist.

R' Isaac is known for his lengthy and erudite commentary on *Semag* (Venice, 1547). Only a portion of it appears in the printed edition, the bulk of it remaining in manuscript.

R' Tevel of Nuremberg was R' Isaac's teacher.

The Tosafists (Baalei HaTosafos)

Biographical information regarding most of the *Baalei HaTosafos* is almost nonexistent. About many of the others very little is known. Fifty-three of the *Baalei HaTosafos* are listed below (in alphabetical order of their first names), along with the fragmentary biographical information available. Those Tosafists about whom more is known are given separate entries on the pages noted.

R' Avigdor Katz; ר' אֲבִיגְדוֹר בֶּן אֵלִיָהוּ פֶּ"ץ; Vienna, Austria, c. 1250; author of *Pesakim UPashatim* (ms.); disciple of *R' Simchah of Speyer and *R' Eliezer of Verona; correspondent of *R' Yitzchak of Vienna; teacher of *R' Tzidkiyah HaRofei.

R' Avraham of Orleans; ר' אַבְרָהָם בֶּן יוֹסֵף; Orleans, France, c. 1200; son of *R' Yosef Bechor Shor; father-in-law of *R' Yèhudah of Paris

R' Baruch ben Shmuel; ר' בָּרוּךְ בֶּן שְׁמוּאֵל; d. Mainz, Germany, 1221; author of *Sefer HaChochmah* (not extant), *Tosafos* on various tractates and liturgy; disciple of *R' Eliezer of Metz and *R' Moshe ben Shlomo; served on *beis din* of Mainz

R' Baruch ben Yitzchak; ר' בָּרוּךְ בֶּן יִצְחָק; b. Worms, Germany, c. 1170; d. Eretz Yisrael, c. 1240; author of *Sefer HaTerumah;* disciple of *R' Yitzchak of Dampierre (Ri)

R' Chaim HaKohen; ר' חַיִּים בֶּן חֲנַנְאֵל הַכֹּהֵן; Paris, France, c. 1170; disciple of *Rabbeinu Tam; grandfather of *R' Moshe of Coucy

R' Chizkiyahu ben Yaakov; ר' חִזְקִיָהוּ בֶּן יַעֲקֹב; d. Bachrach, Germany, 1283; Rabbi of Magdeburg, Germany; correspondent of *R' Yitzchak of Vienna, *R' Avigdor Katz and *R' Yechiel of Paris; uncle and teacher of *Maharam of Rothenburg

R' Elchanan ben Yitzchak of Dampierre; ר' אֶלְחָנָן בֶּן יִצְחָק מִדַּנְפִּיר; martyred, Dampierre, France, 1184; son and disciple of *R' Yitzchak of Dampierre (Ri); authored a commentary on tractate *Avodah Zarah,* and *Tikkun Tefillin* and *Sod HaIbbur* on halachah; teacher of *R' Yechiel of Paris and *R' Peretz of Corbeil; when R' Elchanan was killed his father assumed responsibility for the education of his son, Shmuel

R' Eliezer ben Nassan (Ravan); see entry p. 129

R' Eliezer ben Yitzchak; ר' אֱלִיעֶזֶר בֶּן יִצְחָק; Prague, Bohemia, (Czechoslovakia), c. 1190; disciple of *Rabbeinu Tam

R' Eliezer of Metz; see entry p. 131

R' Eliezer of Touques; ר' אֱלִיעֶזֶר מְטוּקְ; Toques, Normandy, France, c. 1280; edited the *Tosafos* of *R' Shimshon of Sens, the Rabbis of Evreux, and many others, the result comprising most of the *Tosafos* as they appear in our present editions; disciple of *R' Yitzchak of Vienna

R' Eliezer of Verona; ר' אֱלִיעֶזֶר בֶּן שְׁמוּאֵל; Verona, Italy, c. 1225; disciple of *R' Yitzchak of Dampierre (Ri); colleague of *R' Yeshayah of Trani; correspondent of *Ravyah, *Rokeach and *R' Yitzchak of Vienna; teacher of *R' Avigdor Katz

R' Eliyahu Menachem of London; ר' אֵלִיָהוּ מְנַחֵם בֶּן משֶׁה מִלּוֹנְדוֹן d. London, England, c. 1284; appointed chief rabbi of England by King Henry

III, but removed from that post in 1255 after refusing to press his brethren for the heavy taxes imposed by the king; authored a commentary on *Seder Zaraim* often cited by *Tosafos Yom Tov*

R' Eliyahu of Paris; see entry p. 129

R' Eliyahu of York; ר' אֵלִיָהוּ מִיוֹרק; martyred, York, England, 1190; disciple of *Rabbeinu Tam

R' Ephraim of Regensburg; ר' אֶפְרַיִם בֶּן יִצְחָק מֵרֶגֶנְשְׁבּוּרג; d. Regensburg, Germany, 1175; author of *Arbaah Panim* (not extant), a commentary on Talmud, and liturgical poems; disciple of *Rabbeinu Tam and *Riva; colleague of *R' Yitzchak ben Mordechai and R' Moshe ben Yoel on the *beis din* of Regensburg; sometimes called R' Yakir for in *Jeremiah* 31:20, Ephraim, son of Joseph, is referred to as *Haben yakir li Ephraim* ["Ephraim is my beloved (yakir) son"]

R' Menachem of Joigny; ר' מְנַחֵם בֶּן פְּרֵץ מִיּוֹאַנִי; Joigny, France, c. 1180; disciple of *Rabbeinu Tam; prominent participant in conclave of 1160 in Troyes

R' Meshullam of Melun; see entry p. 130

R' Moshe ben Shlomo; ר' מֹשֶׁה בֶּן שְׁלֹמֹה; Mainz, Germany, c. 1180; author of *Sefer HaDinim* (not extant); disciple of *Rabbeinu Tam; teacher of *R' Elazar Rokeach of Worms; member of the *beis din* of Mainz;

R' Moshe of Coucy; see entry p. 137

R' Moshe of Evreux; ר' מֹשֶׁה בֶּן שְׁנָאוּר מֵאִיבְרָא; Evreux, Normandy, France, c. 1230; disciple of *Ritzba and *R' Shimshon of Sens; correspondent of *R' Yechiel of Paris and *R' Nasanel of Chinon; teacher of *R' Yonah of Gerona; along with his brothers R' Shmuel and R' Yitzchak, he headed an independent Tosafist academy at Chateau Thierry, and the three became known as *Rabbanei Eivra* ["the Rabbis of Eivra"]; composed *Tosafos* [known as *Tosafos Evreux*] on *Rif's *Sefer HaHalachos* rather than directly on the Talmud — perhaps this was due to the lack of Talmudic volumes following the burning of the Talmud in 1244 [see Historical Introduction]

R' Moshe of Kiev; ר' מֹשֶׁה מִקִיוֹב; Kiev, Russia, c. 1150; corresponded with *R' Shmuel ben Eli of Baghdad regarding decisions of the Geonim and transmitted these decisions to the Tosafists; disciple of *Rabbeinu Tam

R' Moshe of Pontoise; ר' מֹשֶׁה בֶּן אַבְרָהָם מִפּוֹנְטְיִיזָא; Pontoise, France, c. 1180; disciple of *Rabbeinu Tam

R' Moshe Tachau; ר' מֹשֶׁה בֶּן חִסְדָּאי תַּכוּ; Regensburg, Germany, c. 1230; author of *Kesav Tamim;* cited by *Ramban as R' Moshe of Poland; correspondent of *R' Simchah of Speyer and *R' Yitzchak of Vienna

R' Nasanel of Chinon; ר' נְתַנְאֵל מִקִינוֹן; Chinon, France, c. 1220; disciple of *R' Yitzchak of Dampierre (Ri); colleague of *R' Yechiel of Paris; correspondent of *R' Moshe of Evreux

R' Peretz of Corbell; ר' פֶּרֶץ בֶּן יִצְחָק הַכֹּהֵן; d. Corbeil, France, c. 1295; author of *Tosefos R' Peretz* and glosses on *Semak and *Tashbatz; disciple of *R' Yechiel of Paris and *R' Shmuel of Evreux; correspondent of *Maharam of Rothenburg; teacher of *R' Shimshon ben Tzaddok and *R' Mordechai ben Hillel

R' Peter ben Yosef; ר' פֶּטֶר בֶּן יוֹסֵף; martyred, Carinthia, Austria, 1146; author of glosses on *Sefer HaYashar;* disciple of *Rashbam and *Rabbeinu Tam

R' Shimshon HaZaken; ר' שמשון ;בֶּן יוֹסֵף הַזָּקֵן; martyred, Falaise, France, c. 1140; his halachic decisions are cited by *Ravyah, Or Zarua and Hagaos Maimoniyos; brother-in-law and correspondent of *Rabbeinu Tam; grandfather of *Ritzba

R' Shimshon of Coucy; ר' שמשון בֶּן שמשון מקוצי; Coucy, France, c. 1200; often cited in our editions of Tosafos as HaSar MiCoucy; his decisions are cited in Or Zarua, Semag, Orchos Chaim and Piskei Recanati; nephew and disciple of *R' Yitzchak of Dampierre (Ri); brother-in-law of *R' Moshe of Coucy

R' Shimshon of Sens; see entry p. 136

R' Shmuel ben Meir; see entry p. 126

R' Shmuel ben Natronal (Rashbat); ר' שמואל בֶּן נוֹטרנָאִי (רשב"ט); martyred, Neuss, France, 1197; sometimes called Rabbeinu Shevet; son-in-law and disciple of *Ravan; lived in Bonn, Mainz, Cologne and Regensburg, Germany, before settling in France

R' Shmuel of Falaise (Sir Morel); ר' שמואל בֶּן שלמה מפלייזא; Falaise, France, c. 1250; disciple of *R' Yehudah of Paris and *R' Baruch ben Yitzchak; authored the Tosafos found in present editions of tractate Avodah Zarah; correspondent of *R' Yitzchak of Vienna teacher of *Maharam of Rothenburg

R' Shmuel of Jonville; ר' שמואל בֶּן אַהֲרֹן; Jonville, France, c. 1190; disciple of *Rabbeinu Tam

R' Simchah of Speyer; ר' שמחה בֶּן שמואל; Speyer, Germany, c. 1200; disciple of *R' Eliezer of Metz; colleague and correspondent of *Ravyah; authored a commentary to tractate Horayos and other Talmudic novellae, and three Halachic works Seder Olam, Tikkun Shtaros and She'arim, none of these works are extant; teacher of *R' Yeshaye of Trani and *R' Yitzchak of Vienna

R' Yaakov ben Meir (Rabbeinu Tam); see entry p. 127

R' Yaakov of Orleans; ר' יעקב מאורלינש; martyred, London, England, 1189; sometimes called Rabbeinu Tam of Orleans; author of a commentary on Torah (ms.); disciple of *Rabbeinu Tam

R' Yaakov Yisrael ben Yosef; ר' יעקב ישראל בֶּן יוֹסֵף; France, c. 1180; disciple of *Rabbeinu Tam

R' Yechiel of Paris; see entry p. 138

R' Yehudah ben Klonimos (Ribak); see entry p. 132

R' Yehudah of Paris (Sir Leon); see entry p. 135

R' Yitzchak ben Asher I (Riva); see entry p. 129

R' Yitzchak ben Asher II; ר' יצְחָק בֶּן אַשֵׁר הֶבָּחוּר; martyred, Speyer, Germany, 1196; he was born of the day his grandfather *R' Yitzchak ben Asher I died and was named after him; disciple of *Rabbeinu Tam; teacher of *Ravyah

R' Yitzchak ben Avraham (Ritzba); see entry p. 133

R' Yitzchak ben Meir (Rivam); see entry p. 127

R' Yitzchak ben Mordechai; ר' יצְחָק בֶּן מָרְדְּכַי; Regensburg, Germany, c. 1170; disciple of *Rabbeinu Tam and *Riva; teacher of *R' Yitzchak of Vienna; head of beis din that included *R' Ephraim of Regensburg and R' Moshe ben Yoel

R' Yitzchak HaLavan; ר' יצְחָק בֶּן יַעֲקֹב הַלָּבָן; Prague, Bohemia (Czechoslovakia), c. 1180; author of commentary on tractates Yoma and Kesubos (ms.); disciple of *Rabbeinu

Tam; brother of *R' Pesachyah of Regensburg

R' Yitzchak of Corbeil; see entry p. 139

R' Yitzchak of Damplerre (RI); see entry p. 132

R' Yom Tov of Falaise; ר' יוֹם טוֹב בֶּן יְהוּדָה; Falaise, France, c. 1250; son and disciple of *R' Yehudah ben Nassan (Rivan)

R' Yom Tov of Jolgny; ר' יוֹם טוֹב בֶּן יִצְחָק מִיוֹאַנִי; martyred, York, England, 1191; author of liturgical poems [Omnan Kein of the Yom Kippur evening service is one of his compositions]; disciple of *Rabbeinu Tam

R' Yosef Bechor Shor; ר' יוֹסֵף בֶּן יִצְחָק בְּכוֹר שׁוֹר; Orleans, France, c. 1175; author of liturgical poems and a commentary on Torah; disciple of *Rabbeinu Tam; father of *R' Avraham of Orleans

R' Yosef Poras (RI Poras); ר' יוֹסֵף בֶּן מֹשֶׁה פּוֹרָת (ר"י פור"ת); Troyes, France, c. 1140; disciple of *Rashbam; correspondent of *Rabbeinu Tam

~ Provence

Provence

R' Moshe HaDarshan

ר' מֹשֶׁה (בֶּן יַעֲקֹב) הַדַּרְשָׁן

Narbonne, Provence, 11th cent.

Talmudist, Author.

The earliest known scholar from Provence whose works are cited by later authorities. *R' Nassan ben Yechiel, author of *Aruch*, was his disciple and cites him several times in that work. A great grandson of R' Abun, who was reputedly the first rosh yeshivah in Narbonne, R' Moshe inherited that post from his father, R' Yaakov ben Moshe ben Abun. R' Moshe composed an anthology of midrashim arranged on the verses of the Torah (similar to *Yalkut Shimoni)* interspersed with his original insights and spiced with allusions and *gematria.* *Rashi in his commentary to Torah (see *Numbers* 15:41) refers to this work as the *Yesod* of R' Moshe HaDarshan. The authors of the Midrashic works *Lekach Tov* and *Midrash Agaddah* (Vienna, 1894) may have used R' Moshe's *Yesod.* The authorship of the midrashic work *Midrash Rabbasi* (Jerusalem, 1943) is the subject of much scholarly debate, some assigning it to R' Moshe while others asserting that it is merely based on his *Yesod.* In his *Sefer HaYashar,* *Rabbeinu Tam lists R' Moshe and his brother R' Levi as foremost halachic authorities in their land. In the commentary to I Chronicles (4:31) ascribed to Rashi, R' Shlomo, a son of this R' Levi, is cited. A son of R' Moshe, *R' Yehudah HaDarshan, is reputed to have taught *R' Menachem ben Chelbo and is cited in Rashi's commentary to *Jeremiah* (31:21).

R' Yitzchak ben Mervan HaLevi

ר' יִצְחָק בֶּן מֶרְוָן הַלֵּוִי

*Narbonne, Provence,
late 11th-early 12th cent.*

Talmudist and Teacher.

Under the leadership of R' Yitzchak, Narbonne's Talmudic academy produced such outstanding scholars as *Ravad II, and *R' Moshe ben Yosef HaLevi. R' Yitzchak's disciples and other authorities such as *R' Yosef ibn Migash quote his halachic decisions, and many codifiers followed his opinion.

R' Moshe ben Yosef HaLevi

ר' מֹשֶׁה בֶּן יוֹסֵף [בֶּן מֶרְוָן] הַלֵּוִי

Narbonne, Provence, c. 1140

Talmudist and Teacher.

Under the leadership of R' Moshe, the nephew, disciple, and successor of *R' Yitzchak ben Mervan HaLevi, the Talmudic academy of Narbonne continued to produce outstanding pupils, among them, *Ravad III and *Razah. The latter mentions R' Moshe's interpretations quite frequently in his *Sefer HaMaor.*

R' Moshe's colleague, *Ravad II, consulted him on all difficult questions and would not issue a major decision without his consent.

R' Meshullam ben Yaakov of Lunel

ר' מְשׁוּלָם בֶּן יַעֲקֹב מִלּוּנֵיל

d. Lunel, Provence, 1170

Scholar.

*R' Binyamin of Tudela, who visited Lunel, a city noted for its scholars, in 1165, reported R' Meshullam to be at the head of the scholars of this city. He frequently corresponded with his colleague *Ravad II concerning halachic matters, and encouraged *R' Yehudah ibn Tibbon to translate *R' Bachya's Chovos HaLevavos [Duties of the Heart] from Arabic into Hebrew. R' Binyamin of Tudela relates that R' Meshullam's five sons were prominent scholars, especially *R' Asher 'who is a great scholar in Talmud.' Another son, R' Aharon (not to be confused with *R' Aharon HaKohen, author of Orchas Chaim), defended *Rambam's view reconciling philosophy and Judaism against *Ramah's criticisms. R' Aharon wrote two lengthy letters refuting Rama's claims (see Igros Rama), and he was probably among the 'Sages of Lunel' (headed by *R' Yehonasan HaKohen) who addressed a series of halachic questions to Rambam concerning his Mishneh Torah. Rambam had high praise for these sages, prefacing his reply to them with the remark that the questions attested to the erudition of their authors.

R' Yosef Kimchi

ר' יוֹסֵף (בֶּן יִצְחָק) קִמְחִי

b. Spain, c. 1105
d. Narbonne, Provence, c. 1170

Bible Commentator and Grammarian.
Persecutions by the fanatical Almohad sect of Moslems (see Historical Introduction) forced R' Yosef to flee Spain. He resettled in Narbonne, Provence, where he earned his livelihood as a teacher.

R' Yosef wrote Bible commentaries explaining the plain meaning of the text and stressing grammar and punctuation. His interpretations of the Torah (Sefer HaTorah), the Prophets (Sefer HaMiknah), Job, and Song of Songs have not been published. Some remain in manuscript, and others are only known through citations in the works of other commentators. Only Sefer Chukah

(Breslav, 1868) on Proverbs and a commentary on Job (in Tikvas Enosh, Berlin, 1868) has been published.

In Sefer HaBris, cast in the form of a dialogue between a loyal Jew and an apostate (in Milchemes Chovah, Constantinople, 1710), R' Yosef refutes the arguments of non-Jews against the Jewish religion, and the misinterpretations of Biblical verses quoted by Christians in support of their faith.

R' Yosef wrote several works on Hebrew grammar. His Sefer HaZikaron (Berlin,1888) follows the general rules of *Ibn Chayug and *Ibn Janach, but contains some original insights which were accepted by succeeding generations, such as his classifications of the greater and lesser vowels, and his identification of eight verb classes.

In Sefer HaGalui (Berlin, 1887), he refutes *Rabbeinu Tam's Sefer Hachraos which favored the grammatical theories of *R' Menachem ben Saruk over those of *R' Donash ben Labrat. R' Yosef's other grammatical work, Chibur HaLeket, has not been published.

R' Yosef's translations from Arabic into Hebrew include Chovos HaLevavos [Duties of the Heart] by *R' Bachya ibn Pakudah, which was replaced by the more literal translation of *R' Yehudah ibn Tibbon, Mivchar HaPeninim, attributed to *R' Shlomo ibn Gabirol, which had also been translated by *R' Yehudah ibn Tibbon, but which R' Yosef put into metrical form under the title Shekel HaKodesh (Oxford, 1919).

R' Yosef was the father of *Radak and *R' Moshe Kimchi.

R' Avraham Av Beis-Din (Ravad II)

ר' אַבְרָהָם (בֶּן יִצְחָק) אַב בֵּית דִּין
(רַאב"ד הַשֵּׁנִי)

b. Montpellier, Provence, c. 1110
d. Narbonne, Provence, 1179

Talmudist, Halachist, and Teacher.
R' Avraham studied under *R'

Yitzchak ben Mervan HaLevi in Narbonne. He later traveled to Spain, where he studied under *R' Yehudah of Barcelona. Upon his return to Narbonne the powerful communal leader, R' Todros ben Moshe, appointed him *Av Beis-Din* [chief rabbinical justice] of Narbonne; hence the acronym *Ravad* (= **R'** **A**vraham **A**v **B**eis **D**in).

Ravad II directed the Narbonne talmudic academy and numerous scholars of the Provence area flocked to him. Most notable among them were *Ravad III, who eventually became his son-in-law, and *R' Zerachyah HaLevi, author of *Sefer HaMaor.*

His halachic compendium mostly concerning daily observance — *Sefer HaEshkol,* of which there are two differing printed editions (ed. Auerbach, Halberstadt, 1868; ed. Albeck, Jerusalem, 1935-38) — had a great impact on succeeding generations. Its influence is felt especially in the halachah works of other Provencal scholars, such as *Orchas Chaim* and *Kol Bo.*

Of his entire commentary to Talmud, only fragments of his writings on Tractate *Bava Basra* have survived, but many of his opinions are found in works of *Razah, *Ramban, and *Ran. As *Av Beis Din,* he also wrote numerous responsa, of which only a fraction is still extant *(Teshuvos R' Avraham ben Yitzchak,* Jerusalem, 1962).

Sefer Halttur refers to Ravad II as *HaChasid HaKadosh* ["the holy saint"] because of his extreme piety. He is also reputed to be one of the earliest Kabbalists to whom Elijah the Prophet appeared and revealed teachings of Kabbalah.

R' Yosef ibn Flat

ר' יוֹסֵף אִבְּן פְּלַאת

b. Spain or N. Africa
d. Provence or Syria late 12th cent.

Talmudist, Halachist, and Teacher.

From his birthplace R' Yosef came to Provence where he became one of the leading rabbinical figures of that country. *Razah, *R' Asher ben Meshullam and *Ravad III studied under him, and *Ravad II consulted him on religious questions. R' Yosef's thoroughness is evident in one of his responsa to *Ravad II (Jerusalem, 1935), written in Aramaic, in the style of the Babylonian Geonim. His Talmudic responsa are mentioned in *Ittur, Kol Bo, Shittah Mekubetzes,* and elsewhere.

R' Zerachyah HaLevi (Razah)

ר' זְרַחְיָה (בֶּן יִצְחָק) הַלֵּוִי (רז"ה)

b. Gerona, Spain, c. 1125
d. Lunel, Provence, 1186

Talmudist and Halachist.

R' Zerachyah's family, the prominent Yitzhari clan of Gerona, emigrated to Provence, when Razah was yet a child. He studied under *R' Moshe ben Yosef in Narbonne and *R' Meshullam ben Yaakov in Lunel.

R' Zerachyah was a child prodigy, who composed his first work, *Sefer HaMaor,* at the age of nineteen. It contains his criticisms of *Rif's *Sefer HaHalachos.* R' Zerachyah was most apologetic in correcting this giant of Halachah, and maintained that his insights served only to enhance Rif's monumental code through an extensive commentary that examined it in detail.

Sefer HaMoar begins with a poetic prologue, written in Aramaic, which closes with the line, "Do not classify this youth as an empty barrel, for ofttimes aged wine may be found in a new vessel." To this he adds a short rhyme, in Hebrew, in which he explains that the name of his work, *Maor* ["luminary"], was chosen as an allusion to both his own name [*Zerachyah,* from the Hebrew *zarach,* "to shine"] and the name of his city [Lunel, from the French lune, "moon"]. Razah then completes his introduction in prose, apologizing for his brashness in criticizing so great a luminary as Rif, yet justifying himself by citing examples of other young scholars who differed with acknowledged sages, such as *R' Yonah ibn Janach who criticized *R' Yehudah ibn Chayug. R' Zerachyah closes his introduction by adjuring all future copyists to include his apologetic introduction in all copies of his works, lest later generations accuse him of temerity and the rashness of youth. HaMaor is divided into two sections: HaMaor HaGadol ["the greater luminary"] on the orders Nashim and Nezikin; and HaMaor HaKatan ["the lesser luminary"] on tractate Berachos and the order Moed.

Razah's father, R' Yitzchak HaYitzhari, composed a poem of thanksgiving, praising the Creator for blessing him with a son of such great Torah erudition. This poem appears alongside his son's prologue.

Despite his disclaimers and apologetics, Razah was sharply attacked for presenting a work which implies that Rif sometimes erred in his halachic decisions. In his Hasagos, *Ravad III attacked his colleague, Razah, in very sharp language. The similarly youthful *Ramban, who calls R' Zerachyah "the princely cedar," compiled the extensive work Milchamos HaShem in which he attempts to prove that Razah, not Rif, is in error. Sefer HaMaor, together with the Hasagos and Milchamos HaShem, are printed in all current editions of Sefer HaHalachos. R' Ezra Malchi wrote Shemen LaMaor to defend Razah from the arguments of Ramban, and R' Shlomo Ehrenreich wrote Meoros Shlomo, a commentary to Sefer HaMaor.

Like HaMaor, Razah's Sefer HaTzava on Talmudic methodology contradicts many of *Rif's decisions. It and Ram-

ban's glosses on this work were published in Tamim Deim (225-6) and in Chiddushei HaRamban (Jerusalem, 1928).

When Ravad III produced his manual on family purity titled Baalei HaNefesh, Razah composed glosses known as Hasagos HaRazah (printed in Baalei HaNefesh, or as Sela HaMachlokes, Jerusalem, 1965) refuting many of Ravad's views. Razah's remarks are not cutting; they deal only with the work, and not with the author. In his commentary on Tractate Kinnim (Constantinople, 1741, Talmud and Mishnayos, ed. Vilna), he also criticizes Ravad's commentary on this tractate. In HaMaor Razah mentions his Halachic works named Hilchos Shechitah (printed in Chut HaMeshulash v. 2, New York, 1942) and Hilchos Bedikah, a work that has unfortunately not been preserved. Divrei Rivos, containing a disputation with Ravad on a topic relating to monetary law, appears partially in Shita Mekubetzes (Bava Metzia 88) and in a separate publication (New York, 1908).

Despite his many critical writings, Razah was a man of great humility, as attested to by *R' Yehudah ibn Tibbon: "R' Zerachyah, was unique in his generation. Although he was wiser than I, from the day he met me he did not send a letter ... which he did not show me before it left his hand. He even showed me many of his letters to his brother [R' Berachyah] before sending them."

R' Zerachyah also composed liturgical hymns, some of which appear in the machzorim of Carpentras and Algiers.

Among his closest and most outstanding pupils was *R' Shmuel ibn Tibbon.

*R' Yaakov of Marvege once found himself unable to decide between conflicting explanations of various Talmudic topics as understood by *Rashi and Razah. To determine whose line of reasoning to follow, R' Yaakov made a שְׁאֵלַת חֲלוֹם, i.e., he prayed that his dilemma be solved by Divine inspiration which would come in the form of a dream. The answer he received was a vision of the verse [Psalms 112:4]: "זָרַח בַּחֹשֶׁךְ אוֹר לַיְשָׁרִים, Light shines [Zarach] in the darkness for the upright."

R' Moshe Kimchi

ר' מֹשֶׁה (בֶּן יוֹסֵף) קִמְחִי

d. Narbonne, Provence, c. 1190

Bible Commentator and Grammarian.

Upon the death of *R' Yosef Kimchi, R' Moshe, his eldest son, assumed the responsibility of raising and educating his ten year old brother David who later became famous as *Radak. Although the year of R' Moshe's death is not certain, it is clear that he passed away many years before his younger brother, who quotes him frequently, always with the title, "my teacher, my brother, R' Moshe, of blessed memory."

R' Moshe interpreted much of Scripture. His commentaries on Ezra, Nehemiah, and Proverbs are published in the Mikraos Gedolos edition of Tanach, but erroneously ascribed to *Ibn Ezra. His commentary on Job was published separately (in Tikvas Enosh Berlin, 1868). Like his father, R' Moshe is brief and concise, analyzing the plain meaning of the text and its grammatical implications.

R' Moshe also composed grammatical works, among them Mehalech Shvilei HaDaas (Pesaro, 1508), a textbook on grammar which influenced later texts [the initials of this work's title spell the author's name, Moshe]; and Sefer Tachboshes, a work mentioned in Radak's Michlol, but which has not survived. The eminent grammarian, R' Eliyahu HaBachur, composed notes on R' Moshe's Mehalach, which are printed in many editions of that work.

According to some, R' Moshe wrote an ethical treatise, Taanug HaNefesh, which has also been lost.

R' Yehudah ibn Tibbon

ר' יְהוּדָה (בֶּן שָׁאוּל) אִבְּן תִּיבּוֹן

B. Granada, Spain c. 1120
d. Lunel, France c. 1190

Translator.

Because of persecutions of the Jews by the fanatical Almohade sect (see Historical Introduction), R' Yehudah fled his native Granada and settled in Lunel. *R' Binyamin of Tudela mentions that he worked there as a physician, and that some of his patients were of the nobility. In Lunel, R' Yehudah was on very intimate terms with *Razah, *Ravad III, and *R' Meshullam ben Yaakov. At the latter's request, R' Yehudah translated *R' Bachya's Chovos HaLevavos ["Duties of the Heart"] from Arabic into Hebrew, thus launching his career as a translator. Razah held him in great esteem and showed him his poems before using them in correspondence.

During the years 1161 to 1186 he translated many Arabic works into Hebrew, among them: *R' Shlomo ibn Gabirol's Mivchar HaPeninim and Tikkun Middos HaNefesh; Kuzari of *R' Yehudah HaLevi; Sefer HaRikmah and Sefer HaSharoshim of *R' Yonah ibn Janach, and Emunos VeDeios of R' Saadyah Gaon (892-942).

In his introduction to Chovos HaLevavos, R' Yehudah explains that he translates literally, rather than rendering a free translation, in order to accurately preserve the author's ideas. Scholars acclaimed his accurate translations above all others, and R' Yehudah came to be known as the "father of translators." He originated some new word forms in order to convey certain ideas in a clear and concise manner.

None of his original works have come down to us except for his ethical will (Berlin, 1852). Written in 1190 and addressed to his only son *R' Shmuel ibn Tibbon (who also became a famous translator of Jewish classics), this will instructs R' Shmuel in spiritual, material and physical behavior. R' Yehudah also speaks of the extensive library which he left his son, instructing him to protect it from mice and water damage.

R' Yitzchak ben Abba Mari

ר' יִצְחָק בֶּן אַבָּא מָרִי

b. Provence, c. 1122
d. Marseilles, Provence, c. 1193

Author of Ittur.

At the suggestion of the noted Talmudist R' Abba Mari, his seventeen year old son and disciple, Yitzchak, compiled the laws of ritual slaughter and examination of the animal in Hilchos Shechitah VeTreifos. At about the same time he wrote Hilchos Tzitzis on the laws of the tallis at the request of R' Sheshes Benveniste, Nassi ["prince"] of Barcelona.

These works are part of R' Yitzchak's monumental classic Ittur, which he worked on for over a decade. This Halachic compendium consists of three sections. The first discusses jurisprudence, fiscal law, divorce and marriage (Venice, 1608); the second contains the laws of tzitzis, tefillin, circumcision and forbidden foods (Lemberg, 1860). The final section, called Aseres HaDibros ["The Ten Commandments"], examines ten halachic subjects pertaining to the festivals (Lemberg, 1860).

This work draws on the Jerusalem and Babylonian Talmudim and on Geonic responsa. In fact, Ittur is a primary source of Geonic responsa. The work is frequently cited by the codifiers, especially Tur and Beis Yosef. A number of commentaries were composed on

Ittur; Bnei Yaakov (Constantinople, 1704); Tikkun Sofrim Umikra Sofrim (Constantinople, 1756) and one by R' Meir Yonah ben Shmuel (Vilna, 1874; Warsaw, 1883, 1885). R' Yitzchak's notes on *Rif's Sefer HaHalachos, titled Meah Shearim, are printed in the Vilna edition of the Talmud after the code of Mordechai.

In his prologue to Meah Shearim, R' Yitzchak applies to Rif the verse [Malachi 2:7], "The lips of the Kohen guard knowledge; and Torah is sought from his mouth."

R' Yitzchak carried on a cordial Halachic correspondence with *Rabbeinu Tam. *Ravad III was related to R' Yitzchak.

R' Avraham ben David of Posquieres (Ravad III)

ר' אַבְרָהָם בֶּן דָוִד מפּוֹשְׁקֵיירֶשׁ (ראב"ד הַשְׁלִישִׁי)

b. Narbonne, Provence, c. 1120
d. Posquieres, Provence, c. 1197
[Chanukah 4958]

Talmudist and Halachist.

Ravad III studied under *R' Moshe ben Yosef HaLevi, *R' Meshullam ben Yaakov of Lunel, and *Ravad II, who subsequently became his father-in-law, and revered him greatly. While he was young, R' Avraham became one of the rabbinical authorities of Lunel and directed a Talmudical academy in Nimes which became the foremost yeshivah in all of Provence. Later, at Posquieres, he established an outstanding academy, and supported all of his poor students at his own expense. His disciples there included R' Yitzchak HaKohen of Narbonne, *R' Avraham HaYarchi, R' Meir of Carcassonne, and *R' Asher of Lunel.

Although extremely wealthy, Ravad eschewed luxuries in order to repel the evil inclination, and lived a holy and saintly existence. In 1172, Elzear, the lord of Posquieres, who envied Ravad's wealth, slandered him to the public authorities and had him imprisoned. However, Count Roger II of Carcassonne obtained his release and had the lord of Posquieres banished to Carcassonne.

Ravad began writing at an early age. At first he recorded the teachings of his mentors, but soon, being an independent thinker, he found it necessary to disagree with some of their interpretations and offer his own comments. Of his Talmudic commentaries, those to Tractates *Edios* (Talmud, ed. Vilna), *Kinnim*, (Talmud and Mishnah, ed. Vilna) and *Bava Kamma* have been published (London, 1940). However the commentary on *Tamid* attributed to him (Talmud, ed. Vilna) is probably not by him but by a German Tosafist. Ravad also composed commentaries on the halachic Midrashim on Torah, of which only the one on *Sifra* is extant (Vienna, 1862). *Meiri referred to him as "the greatest of commentators," and placed him alongside *Rif, *Rashi and *R' Yehudah of Barcelona as "the patriarchs of the Talmud ... from whom the entire world [of Talmudic commentary] sprang."

While still a student under R' Meshullam, Ravad produced his treatise *Issur Mashehu* (printed together with *Toras HaBayis*, Jerusalem, 1963) on dietary laws. Many more of Ravad's smaller treatises are found in *Tamim Deim*, covering all aspects of religious practice and affairs. An additional volume of Ravad's decisions and responsa was published as *Teshuvos UPesakim LaRavad* (Jerusalem, 1964). A homily by Ravad, printed as *Derashah L'Rosh Hashanah* (London, 1955), contains much halachic material pertaining to the festivals Rosh HaShanah and Yom Kippur.

Ravad continued to develop his capacity as a critic. His glosses perfected many works and clearly illustrated that Talmudic logic must be applied to each individual case, and that one cannot rely upon a codification of laws without studying the Talmudic sources.

In his critical glosses on Rif's *Sefer HaHalachos*, Ravad extols Rif's magnificent stature, and apologizes for his own inability to follow the codifier in all cases. In *Sefer HaZechus*, a reply to Ravad's questions on Rif, *Ramban speaks of Ravad with awe.

When *Razah published *Sefer HaMaor* with its refutations of Rif's decisions, Ravad attacked him in very sharp terms. While making clear that he bore Razah no personal malice, Ravad claimed that much of the better material in HaMaor was misappropriated from what Razah had heard directly from Ravad *(Divrei Rivos)*.

From the death of Razah in 1186 and thereafter, Ravad no longer spoke harshly of him but issued his critiques in much mellower tones. The heated correspondence between Ravad and Razah concerning the interpretation of a difficult Talmudic passage are collected in *Divrei Rivos* (New York 1908; see also *Shitah Mekubetzes, Bava Metzia*).

Ravad harshly criticized *Mishneh Torah*, mainly because *Rambam did not follow the practice of previous codifiers, who listed their sources in order to show clearly how they derived their halachic decisions. Despite its harsh tone, Rambam revered Ravad greatly and accepted much of his criticism. For his part, Ravad testified that *Mishneh Torah* was a monumental accomplishment, gathering and classifying all Halachic material found in Talmudic literature.

In his later years, Ravad composed *Baalei HaNefesh*, (Venice, 1602) a compendium of the laws of family purity, including the laws of *mikveh* construction. This work is extensively quoted and relied upon in *Tur,* and many decisions in *Shulchan Aruch* are based upon it.

A famed kabbalist, Ravad received mystical instruction from Ravad II and from the Prophet Elijah who appeared to him *(Recanati, Naso).* He himself mentions his *Ruach HaKodesh* ("Divine Inspiration" — *Hasagos Hilchos Lulav* 8:5; *Beis HaBechirah* 6:14; *Tamim Deim* ch. 3). A commentary on the kabbalistic *Sefer Yetzirah* is ascribed to his authorship. He transmitted his kabbalistic knowledge to his son, *R' Yitzchak Sagi Nahor.

R' Asher ben Meshullam

ר' אָשֵׁר בֶּן מְשׁוּלָם

d. Lunel, Provence, c. 1200
Talmudist.

*R' Binyamin of Tudela, who visited Lunel in 1165 reported that R' Asher (mentioned in Tosafos to *Bava Kamma* 64a as Rosh of Lunel) studied day and night in seclusion, fasting all day and never partaking of meat.

R' Asher composed *Hilchos Yom Tov,* which is mentioned in *Tamim Deim,* and *Sefer HaMatanos* which is not extant. He studied under *R' Yosef ibn Flat, and was on cordial terms with *R' Yehudah ibn Tibbon. R' Asher corresponded with the eminent Tosafist *Ri HaZaken. R' Asher's father, *R' Meshullam ben Yaakov, was known as the head of the Lunel scholars.

R' Asher ben Meshullam is often confused with *R' Asher ben Shaul, author of *Sefer HaMinhagos,* who was also a resident of Lunel.

R' Yitzchak Sagi Nahor

ר' יִצְחָק (בֶּן אַבְרָהָם) שַׂגִּי נָהוֹר

Posquieres, Provence, c. 1200
Kabbalist.

Because R' Yitzchak was born blind, he was called *Sagi Nahor* ["full of light,"

a euphemism for sightlessness]. Notwithstanding his handicap, R' Yitzchak was the principal disseminator of Kabbalah in Provence and Spain, and *R' Bachya *(Vayeishev)* called him "the father of Kabbalah." R' Yitzchak was instructed in these mystical teachings — which had been handed down from teacher to elite disciples orally ever since Moses received them on Mount Sinai — by his father, *Ravad III. *R' Menachem Recanati *(Naso — Birkas Kohanim)* reports that Elijah the Prophet also taught R' Yitzchak. R' Yitzchak in turn revealed these teachings to several disciples, among them *R' Ezra and *R' Azriel of Gerona, and systematized some of the material for easier comprehension. These two disciples were especially instrumental in publicizing their master's system in Spain, where it finally found its way to *Ramban. R' Yitzchak's disciples also recorded his interpretations, some of which have been preserved in manuscript, among them a commentary to *Sefer Yetzirah* and one on prayers.

R' Yehonasan of Lunel

ר' יְהוֹנָתָן (בֶּן דָּוִד הַכֹּהֵן) מִלּוּנִיל

b. Provence, c. 1150
d. Eretz Yisrael, c. 1215
Head of the Lunel Scholars.

R' Yehonasan, a disciple-colleague of *Ravad III, was a leading Talmudist in the golden age of Torah in Provence. He greatly revered *Rambam, and after studying *Mishneh Torah,* addressed twenty-four questions to its author in the name of the Sages of Lunel. Rambam gladly replied to R' Yehonasan's inquiries, pleased that his work was being studied in such an erudite manner. Some say that R' Yehonasan composed a work refuting all of *Ravad III's criticisms of *Mishneh Torah.*

At the request of R' Yehonasan,

Rambam sent him a copy of his philosophical *Moreh Nevuchim* ["*Guide to the Perplexed*], written in Arabic, and R' Yehonasan had it translated into Hebrew by *R' Shmuel ibn Tibbon.

Of R' Yehonasan's running commentary to *Rif's *Sefer HaHalachos,* Tractate *Eruvin* is published together with the Halachos in the standard editions of the Talmud, and Tractate *Chullin* was published separately in *Avodas HaLeviim* (Frankfurt, 1871). Recently more segments of this work have become available (on the Tractates *Berachos, Rosh Hashanah, Yoma, Succah, Taanis, Megillah, Moed Kattan, Kiddushin, Bava Kamma, Bava Metzia, Sanhedrin, Avodah Zarah, Makkos* and *Shevuos*), as well as a commentary on the Talmud, Tractate *Horayos.* R' Yehonasan's Halachic decisions appear frequently in the works of succeeding generations. According to tradition, R' Yehonasan emigrated to *Eretz Yisrael* in 1211, together with three hundred Tosafists.

R' Avraham HaYarchi

ר' אַבְרָהָם (בֶּן נָתָן) הַיַּרְחִי

b. Avignon, Provence, c. 1155
d. Toledo, Spain, 1215

Author of *Manhig.*

R' Avraham was a disciple of *Ravad III; the Tosafist *Ri of Dampierre; Ri's son, R' Elchanan; and *R' Yitzchak ben Abba Mari of Marseilles, author of *Ittur,* who was also a relative. The surname HaYarchi [from *yare'ach,* "moon"] alludes to his birthplace Lunel [from the French *lune,* "moon"]. R' Avraham often signed אֲבֵּ"ן הַיַּרְחִי [Even HaYarchi], an acronym for Avraham ben Nassan HaYarchi.

He is also known to have signed legal documents, notably a *get* ["writ of divorce"], together with *Ramah.

At an early age, R' Avraham took to traveling, and he experienced much privation during these years. Besides visiting all the major cities of France and Provence, he spent some time in Germany, and finally made his way to Spain.

In 1204 he settled in Toledo, where his vast knowledge gained him the patronage of the rich and prestigious R' Yoseph ibn Shushan, and his sons R' Shlomo and R' Yitzchak. In his comfortable new surroundings, R' Avraham compiled his *Manhig Olam,* better known as *Sefer HaManhig* (Constantinople, 1519), and dedicated it to the Ibn Shushan family for their great kindness.

The *Manhig* is a manual of all laws governing Jewish life. The authorities preceding him are quoted, and interesting details concerning the customs practiced in the various places R' Avraham visited in his travels are also furnished, including his own halachic decisions rendered there. The kabbalistic material contained in *Manhig* proves that its author was well versed in mystical lore.

R' Avraham was a strong opponent of philosophy, and it was he who delivered the reply of *R' Shimshon of Sens to *R' Meir Abulafia denouncing philosophical pursuits.

He also wrote responsa and a commentary to Tractate *Kallah* (Tiberias, 1906). In Spain, R' Avraham learned enough Arabic to translate into Hebrew a responsum of R' Saadyah Gaon. Some ascribe a work titled *Machzik HaBedek,* not extant, to R' Avraham, but there is doubt as to whether this work ever existed.

R' Moshe HaKohen (Ramach)

ר' מֹשֶׁה הַכֹּהֵן (רמ"ד)

Lunel, Provence, 12th century
Author of *Hasagos* on *Mishneh Torah.*

Kesef Mishneh cites Ramach's *Hasagos* [criticisms] on *Rambam's *Mishneh*

Torah, and part of the Hasagos have been published (Jerusalem, 5629). According to Sefer Yuchasin, Rambam personally replied to R' Moshe's criticisms, but these replies are not extant. R' Moshe is sometimes cited by *Ran and *Rivash.

R' Yehudah ben Berechyah (Ribav)

ר' יְהוּדָה בֶּן בְּרֶכְיָה (ריב״ב)

Provence, late 12th cent.

Author of Shitas Ribav.

R' Yehudah's commentary on *Rif's Sefer HaHalachos, titled Shitas Ribav, is printed on our Talmud editions on tractate Berachos and most of the tractates of Seder Moed. It quotes earlier commentators and codifiers, especially his father's brother, *Razah.

R' Shmuel ibn Tibbon

ר' שְׁמוּאֵל (בֶּן יְהוּדָה) אִבְּן תִּיבּוֹן

b. Lunel, Provence c. 1150
d. Marseilles, Provence c. 1230

Translator.

R' Shmuel, the son of *R' Yehudah ibn Tibbon, continued in his father's footsteps as a classical translator. Many technical and conceptual terms used freely by later authors were coined or hebraized by R' Shmuel, e.g. the word ofek for horizon (from the Arabic). A list of such words appears at the end of Moreh Nevuchim.

At the request of *R' Yehonasan of Lunel, R' Shmuel translated *Rambam's Moreh Nevuchim ["Guide for the Perplexed"] from Arabic into Hebrew. After finishing part of the work, R' Shmuel sent a copy to Rambam for approval, and he included a number of questions and a request for permission to come to Cairo and study under Rambam himself.

Rambam's reply, dated 8 Tishrei 4960 (1199), expressed satisfaction with R' Shmuel's translation and lauded his aptitude and knowledge. After replying to all of his questions, Rambam advised him not to make the trip to Egypt, because Rambam's heavy schedule would leave him no time to study with R' Shmuel. Rambam also expressed his opinion that a literal translation would be burdensome for the reader, and a free translation conveying the ideas would be preferable. Following his father's precedent, however, R' Shmuel is quite literal in his translation. It retains a faithfulness to the original not displayed by any other translators of this work, and therefore became the accepted version, favored over *al-Charizi's free translation.

Although his work was considered a great contribution, R' Shmuel did not escape reproach during the great controversy over the Rambam's philosophical works some decades later. His chief accuser was *R' Yehudah Alfakhar.

An enthusiastic admirer of Rambam and follower of his views, R' Shmuel also translated other of his works: Maamar Techiyas HaMeisim and Igeres Teiman; the commentary on tractate Avos with its introduction Shemonah Perakim; and the last chapter of the Mishneh commentary on tractate Sanhedrin. He also translated philosophical works of Arab authors.

Among R' Shmuel's original works is Maamar Yikavu HaMayim (Pressburg, 1837), a very lengthy allegoric-philosophic interpretation of a Biblical verse (Genesis 1:9). His philosophical commentary on Ecclesiastes is still in manuscript, and he refers to a similar commentary on Song of Songs. In his Yikavu HaMayim he mentions a work entitled Ner HaChofesh, believed to be an allegoric-philosophic commentary on most of the Scriptures.

R' Shmuel resided in various communities, including Beziers and Arles in

Provence and Barcelona and Toledo in Spain. In 1213 he was in Alexandria, Egypt, and he finally settled in Marseilles. His son, *R' Moshe ibn Tibbon, and his son-in-law, R' Yaakov Anatoli, carried on his pursuit of philosophy and the art of translation.

R' David Kimchi (Radak)

ר' דָוִד (בֶּן יוֹסֵף) קִמְחִי (רד"ק)

b. Narbonne, Provence, 1160
d. Narbonne, Provence, 1235

Bible Commentator and Grammarian. *R' Yosef Kimchi died when his youngest son, David, was only ten, and David was raised and educated by his elder brother, *R' Moshe Kimchi.

Radak's Scriptural commentary reportedly covered all of Scripture, but we possess only that to Genesis, the Prophets, Psalms, Proverbs, and Chronicles. His interpretations stress the plain meaning of the text and the continuity of the verses, yet he does not omit exegetical Midrashic teachings. He notes all grammatical and historical data. At times he introduces philosophical explanations. The occasional polemics against Christianity in his commentaries were censored, but were later published separately under the title Teshuvos HaNotzrim (Altdorf, 1644). He also argued against Christianity in Vikuach (Constantinople, 1710). The popularity of Radak's commentary gave rise to a popular paraphrase of the Mishneh (Avos 3:17), "Without kemach ["flour," a play on R' David's surname Kimchi], one cannot learn Torah." Radak also wrote Et Sofer (Lyck, 1864) on Masoretic notes and accents.

His famous work on Hebrew grammar is Sefer Michlol. The first part contains rules of Hebrew grammar adapted from the works of *Ibn Chayug, *Ibn Janach, and his father. The second part, a dictionary of Scripture, was first published in 1590 in Naples, Italy, as Sefer HaShorashim and several times thereafter.

Michlol was attacked by other grammarians such as *R' Yosef Caspi and *R' Profiat Duran for omitting in-depth analysis. The book, however, was defended by R' Eliyahu Bachur, who added his comments and popularized it; it also became a text used by non-Jews such as Reuchlin who wished to study Hebrew.

In the great controversy concerning Rambam's philosophical views and works which raged in Montpellier (see Historical Introduction), Radak strongly defended Rambam and favored philosophical pursuit as long as it did not lead one astray from religion. He sent letters to *R' Yehudah Alfakhar to gain his support, but met with no success.

R' Meir of Trinquetaille

ר' מֵאִיר (בֶּן יִצְחָק) מִטְרִנְקְטַיילִיש

Carcassonne, Trinquetaille, and Arles,
Provence, c. 1200

Author of Sefer HaEzer.

R' Meir was born in Carcassonne. His father, R' Yitzchak, wished him to be in a complete Torah environment and therefore brought him to study under *Ravad III. He studied under this master so intensely, that he was soon regarded not only as a pupil, but as a colleague.

R' Meir authored Sefer HaEzer (not extant) defending *Rif against refutations of *Razah. His son was *R' Nassan of Trinquetaille.

R' Meshullam of Bezier

ר' מְשׁוּלָם (בֶּן מֹשֶׁה) מִבֶּדְרַשׁ

d. Bezier, Provence, c. 1238

Author of Sefer HaHashlamah.

R' Meshullam studied under his father, R' Moshe ben Yehudah of Lunel, son-in-law of *R' Meshullam ben Yaakov. When his mother died and his father remarried, R' Meshullam was forced to fend for himself, and he set out for Bezier.

He is best known for his *Sefer HaHashlamah*, designed to complete *Rif's *Sefer HaHalachos*, which omits many Talmudic discussions. R' Meshullam cites most of the codifiers who preceded him, and renders his own halachic decisions, which do not always concur with that of Rif. *Sefer HaHashlamah* is quoted by some of the commentators, especially *Meiri, who calls him, "the great rabbi, father of all who dwell in the tents [of Torah]." With the passage of time, R' Meshullam's work was all but forgotten. In 1885, R' Yehudah Lubetzky published the first printed edition of this work on most of Seder *Nezikin*. Recently his entire work on Rif has been published (except for Tractate *Kesubos* and *Halachos Ketanos*). Some tractates have appeared in two or three different editions. The commentary printed in the margin of the Vilna edition of Tractate *Yevamos* as *Tosefos Chad MeiKama'ei* is in reality a part of *Sefer HaHashlamah*.

R' Nassan ben Meir of Trinquetaille

ר' נָתָן בֶּן מֵאִיר מִטְרִנְקְטַיילִיש

Trinquetaille and Arles, Provence, c. 1230
Talmudist and teacher.

R' Nassan studied under his father, *R' Meir ben Yitzchak, author of *Sefer HaEzer*. R' Nassan's own works include *Shaar HaTefisah* on Halachah, which he sent to *R' Shmuel HaSardi, and a Torah commentary, known to us only from citations in the works of other authors.

Some of the most famous personalities of Provence and Spain were R' Nassan's disciples, among them, *Ramban and *R' Meir of Narbonne. R' Nassan's grandson, *R' Eshtori HaParchi, mentions his grandfather frequently in *Kaftor VaFerach*.

R' Meir of Narbonne (HaMeili)

ר' מֵאִיר (בֶּן שִׁמְעוֹן) מִנַּרְבּוֹנָא (הַמְעִילִי)

b. Narbonne, Provence, c. 1190
d. Toledo, Spain 1263
[8 Marcheshvan 5024]

Halachist.

R' Meir, a disciple of his father, R' Shimon; his uncle, *R' Meshullam of Bezier; and *R' Nassan ben Meir of Trinquetaille, maintained a correspondence with his colleague, *Ramban.

R' Meir compiled *Sefer HaMeoros* on the halachic material of tractates *Berachos, Chullin,* order *Moed,* and the laws of writing a *Sefer Torah, tefillin* and *mezuzos.* This has been published recently by R' M. Y. Blau, in addition to works on *Bava Kama, Yevamos* and *Kesubos.*

Another work by R' Meir, *Milchemes Mitzvah,* is presumably, as indicated by its name, a defense against attacks on Judaism. Excerpts from this treatise indicate that it contained, among other topics, a copy of a letter from R' Meir to the French king (probably Louis IX, who reigned 1226-70) outlining the king's unfairness in promulgating anti-Jewish legislation. Both the contents and the tenor of this letter are unique. R' Meir upbraids the king for his ingratitude, pointing out that on many occasions the taxes paid by his Jewish subjects had saved their royal masters, and that a Jewish soldier had sacrificed his own life to save Charlemagne during the latter's siege of Narbonne. Charlemagne had not forgotten this favor and assigned a substantial portion of Narbonne to the Jews and had the edict recorded in the official records of the city. R' Meir further reminds the king that he too is human and will have to answer for his deeds before the Heavenly Tribunal. The accusatory tone of this epistle and its boldness is startling, and attests to its author's strength of character, courage, and compassion for his oppressed people. Another part of this work records a religious dispute held by R' Meir with an eminent churchman. This clergymen was so impressed by R' Meir's arguments that he remained his lifelong admirer and friend, and, when he was subsequently appointed to the college of cardinals, he used his influence to better the Jews' lot. Another portion of this work deals with the interpretation of key passages of the prayers, and halachos relating to them.

R' Meir mentions some additional works which have not come down to us: Chibbur HaDerashos, sermons for the festivals; Maorah, commentary to the Torah; and Meishiv Nefesh, an answer to a critique of *Rambam's philosophical approach to Judaism in the first two chapters of Hilchos Yesodei HaTorah.

R' Asher ben David

ר' אָשֵׁר בֶּן דָּוִד

Provence, c. 1250

Kabbalist.

R' Asher was a grandson of *Ravad III, and studied under his own father R' David, and under his uncle, the prominent kabbalist *R' Yitzchak Sagi Nahor. R' Asher authored the kabbalistic works Sefer HaYichud and Tikkun Yud-Gimmel Middos. Only fragments have been published, while the bulk of the work remains in manuscript.

R' Asher ben Shaul

ר' אָשֵׁר בֶּן שָׁאוּל (מִלּוּנֵיל)

Lunel, Provence, c. 1250

Author of Sefer HaMinhagos.

R' Asher, like his older brother, R' Yaakov Nazir, delved into kabbalistic literature. He wrote Sefer HaMinhagos (Jerusalem, 1935) on the customs of Provence.

R' Chizkiyah Chizkuni

ר' חִזְקִיָּה (בֶּן מָנוֹחַ) חִזְקוּנִי

Provence, c. 1250

Torah Commentator.

R' Chizkiyah, about whose personal life almost nothing is known, composed a Torah commentary, Chizkuni (Venice, 1524), which has been reprinted many times. A new critical edition, based on what is thought to be the author's original manuscript, has recently been published (Jerusalem, 1981). Although R' Chizkiyah himself testifies that his work was culled from twenty earlier commentaries, he almost invariably does not cite his sources. Explaining this omission in his poetic preface, the author says that he found many students who prejudge the words of the commentators, passing over those whom they consider inferior scholars and dwelling only on what is quoted in the name of those whom they regard as wealthy in Torah knowledge. Seeing this attitude as a slur on Torah scholars, R' Chizkiyah elected to omit the names so that his readers would "not look at the barrel, but at the wine poured from it." A noteworthy exception to the omission of sources is R' Chizkiyah's consistent citation of *Rashi by name. Indeed, Chizkuni often expands on Rashi's interpretations and is considered the first of scores of supercommentaries which have been written to elucidate the teachings of Rashi. A seeker of the plain meaning of Scripture, R' Chizkiyah often follows the interpretations of *R' Avraham ibn Ezra and *Rashbam.

R' Reuven ben Chayim

ר' רְאוּבֵן בֶּן חַיִּים

Narbonne, Provence, c. 1260

Halachist.

R' Reuven studied under *Ravad III's disciple, R' Yitzchak HaKohen of Narbonne, and in turn transmitted his Torah knowledge to *Meiri.

Sefer HaTamid, R' Reuven's exposition of the prayers, is first mentioned by *R' Aharon of Lunel in *Orchos Chayim*. Only part of the manuscript has survived, and it was recently reprinted (Jerusalem, 1967).

Meiri said of R' Reuven: "I am as the smallest of his fingers, the remnants of his handiwork ... he was proficient in all aspects of the Talmud with a marvelous expertise ..."

R' Mordechai ben Yosef (of Avignon)

ר' מָרְדְּכַי בֶּן יוֹסֵף (מֵאֲוִיגְנוֹן)

Avignon, Provence, 13th century

Talmudist.

R' Mordechai's *Beis Shearim* on the laws of marriage contracts, *Shaarei Nedarim* on vows, and *Issur VeHeter* or *Eiver Min HaChai* on dietary laws have been lost. They are known only through *Shaarei Zion, Orchos Chaim, Ma'aseh Rokeach* and *Sefer HaBatim* on *Rambam (the latter work by his disciple *R' David HaKochavi). Still extant in manuscript is his defense of Judaism against the attacks of the apostate Pablo Christiani.

In 1215 a papal decree was issued ordering Jews in the Ashkenazic communities to wear the "badge of shame" on their clothing, and the law was instituted in Provence about 1270. R' Mordechai appeared with a delegation before Charles I in 1276 and succeeded in having the decree abolished in Provence.

R' Moshe ibn Tibbon

ר' משֶׁה (בֶּן שְׁמוּאֵל) אִבְּן תִּיבּוֹן

b. Marseilles, France, c. 1200
d. Marseilles, France, c. 1283

Translator.

R' Moshe, the son of *R' Shmuel ibn Tibbon, followed the family tradition of translating classics from Arabic into Hebrew. R' Moshe's most notable translation is of *Rambam's *Sefer HaMitzvos* (Constantinople, 1517). R' Moshe also translated some of Rambam's Mishnah commentary, a fragment of which was published (Berlin, 1847), and some of Rambam's medical and philosophical treatises. He also translated Aristotelian works of Arabic philosophers.

As an original writer, he produced a philosophic commentary on Song of Songs (Lyck, 1874), and a Torah commentary mentioned by bibliographers, which has not survived. Three works — *Sefer Peah,* an allegoric exposition of the *Aggadah* in the Talmud which refutes arguments of Christian scholars; *Olam Katan,* a philosophic treatise on the immortality of the soul; and *Sefer HaKinyanim* or *HaTaninim* — are still in manuscript.

R' Moshe earned his livelihood as a physician.

His son, R' Yehudah, wrote a commentary to Rambam's *Moreh Nevuchim.*

R' Manoach

ר' מָנוֹחַ

Narbonne and Bezier, Provence, 13th cent.

Talmudist.

R' Manoach studied under *R' Reuven ben Chaim and *R' Meir of Narbonne.

Kesef Mishneh frequently quotes *Sefer HaMenuchah,* R' Manoach's commentary on *Rambam's *Mishneh Torah*. Originally, only a part of *Sefer HaMenuchah* was published (Constantinople, 1718). In recent times more parts of his commentary have been published (Jerusalem, 5730; Rambam, ed. Frankel). The extant parts of *Sefer HaMenuchah* cover significant parts of *Sefer Ahavah* and *Zemanim*. According to some authorities, R' Manoach's father was named Yaakov. Others, however, believe that the author of *Sefer HaMenuchah* is the R' Manoach ben Shimon mentioned by *Rivash and *Ohel Moed*.

R' David ben Levi

ר' דָּוִד בֶּן לֵוִי

Provence, 13th cent.

Author of *Sefer HaMichtam*.

R' David studied under his father R' Levi bar Beniveste and R' Shmuel Skili (or R' Shmuel Shekel). R' David composed *Sefer HaMichtam*, a commentary to the passages of the Talmud (or to the *Rif) pertaining to halachah. Judging from quotations of this work and certain extant remains, it would appear that this work was only on Seder *Mo'ed*. It is extensively cited in the works of contemporary Provencal scholars, such as *Orchos Chaim* and *Kol Bo*.

Substantial protions of this work have recently come to light *(Berachos, Pesachim, Succah, Beitzah, Taanis, Megillah and Mo'ed Kattan)*. Appended to the edition of *Sefer HaMichtam* on *Pesachim* (New York, 1959) is a collection of responsa by various Provencal scholars, among them some by R' David.

R' Menachem HaMeiri

ר' מְנַחֵם (בֶּן שְׁלֹמֹה) הַמְּאִירִי

b. Provence, c. 1249
d. Perpignan, Provence c. 1306

Talmud Commentator.

Meiri, who, until modern times, was virtually unknown to any but the most erudite scholars is today one of the most quoted authors wherever Talmud is studied. This resurgence of Meiri's popularity is due to the rediscovery and publication of his monumental *Beis HaBechirah*, a classic work on the orders *Moed, Nashim* and *Nezikin*, and the tractates *Berachos, Chalah, Chulin, Tamid, Mikvaos* and *Niddah*. Meiri's commentary is unique in its lucid and facile presentation and in its very method and arrangement. Strictly speaking, *Beis HaBechirah* is not a commentary at all, but a digest of the comments of the Gemara to the Mishnah, arranged in the form of a commentary to the Mishnah. This digest, however, is given together with all the pertinent differing interpretations of the greatest authorities up to and including his time.

Meiri quotes his predecessors not by name, but by original honorary titles. Thus *Rif is called *Gedolei HaPoskim* — the greatest decisor; *Rashi, *Gedolei HaRabbanim* — the greatest teacher; *Rambam, *Gedolei HaMechabrim* — the greatest codifier; *Ravad III, *Gedolei HaMeforshim* — the greatest expositor; *Razah, *Gedolei HaRishonim* — the greatest of the early ones; and Meiri's contemporary *Rashba, *Gedolei HaDor* — the greatest of the generation. After the appearance in print of *Beis HaBechirah* to *Megillah* (Amsterdam, 1769), a few other individual parts of the work were published. It was not, however, until very recent times that a concerted effort was made to publish the entire work. Recently, a new annotated edition of the complete commentary has been published (Jerusalem, 1968).

In addition to *Beis HaBechirah* (which he completed in fifteen years), Meiri also composed novellae to many tractates in the form of comments on the *Gemara* in the style of the classic Spanish commentators.

Among Meiri's other work are *Chibbur HaTeshuvah* on repentance; *Magen Avos* (London, 1909) defending the customs of Provence; *Kiryas Sefer* (Smyrna, 1863; 1881) covering the laws of writing a *Sefer Torah* and notes on the *Mesorah*; *Kesav Da'as*, cited in his *Beis HaBechirah*, which has not been found; and *Beis Yad* (Jerusalem, 1912) concerning the laws of washing the hands upon arising and before eating.

Meiri introduces his commentary to *Avos* with a lengthy prologue which traces the line of Torah scholarship, link by link, from Biblical times to his own day. This prologue was inspired by the beginning of *Avos* itself, which opens by recording the chain of tradition and Torah leadership from Moses to Joshua, through the elders and prophets, the Men of the Great Assembly, and finally the Tannaim [Rabbinical authorities of the Mishnaic era]. Meiri's introduction became a valuable historical source and the forerunner of a genre of books dedicated to this pursuit [e.g., *Shaarei Zion* by R' Yitzchak de Lattes; *Sefer HaYuchsin* by R' Avraham Zacuto].

According to R' Yitzchak de Lattes, Meiri also composed a commentary covering all of Scripture; however, only his interpretations of Psalms (Jerusalem, 1936) and Proverbs (Leiria, 1492) have survived.

By his own account, Meiri was descended from the greatest Provencal Talmudists, *R' Meshullam of Bezier, *R' Moshe ben Yosef, *Ravad II and *Ravad I.

In the great controversy that surged in Provence during this period (see Historical Introduction), Meiri defended the study of philosophy and the sciences, but stipulated that this study should be delayed until one has mastered the Talmud. Meiri was the disciple of *R' Reuven ben Chaim. He maintained an active halachic correspondence with *Rashba.

R' Abba Mari HaYarchi

ר' אַבָּא מָרִי (בֶּן מֹשֶׁה) הַיַּרְחִי

b. Lunel, Provence, c. 1240
d. Perpignan, Provence, c. 1315

Talmudist.
*R' Abba Mari, a descendant of *R'

Meshullam ben Yaakov of Lunel, was a Talmudist acquainted with philosophy. When he moved to Montpellier, he found the study of Talmud being neglected by the young, who devoted most of their time to philosophy and science. He also heard the allegoric-philosophical Torah lectures of R' Levi ben Chaim and R' Yaakov Anatoli which introduced Greek philosophy into the interpretation of Torah verses, ranking Aristotle with Moses.

To counter the threat of these practices in his native homeland, R' Abba Mari wrote many letters to the leading authorities of Provence condemning the study of philosophy and urging them to save their communities from spiritual destruction. *Rashba, the greatest sage of the period, wholly supported R' Abba Mari in his endeavors, and Rashba's support gained R' Abba Mari many adherents.

R' Abba Mari moved to Arles and then to Perpignan, where he published *Minchas Kenaos* (Pressburg, 1838), a collection of all the correspondence involved in this controversy, with an introduction concerning principles of faith, such as Divine providence, G−d's sovereignty, and His creation of the world.

The name HaYarchi alludes to his birthplace, Lunel [*lune* is French for moon; יָרֵחַ, *Yare'ach*, is the Hebrew equivalent].

R' Machir ben Abba Mari

ר' מָכִיר בֶּן אַבָּא מָרִי

Provence, late 13th-early 14th centuries
R' Machir's encyclopedic Midrash, *Yalkut HaMachiri*, covering the Later Prophets, Psalms, Proverbs, and Job, draws on the Jerusalem and Babylonian Talmuds, *Tosefta*, the various halachic Midrashim and *Pirke deR' Eliezer*. His introduction indicates that it was written in his old age. Only parts of this work

have been preserved. The existing portions include fragments on: Isaiah (Berlin, 1894), Psalms (Berdychev, 1899), the Book of the Twelve Prophets, and Proverbs (Jerusalem, 1967).

R' Yedayah HaPenini

ר' יְדַעְיָה (בֶּן אַבְרָהָם) הַפְּנִינִי

d. Bezier, Provence, c. 1315

Author of *Bechinos Olam.*

R' Yedayah studied under his father, the Hebrew poet R' Avraham of Bezier, and under *R' Meshullam of Bezier. He was greatly interested in philosophy, and subscribed to the views of *Rambam.

At the age of seventeen, he composed *Sefer HaPardes* (Constantinople, 1515), which takes a philosophical approach to ethics. One year later he wrote *Ohev Nashim,* a refutation of *Minchas Yehudah Sonei Nashim,* Yehudah ibn Shabsai's satire against women and marriage.

R' Yedayah's best known work is *Bechinos Olam* (Mantua, 1476), which depicts poetically and philosophically the value of spiritual gain and downplays worldly pursuits. *Bechinos Olam* is quoted in *Akeidah* and by Abarbanel, but it was strongly opposed by the celebrated Italian kabbalist R' Avi-Ad Sar Shalom (preface to *Emunas Chachamim).* Eighty editions were printed of this book, and it has been translated into English, French, Latin, German, and Yiddish and also interpreted by many commentators.

When in 1305, *Rashba pronounced a ban of excommunication against anyone studying philosophy and science before the age of twenty-five (see Historical Introduction), R' Yedayah addressed an apologetic letter to the sage in defense of philosophy and science. This letter, called *Igeres Hisnatzlus,* is incorporated in Rashba's responsa (vol. 1, resp. 418).

Among R' Yedayah's other works are *Bakashas HaMemin* [lit., "supplication of the letter 'mem' "], a poetic prayer, every word of which begins with the letter מ (Soncino, 1488); philosophical commentaries to Midrashim *(Midrash Rabbah,* Rodelheim, 1854); *Leshon HaZahav,* a commentary to Psalms (Venice, 1599) and Tractate *Avos* (Jerusalem, 1970); and a supercommentary to *Ibn Ezra's Torah commentary. He wrote various philosophical and scientific works — some are extant in manuscript and others are known only from citations in his other works.

R' David HaKochavi

ר' דָּוִד (בֶּן שְׁמוּאֵל) הַכּוֹכָבִי

b. Estella, Navarre (Spain), c. 1260
d. Provence, c. 1330

Dayan.

R' David was a disciple of *R' Mordechai ben Yosef, author of *Shaarei Nedarim.* In 1305, R' David was appointed a member of the Avignon *Beis Din.*

R' David wrote *Kiryas David* ("The City of David"), comprising a series of treatises. One of these is *Migdal David* ("The Fortress of David"), in which the author explains the reasons for some of the *mitzvos,* expounds on some of the difficult topics in Scripture, and illuminates some of the obscure passages in the aggadic portions of the Talmud. In his words, the *Migdal* was intended to protect the people in the 'City of David' against the attacks of their enemies.

This portion of R' David's work is extant in manuscript only. Another, more widely known part of this work is *Sefer HaBattim* ("the Book of Houses"), i.e. the houses within the "City of David." This is a compendium of laws arranged according to *Rambam's code, in which R' David collected the various conflicting views of the authorities preceding him, from the geonic era to his day. This work is quoted by *Maggid Mishneh, Kessef Mishneh* and others. The known extant remains of this work has been published in two volumes (New York 1979, 1980). Yet another portion of this work is *Rechavah*, in which R' David explores in depth some of the topics summarized in *Sefer HaBattim*. No portion of this work is known to have survived. R' Yitzchak deLattes *(Shaarei Zion)* says ecstatically of R' David's 'City,' 'there is nothing like it in this country!'

The author of *Ezras Nashim (Shitas HaKadmonim, Kiddushin)*, R' Yaakov ben R' Moshe of Bagnols (Provence) was R' David's grandson.

The name *HaKochavi* is derived from R' David's birthplace Estella, meaning star *(kochav in Hebrew)*.

R' Aharon HaKohen of Lunel

ר' אַהֲרֹן (בֶּן יַעֲקֹב) הַכֹּהֵן מִלּוּנֵיל

b. Narbonne, Provence
d. Majorca, Spain
c. 1325

Halachist.

R' Aharon was the scion of a prominent rabbinic family. His great-grandfather, R' Yitzchak HaKohen, a disciple of *Ravad III, composed a commentary on the Jerusalem Talmud (on the greater part of three sedarim), and his grandfather, R' David, wrote a treatise on dietary laws.

R' Aharon was born in Narbonne but spent many years wandering before settling in Majorca. He was known as R' Aharon of Lunel because of his family roots in that city. When in 1306 Philip IV expelled the Jews from France, R' Aharon was forced to wander from place to place. Although he was a recognized halachic authority, R' Aharon wrote that he was often at a loss to reply to questions put to him — a result of both his wearisome travels in

search of a home, and the lack of books for study and research.

This convinced him to compile *Orchos Chaim,* a compendium of the opinions of the codifiers on the laws of prayer, Sabbath, and holidays (part 1, Florence, 1750); marriage, and divorce, and dietary regulations (part 2, Berlin, 1902). His main sources were *Rambam, *Semak, *Rashba, *Tashbatz, Sefer HaTerumah,* and the early halachic authorities and geonic responsa. *Beis Yosef* cites *Orchos Chaim* over two hundred times. An abridged form of *Orchos Chaim* is the popular halachic compendium *Kol Bo* (Naples, 1590), whose authorship is uncertain. Some claim it to be an earlier work of R' Aharon's and the forerunner of *Orchos Chaim.*

R' Aharon finally found refuge on the Spanish island of Majorca, where he became acquainted with the rabbi of the community, R' Shem Tov Falco, a scholar in his own right who is mentioned by *Rashba and others. Both the customs of Majorca and the decisions of its rabbi are recorded in *Orchos Chaim.*

R' Yosef Caspi

ר' יוֹסֵף (בֶּן אַבָּא מָרִי) כַּסְפִּי

b. Argentiere, Provence, 1280
d. Majorca, Spain, 1340

Philosopher, Commentator, Grammarian.

R' Yosef was greatly intrigued by philosophy, and considered *Rambam his mentor, always bemoaning the fact that he did not live in the great teacher's era. In quest of knowledge, he traveled to Egypt to study philosophy from Rambam's descendants. He was most disappointed to discover that these devoted Talmudists did not occupy their time with philosophical studies. To himself and his futile journey, R' Yosef applied the words of Isaiah (31:1): "Woe unto them that descend to Egypt for assistance." Being financially secure, he was able to continue his journey to Fez, Morocco, and then to Provence. Eventually, he settled in Spain.

At the age of seventeen, R' Yosef began to write, and produced about forty books. R' Yosef named each of his works with a two word phrase, the second word being *kesef*, the Hebrew word for silver, an allusion to his birthplace, *Argentiere*, [from the French word for silver, *argent*]. He himself catalogued his writings in *Kevutzas HaKesef*.

At Arles, Provence, in 1317, he composed *Tiras Kesef*, which interprets miracles as natural occurrences and reconciles philosophy with religion and kabbalah. This treatise evoked stern opposition from many a Talmudist, and evoked a letter of reproof from R' Klonimos ben Klonimos.

R' Yosef also composed *Adnei Kesef*, a commentary on Prophets; and *Chatzotzros Kesef*, a commentary on Proverbs and Ecclesiastes. In the field of language, he composed a dictionary, *Sharsharos Kesef*; a grammatical essay, *Resukos Kesef*; and a commentary on *Ibn Janach's *Sefer HaRikmah*.

Among his philosophical works, the most popular is his commentary to *Rambam's *Moreh Nevuchim*, divided into two parts, *Amudei Kesef* and *Maskiyos Kesef*. *Tzror HaKesef* contains a summary of Arab philosophy, and *Terumas Kesef* is based on Aristotle's attitude to ethical conduct. In his will, titled *Tzava'as Kesef*, which contains his concepts of Judaism and fulfillment of the commandments, he stresses that without strict observance of *mitzvos* it is impossible to comprehend the deeper meanings of Torah. Nevertheless, Caspi's works and philosophical attitude met with strong opposition even in successive generations, and *Rashbatz

and Abarbanel often criticized his writings.

R' Levi ben Gershon (Ralbag)
ר׳ לֵוִי בֶּן גֵּרְשׁוֹן (רלב״ג)
b. Bagnols, Provence, 1288
d. France, 1344

Bible Commentator, Talmudist, Philosopher, Astronomer.

Ralbag is best known for his commentary to Scripture, which first explains the literal meaning of the text, and then sums up the philosophical ideas and moral maxims contained in each section.

Ralbag's most famous work is *Milchamos HaShem* (Riva diTrento, 1560), a philosophical treatise strictly adhering to Aristotelian thought. Ralbag's rigid Aristotelianism led him to rationalize many of the miracles in the Bible, and to accept an untraditional view of the world's antiquity. The philosophy underlying this work and his Bible commentary was sharply criticized by the most prominent authorities, such as *Rivash, Abarbanel, and *Messer Leon, who claimed they deviated from the true spirit of Judaism, and border on heresy.

*R' Chisdai Crescas devoted considerable space in his *Or Hashem* to refute Ralbag's views on various issues. Maharal of Prague devotes an entire essay (preface to *Gevuros HaShem*) to a rebuttal of Ralbag's view that miracles cannot involve changes in the heavenly bodies.

Much different, however, was the rabbinical reaction to Ralbag's Talmudic works: *Shaarei Zedek* (Leghorn, 1800), a commentary on the thirteen halachic rules of the *tanna*, R' Yishmael; *Mechokek Safun*, an interpretation of the aggadic material in the fifth chapter of Tractate *Bava Basra*; a commentary to Tractate *Berachos*; and two responsa. All these are mentioned respectfully in the works of later generations, but none of them (except *Shaarei Zedek)* are extant.

Although critical of his philosophical pursuits, subsequent generations of Talmudical scholars *(Teshuvos Rashbatz* 1:134) acknowledged R' Levi's stature as a Talmudic scholar and his strong orthodoxy in observance of the commandments.

Ralbag composed an extensive treatise on astronomy, which includes astronomical tables and describes an instrument [the Jacob Staff] that Ralbag invented for precise observation of the heavenly bodies. The work was eventually translated into Latin, and had such a great influence on non-Jewish astronomers that a crater on the moon has been named "Rabbi Levi" [approx. 35° S. lunar lat., 23° E. lunar long.] in his honor.

His other works include *Maaseh Choshev,* a treatise on algebra, and some works on medicine, which was probably his profession.

R' Eshtori HaParchi

ר' אֶשְׁתּוֹרִי (בֶּן מֹשֶׁה) הַפַּרְחִי

b. Provence, c. 1280
d. Eretz Yisrael, c. 1345

Talmudist, Halachist, Scholar.

Disciple of his father, R' Moshe, *Rosh, and his relative R' Yaakov ben Machir ibn Tibbon.

During his wanderings following the expulsion from France (see Historical Introduction), R' Eshtori composed several works: *Batei HaNefesh* on ethics; *Shoshanas HaMelech* on the sciences mentioned in the Talmud; and *Shaar HaShamayim,* novellae on the Talmud, which have not been preserved but are cited in his *Kaftor VaFerach.*

R' Eshtori spent some time in Spain and thereafter emigrated to *Eretz Yisrael,* where he finally found peace. He immersed himself in the halachic material concerning *Eretz Yisrael* and the history of the Holy Land. For seven years, R' Eshtori toured *Eretz Yisrael* to learn its geography accurately. Then he settled in Beis Shean, where, in a quiet and undisturbed atmosphere, he compiled *Kaftor VaFerach* (Venice, 1546) concerning the holiness of the land and the status of all of its cities and boundaries according to the Talmud, the Midrash, and halachic authorities, including those of his grandfather, *R' Nassan ben Meir of Trinquetaille. This work was praised by the leading rabbinical authorities, including *Radvaz, R' Betzalel Ashkenazi, R' Yosef Karo, Rama, and many others.

R' Eshtori also translated some treatises on medicine from Latin into Hebrew.

Some historians claim that the unusual name Eshtori is a pseudonym taken from the words אִישׁ הַתּוּרִי ["explorer"]. This theory is belied by the fact that he signed all his works, even those composed before his wanderings began, with this name.

Italy

Italy

R' Shabsai Donolo

ר' שַׁבְּתַי (בֶּן אַבְרָהָם) דונולו

b. Oria, Italy, 913
d. after 982

Scholar.

At the age of twelve, R' Shabsai and his entire family were taken prisoner by Arabs. He was later ransomed by relatives at Otranto, while the rest of his family was carried off to Palermo (Sicily) and North Africa. Despite the hardships he suffered, his thirst for knowledge did not abate and he wandered about in search of someone to instruct him in astrology. His teacher in this field was an Arab from Baghdad named Bagdesh, whose theories R' Shabsai later synthesized with those of the Greek and Indian astrologers, whose books he possessed.

His main contribution was his commentary to Sefer Yetzirah, titled Chachmuni and based on astrology and astronomy (Leipzig, 1845). This work is cited by *Rashi (Eruvin 56a).

R' Shabsai was also an acclaimed physician, and wrote a medical treatise entitled Sefer HaYekar and other works in this discipline (Kisvei HaRefuah LeR' Shabsai Donolo, Jerusalem, 1949).

R' Klonimos of Lucca

ר' קלונימוס (בֶּן מֹשֶה) מלוקה

Lucca, Italy, 10th cent.

Talmudist, Halachist.

This scion of the famous Klonimos clan, which had been influential in the development of scholarship in Italy and Germany-France since the eighth century, carried on the family tradition. Some of his extensive responsa have been preserved and published under the title Teshuvos R' Klonimos of Lucca (Berlin, 1891). *R' Gershom Meor Ha-Golah referred to him with great reverence and praised his liturgical compositions, among which is Malchuso BeKehal Adaso recited during the Yom Kippur Shacharis service in Ashkenazic communities. Tosafos (Menachos 109b) reports that, "R' Klonimus, the father of *R' Meshullam, at the time of his death ... emended three passages as if through prophecy ..."

Tradition records that an ancestor of R' Klonimos was brought by one of the French kings to establish a Torah academy in Mainz, in order to bolster the Jewish communities in that region, but the records are unclear as to when this happened. *R' Elazar of Worms — author of Rokeach — himself a member of the Klonimos family, reports that the kabbalistic interpretations of the prayers were handed down in his family for many generations and were given to his ancestor R' Moshe (ostensibly the scholar transported to Mainz by the king) by an otherwise unknown Babylonian scholar. These kabbalistic "secrets" finally were transmitted to *R' Shmuel of Speyer and to his son *R' Yehudah HaChassid (both members of the Klonimos family). In turn, R' Yehudah HaChassid taught them to his kinsman R' Elazar of Worms, who had also received some of these secrets independently.

R' Meshullam of Lucca

ר' מְשׁוּלָם (בֶּן קְלוֹנִימוֹס) מִלּוּקָה

b. Lucca, Italy, c. 950
d. Mainz, Germany, c. 1020

Talmudist, Halachist, Liturgist.

The son of *R' Klonimos of Lucca, he was called R' Meshullam the Great. He studied under R' Shlomo HaBavli (d. 990) and corresponded extensively with R' Sherira Gaon (907-1007) of Babylon, and with his son R' Hai Gaon (939-1038). He also kept in close contact with *R' Shimon the Great of Mainz, and many times responded to inquiries of the Mainz Beis Din. He is cited by *Rashi (Zevachim 45b), and his responsa have been collected from various early sources and published (Berlin, 1893).

Many of R' Meshullam's liturgical compositions are in the Yom Kippur *Machzor*. However, his commentary on Tractate *Avos*, referred to in the *Aruch*, has been lost.

R' Meshullam is reported to have engaged in religious disputations with the Karaite sect. The Karaites disregarded Talmudic interpretation to Scripture, and based their laws on a superficially understood plain meaning of Scripture. R' Meshullam proved, using Scriptural references only, that it is permissible to let a light or fire burn in one's home on the Sabbath. This is contrary to the Karaite interpretation of *Exodus* 35:3. Similarly, he proved from *Ezekiel* 46:3 that it is permissible to leave one's house on the Sabbath, thus contradicting the Karaite interpretation of *Exodus* 16:29.

Towards the end of his life, R' Meshullam settled in Mainz, Germany.

R' Eliyahu ben Shemayah

ר' אֵלִיָּהוּ בֶּן שְׁמַעְיָה

Bari, Italy, late 10th-early 11th cent.

Talmudist, Paytan.

R' Eliyahu's *selichos* are particularly popular and many of them appear in various Ashkenazic rites. Forty of these poems have been preserved. In them he describes the plight of Israel in exile and their hope for speedy redemption.

R' Achimaatz ben Paltiel

ר' אֲחִימַעַץ בֶּן פַּלְטִיאֵל

b. Capua, Italy, 1017
d. Oria, Italy, c. 1065

Talmudist, Paytan.

Scion of the family of R' Amitai, the forerunner of all Italian scholars and liturgical poets (see Historical Introduction), R' Achimaatz wrote a family chronicle in the form of an epic poem, tracing his genealogy and recounting various incidents he had received as family tradition. Many miraculous occurrences are recorded, and his ancestors are portrayed as great kabbalists. The chronicle is also of great historic value, shedding much light on the origins and conditions of the Jewish communities of southern Italy, their leaders, and their ties with Eretz Yisrael and Babylon. This work was recently published (Jerusalem, 1944, 1974; New York, 1924) as *Megillas Achimaatz*.

R' Matzliach

ר' מַצְלִיחַ (בֶּן אֵלִיָּהוּ)

Sicily, Italy, c. 1060

Talmudist.

R' Matzliach traveled to Babylon to study under the Geonim there. He was thoroughly acquainted with the ways and customs of his teacher, R' Hai Gaon (939-1038), and at the request of *R' Shmuel HaNaggid composed a biography of the illustrious Gaon.

His star pupil was *R' Nassan ben Yechiel, author of the *Aruch*.

R' Klonimos of Rome

ר' קְלוֹנִימוֹס (בֶּן שַׁבְּתַי) אִישׁ רוֹמִי

b. Rome, Italy
d. Worms, Germany, 1096

Talmudist, Halachist, Liturgist.

In 1064, R' Klonimos was called to

Worms to succeed *R' Yaakov ben Yakar as head of the Talmudic academy there. *Rashi cites him (Beitzah 24b) and lauds his erudition. The halachic decisions of R' Klonimos also appear in the works of Rashi and his school. R' Klonimos died a martyr during the first crusade.

R' Nassan ben Yechiel

ר' נָתָן בֶּן יְחִיאֵל

b. Rome, Italy, c. 1035
d. Rome, Italy, after 1102

Halachist, Commentator, Lexicographer.

Most of the biographical facts known about R' Nassan are gleaned from the cryptic poem which he appended to his masterwork, Aruch. In metered rhyme, heavily embellished with Scriptural and Talmudic allusions, he describes his unwavering faith in the Supreme Judge, despite the loss of four sons in early childhood. Regarding his only surviving son, Reuven, he writes prayerfully, "May Reuven live ..." [Deuteronomy 33:6], and, "He shall live on ..." [Psalms 49:10].

During the lifetime of his father, R' Yechiel, dean of the Talmudic academy of Rome (see Historical Introduction), R' Nassan earned his livelihood selling linen for shrouds. Upon R' Yechiel's passing, his three surviving sons, R' Nassan, R' Daniel and R' Avraham, succeeded their father as heads of the academy. In this position, R' Nassan actively looked after his community's spiritual needs. In 1088 he erected a mikveh ["ritualarium"] for public use, and in 1102, one year after he finished writing his Aruch, construction was completed on a magnificent synagogue built by him and his brothers. Sometime during this period he "proclaimed a vow to the Almighty and fulfilled it" by engaging Shmuel, the scribe of Otranto, to write a Torah scroll, with scrupulous exactitude and beautiful calligraphy.

R' Nassan studied Talmud under his father, as well as *R' Moshe HaDarshan and *R' Matzliach. Many halachic questions were addressed to him.

In the Aruch, — a compendium of words found in the Babylonian and Jerusalem Talmudim, Tosefta, Midrashim and Targumim — R' Nassan traces the root of each word, renders the accurate Talmudic text in which the word is found, and often presents a complete analysis of the cited passage. The Aruch draws on works of the famous Talmudic authorities R' Hai Gaon, *R' Gershom Meor HaGolah, *R' Chananel, and *R' Nissim, and on the Halachic compendiums of the Geonim, such as the Sheiltos. Thus it is itself a complete Talmudic commentary, unique in that it follows alphabetical order. This monumental work, completed in 1101, was universally accepted and used by all Ashkenazic and Sefardic scholars. *Rashi mentions the Aruch on one occasion (Shabbos 13b) and addressed an inquiry to its author. R' Nassan was also well educated in secular studies, including medicine, and was versed in many languages.

R' Shlomo ben HaYasom

ר' שְׁלמה בֶּן הַיָּתוֹם

Southern Italy, or Sicily,
late 11th-early 12th cent. (?)

Talmudist.

Although R' Shlomo compiled a commentary to many tractates of the Talmud, only his notes on Tractate Moed Katan survive. His commentary is one of the earliest that explains the sequence of topics, discusses the chronological order of the Talmudic Sages, and interprets Biblical verses quoted by the Talmud. R' Shlomo quotes *R' Gershom Meor HaGolah and

*Rashi, and cites the customs of the city of Hebron (Eretz Yisrael). He, in turn, is quoted by *Rid and Shibolei HaLeket.

R' Tovyah ben Eliezer

ר' טוֹבִיָה בֶּן אֱלִיעֶזֶר

Kastoria, Greece,
late 11th-early 12th cent.

Liturgist, Commentator.

R' Tovia's major work, Midrash Lekach Tov, is a commentary on the Torah and the five Megillos, incorporating Halachah, Aggadah, and pshat. It is cited by R' Avraham ibn Ezra, *Rosh (Hilchos Tefillin), Shibolei HaLeket (ch. 118), *R' Menachem ben Shlomo, *Rabbenu Tam, *Rashbam, Or Zarua, and Ittur. The Torah commentary was published on Leviticus, Numbers and Deuteronomy under the title Pesikta Zutresa. Genesis and Exodus were subsequently published under the author's original title, Lekach Tov, by S. Buber (Vilna, 1884). Of the Megillos, only Ruth (Mainz, 1887) and Lamentations (Frankfurt-am-Main, 1895) have appeared.

The name Lekach Tov ["a goodly lore"; from the description of the Torah given in Proverbs 4:2] alludes to both R' Tovyah's name and his habit of introducing the commentary to each weekly Torah portion with an exposition on a Scriptural verse containing the word tov ["good"] and relating it to the portion.

Some of R' Tovyah's liturgical hymns are still extant, and one is printed in the Buber edition of Lekach Tov. He is the author of a commentary on R' Elazar HaKalir's liturgy (krovetz) for the Shemoneh Esrei of Tishah B'Av.

R' Menachem ben Shlomo

ר' מְנַחֵם בֶּן שְׁלֹמֹה

Italy, 12th cent. (?)

Grammarian, Author of Midrash Se-chel Tov.

This collection of old Midrashic material, arranged on each verse of the Torah and the five Megillos, is interspersed with halachic notes and original comments.

The work is quoted both for its aggadic substance and for its halachic material. Among the halachists of later generations who cite opinions and decisions of Sechel Tov are *Maharam Mintz, Orchos Chaim, and *Mordechai. Today, Sechel Tov is extant only from Genesis XV through Exodus XIX (Berlin, 1900).

In 1143, R' Menachem wrote a textbook on Hebrew grammar entitled Even Bochan (fragments of which have been published), in which he generally followed the opinions of *R' Menachem ben Saruk. He wrote this work "to bring honor to my Creator; for I have seen how the oppressive poverty imposed upon my people by the yoke of gentile taxation prevents them from delving into the meaning of Scripture ... this book will aid in teaching their sons the service of their Master to enable them to find favor in His eyes. It was also my intention to enlighten my three young sons — Yedidyah, Shealtiel and Yitzchak, a trebled thread blessed unto G–d — how to apply sechel [intelligence] to the understanding of Scripture ...".

R' Shmuel of Rosany (Rushalna)

ר' שְׁמוּאֵל מָרְחָא (רוֹשַׁיינוֹש)

b. Ancona, Italy, c. 1090
d. Italy, c. 1160

Torah Commentator.

The Aruch and *Rashi's commentary are quoted frequently in R' Shmuel's Torah commentary, which presents both the midrashic and plain meaning of the text. This work was recently published (Jerusalem, 1976).

Some identify *Rushaina* with Russia, and believe that R' Shmuel was among the first scholars to live in that land.

R' Yitzchak of Siponto

ר' יִצְחָק (בֶּן מַלְכִּי צֶדֶק) מִסִּיפּוֹנְטוֹ

b. Siponto, Italy, c. 1110
d. Salerno, Italy, c. 1170

Mishnah Commentator.

Called the "great rabbi" by *R' Binyamin of Tudela, R' Yitzchak is famous for his clear, concise Mishnah commentary, which is cited by the later Tosafists. His commentary on Order *Zeraim* is printed in all full editions of the Talmud, and the one on Order *Taharos* is quoted by *R' Shimshon of Sens. He may have written on other orders as well. He corresponded with *Rabbeinu Tam.

R' Yeshayah of Trani I HaZaken (Rid)

ר' יְשַׁעְיָה (בֶּן מָאלִי) דְּטְרָאנִי הַזָּקֵן (רִי"ד)

b. Trani, Italy, c. 1180
d. Trani, Italy, c. 1260

Tosafist, Halachist, Teacher.

Son of R' Mali, one of the foremost scholars of Trani in Southern Italy, R' Yeshayah seems to have traveled to Germany to study under R' Simchah of Speyer. He and his elder colleague, R' Elazar of Verona, a disciple of *Ri HaZaken, were instrumental in introducing the Tosafist method of Talmudic exposition to Italy. Jointly they headed an academy, probably in Verona, where they restored Talmudic scholarship, which had been dormant in Italy for approximately a century while its scholars occupied themselves with secular subjects.

R' Yeshayah's *Tosafos* are distinguished for their startling originality and uncompromising search for truth. He composed as many as six editions of Tosafos to some tractates, sometimes demonstrating the absurdity of a view he himself had espoused earlier. He greatly revered *Rashi and reverently refers to him as *HaMoreh,* the teacher. Many of his *Tosafos* have been printed in various editions and have recently been collected and published in one volume. He also composed a halachic work modeled upon *Rif and arranged on the tractates of the Talmud. All known extant parts of this work (encompassing *Berachos* and most of the orders of *Moed, Nashim* and *Nezikin)* have been published in a multi-volume series as *Piskei Rid* (Jerusalem, 5724-37). Another halachic work, *Sefer HaMachria* (Leghorn, 5539), contains essays on miscellaneous topics. Many scholars feel that the commentary on *Menachos* ascribed to *Rashba (in *Asifas Zekeinim)* was really by R' Yeshayah.

The recognized leader of Italian Jewry in his generation, R' Yeshayah received halachic inquiries from all parts of Italy and Germany. He carried on a halachic correspondence with his teacher, R' Simchah of Speyer, and wrote over twenty responsa to *R' Yitzchak Or Zarua. Some of Rid's responsa have been published (Jerusalem, 1967). *Shibolei HaLeket* cites his halachic decisions over 200 times, and *Maharam of Rothenburg declared his decisions to be as authoritative as those of *R' Gershom Meor HaGolah, Rif, and *Rambam. *Rosh mentions his opinions many times.

The field of Biblical exegesis was also given considerable attention by R' Yeshayah. Here, too, he exhibits the remarkable versatility and wide scope displayed in his Talmudic endeavors. While his commentary to the Torah [discovered by Chida and printed in his *Pnei David* (Leghorn, 1692) and separately (Jerusalem 1972)] is in the style of the Tosafists, centering around the difficulties in the commentary of 'the Teacher' (Rashi), his commentary to the Prophets and Writings adopts the method of the classical Bible exegetes, devoted to analyzing the literal sense of the text. This commentary, which had previously been printed in some editions of Scripture only on the Book of Judges and Samuel, has recently been printed in its entirety, except for most of The Twelve Books and Chronicles (Jerusalem 1959-78). R' Yeshayah speaks of having composed a commentary to *Sifra*. His commentary on the Passover *Haggadah* is cited extensively in *Shibolei HaLeket*.

In his responsa (123), R' Yeshayah mentions a trip he made to *Eretz Yisrael* and, on the basis of his personal observation, rejects a proposed commentary concerning the geographical location of Acre (עכו).

Very little much is known about his disciples. However his grandson *R' Yeshayah of Trani II was a noted scholar, and two famous Torah greats of later generations, R' Moshe Trani (Mabit) and his son R' Yosef (Maharit), were his descendants.

R' Binyamin HaRofei

ר' בִּנְיָמִין (בֶּן אַבְרָהָם) הָרוֹפֵא

b. Italy, c. 1220
d. Rome, Italy, c. 1280

Halachist, Liturgist.

Shibolei HaLeket, written by his younger brother *R' Tzidkiyah HaRofei, mentions R' Binyamin's decisions and notes. *Sefer Yedidus,* containing R' Binyamin's halachic analysis, has been lost, along with his Siddur and *Seder HaIbbur,* concerning the laws pertaining to the setting of the calendar. All, however, are quoted in other works.

R' Binyamin abridged *Sefer Yereim* (of *R' Eliezer of Metz), and arranged it in its present form. (The original, unabridged version of this work is now

known as *Yereim HaShalem.*) He also composed glosses on *Rashi's Torah commentary, and on R' Shlomo ben Shabsai's commentary on *Sheiltos.*

In 1239, when the apostate Nicholas Donin assailed the Talmud and appealed to Pope Gregory IX to order its burning, the Jews of Rome prayed and fasted and R' Binyamin composed the penitential hymn *El Mi Anusa L'ezra.* In June of 1242, when several wagonloads of Talmud manuscripts were burned in Paris, he composed a stirring lamentation. This, along with many of his liturgical compositions are found in some manuscript copies of *Machzor Roma.*

He also authored *Masa Gei Chizayon* (Riva di Trento, 1560), a satirical poem directed against the arrogance of the wealthy and the nobility, and *Pirush Alef-Beitin,* on the Aramaic parts of the Shavuos liturgy *(Kovetz al Yad,* 1884).

R' Binyamin was a disciple of R' Meir ben Moshe, rabbi of Rome. In addition to his knowledge of Talmud, R' Binyamin was acquainted with mathematics and astronomy, and fluent in Italian, Greek, Latin, and Arabic.

R' Yehudah HaRofei (Rivevan)

ר' יְהוּדָה (בֶּן בִּנְיָמִין) הָרוֹפֵא (ריבב"ן)

b. Rome, Italy, c. 1210
d. Rome, Italy, c. 1280

Halachist.

He studied under R' Yitzchak of Comirino, and under R' Meir ben Moshe, whom he later succeeded as chief rabbi of Rome. R' Yehudah in turn taught his cousin, *R' Tzidkiyah HaRofei.

R' Yehudah's running commentary on *Rif's *Sefer HaHalachos* covering Order *Moed,* in addition to an independent commentary on Tractate *Shekalim,* are printed in all full editions of the Talmud. He also composed a halachic digest on dietary laws, and completed the *Sheiltos* commentary begun by his relative, R' Shlomo ben Shabsai. R' Yehudah also composed a commentary to many tractates of *Rif's *Halachos,* of which Tractates *Pesachim* (in the periodical *Talpiyos,* 5715) and *Succah (Ginzei Rishonim,* Jerusalem, 1962) have been published.

A member of the prominent Anav (Del Mansi) clan [see Historical Introduction], R' Yehudah is also referred to as R' Yaaleh, an acronym for *Yehudah Anav LeMishpachas HaAnavim* ["Yehudah Anav of the Anav family"], as well as a play on the words *Yehudah Yaaleh* ["Yehudah shall lead" (Judges 1:2)].

R' Tzidkiyah HaRofei

ר' צִדְקִיָה (בֶּן אַבְרָהָם) הָרוֹפֵא

b. Italy, c. 1230
d. Rome, Italy, c. 1300
Author of *Shibolei HaLeket.*

This descendant of the prominent Italian Anav family studied under his cousin, *R' Yehudah ben Binyamin; R' Meir ben Moshe, rabbi of Rome; and R' Avigdor Katz. He also studied under R' Yaakov of Wurzburg, an otherwise unknown scholar. In the famed halachic compendium *Shibolei HaLeket* (Vilna, 1886), R' Tzidkiyah presents laws of prayer, Shabbos, festivals, *kashrus,* circumcision, mourning, monetary matters (such as inheritance and interest), in concise, popular form. An abridged edition of this work had previously been published (Venice, 1546). The full text of the work came to light only in modern times. It was published by S. Buber as *Shibolei HaLeket HaShalem.*

R' Tzidkiyah noted that the book was not an original work, but a compilation of gleanings from *Halachos Gedolos,* *Rif, *Rashi, *Rambam, *Razah, *Rid, and others. Preference was given to those opinions that seemed most halachically correct to the author. *Sefer Tanya* is considered by some an abridgment of *Shibolei HaLeket,* in that most of *Shibolei HaLeket* is quoted in it.

R' Tzidkiyah corresponded with R' Avigdor Katz in Vienna, *Maharam of Rothenburg in Germany, and R' Avraham ben Yosef of Pesaro.

R' Yechiel Anav

ר' יְחִיאֵל (בֶּן יְקוּתִיאֵל) עָנָיו

d. Rome, Italy, c. 1300
Author, Liturgist.

Another member of the Anav (Del Mansi) family, he is reputed to be the author of *Sefer Tanya,* a work similar to, though shorter than, *Shibolei HaLeket,* which drew upon both *Shibolei HaLeket* and its sources, notably *Rivevan.* It was used by the Italian communities as a code of Jewish law for many generations.

He is also the author of *Maalos HaMidos* (Cremona, 1556), on character improvement. Among his liturgical compositions is his hymn of lamentation upon the burning of a Roman synagogue in 1268.

A talented scribe, he copied the Jerusalem Talmud and many rare Hebrew books (among them *R' Shlomo ben HaYasom's work). Some of his manuscripts have been preserved in various libraries.

R' Yeshayah of Trani II (Riaz)

ר' יְשַׁעְיָה (בֶּן אֵלִיָהוּ) מִטְרָאנִי הָאַחֲרוֹן (ריא"ז)

b. Trani, Italy, c. 1235
d. Trani, Italy, c. 1300
Halachist.

Tradition records that *Rid regarded his grandson Riaz as his spiritual heir. Riaz recorded the opinions of his grandfather — although not always subscribing to his view — in his own halachic works.

Riaz composed a halachic compendium on most of the Talmud in the style of Rif. Parts of this work appear in *Shiltei*

HaGiborim, printed as marginal glosses to the Rif, and parts in Me'at Devash (Oxford, 1928). This work has recently been published in its entirety as Piskei HaRiaz, together with the decisions of his grandfather. His longer work, Kuntres HaRayos, which presents the analysis behind the halachic decisions recorded in the compendium, is in manuscript.

Some of the commentaries to Scripture bearing his grandfather's imprimatur have been ascribed by various scholars to R' Yeshayah II, but without sufficient justification.

R' Menachem Recanati

ר' מְנַחֵם (בֶּן בִּנְיָמִין) רִיקַנְטִי

Italy, late 13th-early 14th cent.

Kabbalist, Torah Commentator.

R' Menachem was one of the first Italian kabbalists who committed the mystical teachings to writing. The profound interpretations in his Torah commentary greatly influenced the kabbalistic schools of succeeding generations. *R' Mordechai Yaffe (Levush) considered this volume so important that he composed a running commentary, Levush Aven Yekarah, to clarify R' Menachem's terminology and logic.

In Taamei HaMitzvos, R' Menachem presents kabbalistic reasons for the commandments, and some kabbalistic interpretations of the prayers (Constantinople, 1544). Piskei HaRecanati (Bologna, 1578) is a collection of halachic decisions, mostly belonging to authorities of previous generations (primarily German and French scholars), usually presented without discussion of the sources upon which these decisions were based. This book is cited many times by later authorities such as Magen Avraham and Shach.

*Ramban is frequently quoted in R' Menachem's kabbalistic works, and

referred to as HaRav HaGadol ["the great master"].

R' Aharon Abu-al-Rabi

ר' אַהֲרֹן (בֶּן גֵּרְשׁוֹן) אַבּוּ אַל רַבִּי

Sicily, Italy, c. 1400

Religious Philosopher, Grammarian.

After studying at the northern Italian Talmudic academy of Treviso, he applied himself to the study of the sciences and traveled extensively to Asia, visiting Egypt, Eretz Yisrael, Syria, Turkey, and Crimea. During these travels he came in contact with Karaites, Moslems, and Christians, and defended the Jewish faith with arguments particularly suited to each sect. In Rome he had an audience with the pope, who was quite impressed by his sensible and scholarly answers defending Jewish tradition.

His works on his disputations, on religious philosophy, and on Hebrew grammar, have not survived; they are known to us only through his supercommentary to *Rashi's Torah commentary printed in a rare volume known to bibliophiles as "Knizel" (Constantinople, c. 1525).

R' Eliyahu of Ferrara

ר' אֵלִיָּהוּ מִפֵּירָרָא

b. Italy
d. Eretz Yisrael, c. 1450

Talmudist, Halachist.

At an advanced age, R' Eliyahu set out for Eretz Yisrael. After a stormy journey, during which both his son and grandson were lost, he finally arrived at his destination, and made his way to Jerusalem. In 1434, he was appointed rabbi of the Holy City, and thereafter inquiries were sent to him from Alexandria and Damascus. In his letters to his wife and children, he describes Jerusalem and tells of the river Sambatyon and the ten lost tribes.

R' Yosef Colon (Maharik)

ר' יוֹסֵף (בֶּן שְׁלֹמֹה) קוֹלוֹן (מהרי"ק)

b. Chambery, France, 1410
d. Pavia, Italy, c. 1480

Halachist.

The responsa of Maharik (Venice, 1519) are fundamental works of Halachah and are quoted by all the authorities. He was considered the foremost Italian Talmudist and rabbinical authority of his day. His halachic decisions in all matters were sought by Jews near and far, and many German communities turned to him for guidance. During this period, numerous Jews from southern Germany moved to northern Italy, where they established their own communities. These small new communities considered him their halachic authority. Thus Maharik came to be regarded as one of the most authoritative personalities by both Italian and Ashkenazic Jewry.

R' Yosef was a member of a French family named Trabot which traced its lineage to *Rashi. His father, a scholar who was also R' Yosef's teacher, was referred to by his famous son as "my master, wonder of the generation." In his early youth R' Yosef may have studied under *Maharil, when the latter spent some time in Chambery, on the Italian-French border.

In the last years of his life Maharik served as Rabbi of Pavia.

When he lived in Mantua, R' Yosef maintained close ties with *R' Yehudah Messer Leon, one of the greatest Italian rabbis of the age, who served as rabbi of Mantua at that time. Many responsa by Maharik attest to the friendship between these two men. A later source relates that a fierce controversy (over an unknown matter) turned R' Yosef and R' Yehudah to bitter opponents, and that the strife reached such proportions that the government intervened, banishing both scholars from the city. According to this source this episode was the reason Maharik accepted the rabbinate in Pavia, where he served until his death. But it has recently been proven that no reference to this controversy or its cause exists in the halachic literature of the day, and that the sole source for the story *(Shalsheles HaKabbalah)* is notorious for inacurracy.

Additional responsa by Maharik have been discovered and published recently as *She'elos U'Teshuvos Maharik HaChadashim* (Jerusalem, 1970). Sections of Maharik's novellae to *Semag* and *Rambam's *Mishneh Torah,* recorded by his disciples, have been printed in *Chidushei U'Peirushei Maharik* (Jerusalem, 1971). It also includes *Maharik's* comments to Torah, centering upon the explanation of difficulties in Rashi's commentary. Many comments by Maharik (differing from those in the aforementioned publication) are to be found in the Torah commentary of his celebrated disciple, R' Ovadiah of Bertinoro. He refers to R' Yosef with the acronym מהר"ר (= from the Rav, our Teacher).

R' Yehudah ben Yechiel (Messer Leon)

ר' יְהוּדָה בֶּן יְחִיאֵל (מִיסִיר לֵיאוֹן)

Mantua, Italy c. 1470

Talmudist, Halachist.

As rabbi of Mantua, R' Yehudah issued several edicts, such as banning *Ralbag's Torah commentary, which he felt expressed views contrary to the Torah. To enforce this edict, he threatened to excommunicate any who transgressed it. By so doing, he incurred the wrath of other scholars, who felt that he had no right to assume jurisdiction throughout Italy, since he was not the chief rabbi.

According to an unsubstantiated tradition, bitter conflict erupted between R' Yehudah and *Maharik (see entry for details), which resulted in the intervention of the civil authorities, and the eviction of both scholars from the city in 1475. R' Yehudah repaired to Naples, where he established a Talmudic academy and remained until his death.

He combined deep religious conviction with a broad knowledge of secular subjects. As a philosopher and physician, he was acknowledged even by the gentiles, who conferred upon him the honorary title *Maestro* (or *Messer*). His works include *Livnas HaSapir* on grammar, which remains in manuscript, *Nofes Tzufim* (Vienna, 1863), a textbook on the art of rhetoric, and many unpublished treatises on philosophy and medicine.

The grammarian, R' Avraham de Balmes, author of *Miknah Avraham,* was one of his disciples.

Appendices and Index

◦§ Chronological Perspective

This table enables the reader to ascertain which of the major *Rishonim* were contemporaneous with others who lived in different lands. The listing is according to the centuries and the four areas covered in the book.

	SEPHARDIC LANDS	FRANCE-GERMANY	PROVENCE	ITALY
10TH CENTURY	R' Menachem ben Saruk R' Donash ben Lavrat R' Chushiel	R' Shimon HaGadol		
11TH CENTURY	R' Chanoch ben Moshe R' Nissim ben Yaakov R' Chananel R' Shmuel HaNaggid R' Bachya ibn Pakudah (Chovas HaLevavos) R' Yitzchak al-Fasi (Rif) R' Yitzchak ibn Gias	R' Gershom Meor HaGolah R' Yaakov ben Yakar R' Shlomo Yitzchaki (Rashi) R' Yehudah ben Nassan (Rivan)	R' Moshe HaDarshan	R' Nassan ben Yechiel (Aruch)
12TH CENTURY	R' Yosef ibn Migash (Ri Migash) R' Yehudah Halevi R' Avraham ibn Ezra R' Moshe ben Maimon (Rambam)	R' Shmuel ben Meir (Rashbam) R' Yaakov ben Meir (Rabbeinu Tam) R' Eliezer ben Nassan (Ravan) R' Eliezer of Metz (Yereim) R' Yitzchak of Dampierre (Ri) R' Yehudah HaChassid R' Yitzchak ben Avraham (Ritzba) R' Eliezer ben Yoel Halevi (Ravyah) R' Shimshon of Sens (Rash) R' Elazar Rokeach of Worms	R' Yosef Kimchi R' Zerachyah HaLevi (Razah; HaMaor) R' Avraham ben David (Ravad III)	R' Tovyah ben Eliezer (Lekach Tov)
13TH CENTURY	R' Meir Halevi Abulafia (Ramah) R' Yonah of Gerona (Gerondi) R' Moshe ben Nachman (Ramban) R' Aharon Halevi (Ra'ah) R' Shlomo ibn Aderes (Rashba) R' Yom Tov ibn Asevelli (Ritva)	R' Moshe of Coucy (Semag) R' Yitzchak of Vienna (Or Zarua) R' Meir of Rothenburg (Maharam) R' Mordechai ben Hillel	R' Moshe HaKohen (Ramach) R' David Kimchi (Radak) R' Chizkiyahu Chizkuni R' Menachem HaMeiri R' Yedayah HaPenini (Bechinos Olam) R' Aharon HaKohen of Lunel (Orchos Chaim)	R' Yeshayah of Trani I (Tosefos Rid) R' Yehudah HaRofei (Rivevan) R' Tzidkiyah HaRofei (Shibolei HaLeket) R' Yeshayah of Trani II (Riaz)
14TH CENTURY	R' Bachya ben Asher R' Vidal of Tolosa (Maggid Mishneh) R' David Abudraham R' Nissim (Ran) R' Yitzchak ben Sheshes Perfet (Rivash) R' Yosef Chaviva (Nimukei Yosef)	R' Asher ben Yechiel (Rosh) R' Yaakov Baal HaTurim R' Yaakov Moelin (Maharil)	R' Levi ben Gershom (Ralbag) R' Eshtori HaParchi (Kaftor VeFerach)	R' Menachem Recanati
15TH CENTURY	R' Shimon Duran (Rashbatz) R' Yosef Albo (HaIkkarim)	R' Yaakov Weil (Mahariv) R' Yisrael Isserlein (Terumas HaDeshen)		R' Yosef Colon (Maharik)

❧ Sefarim Composed by the Rishonim

The majority of works written by the *Rishonim* did not appear under any formal title, but were known by such names as *Ramban's Commentary on Torah* (פירוש רמב"ן על התורה) or *Rambam's Mishneh Commentary* (פירוש המשניות להרמב"ם). The following index of extant works lists only those which do not contain the author's name in the title.

In compiling this index the word ספר was omitted whenever it appeared as the first word of the title (e.g., ספר יראים is listed as simply יראים). Additionally the words שו"ת (שאלות ותשובות) and the prefix ה' (ה' הידיעה) although given in the index, have been ignored in the alphabetization (e.g., המפתח is listed under the letter מ).

Page	Name of Author	Name of Work
		א
49	R' Yehudah ben Kuraish	אב ואם
104	R' David Abudraham	אבודרהם
129	R' Eliezer ben Nassan (Ravan)	אבן העזר
73	R' Avraham ibn Ezra	אבן עזרא
101	R' Yehoshua ibn Shuiv	אבן שועיב
144	R' Alexander Zuslein HaKohen	אגודה
153	R' Yaakov Landau	האגור
84	R' Meir HaLevi Abulafia	אגרות הרמ"ה
93	R' Shem Tov ibn Pelquera	אגרת הויכוח
94	R' Shem Tov ibn Pelquera	אגרת המוסר
75	R' Maimon ben Yosef HaDayan	אגרת הנחמה
91	R' Moshe Ben Nachman (Ramban)	אגרת חקודש
74	R' Avraham ibn Ezra	אגרת השבת
93	R' Yitzchak ibn Latif	אגרת התשובה
82	R' Moshe Ben Maimon (Rambam)	אגרת תימן
111	R' Shimon Duran (Rashbatz)	אוהב משפט
97	R' Todros Abulafia	אוצר הכבוד
101	R' Nasanel ben Yeshayahu	אור האפילה
111	R' Shimon Duran (Rashbatz)	אור החיים
139	R' Yitzchak of Vienna	אור זרוע
178	R' Aharon HaKohen of Lunel	אורחות חיים
108	R' Chisdai Crescas II	אור ה'
65	R' Yehudah ibn Balam	אותות העניינים

Page	Name of Author	Name of Work
103	R' Yitzchak of Acco	מאירת עינים
89	R' Yosef ibn Aknin	מאמר בחיוב המציאות
111	R' Shimon Duran (Rashbatz)	מאמר חמץ
170	R' Shmuel ibn Tibbon	מאמר יקוו המים
87	R' Avraham Ben HaRambam	מאמר על הדרשות
83	R' Moshe Ben Maimon (Rambam)	מאמר תחיית המתים
60	R' Shmuel HaNaggid	מבוא התלמוד
85	R' Yehudah al-Charizi	מבוא ללשון הקודש
93	R' Shem Tov ibn Palquera	המבקש
177	R' David HaKochavi	מגדל דוד
102	R' Shem Tov ibn Gaon	מגדל עוז
103	R' Vidal of Tolosa	מגיד משנה
184	R' Achimaatz ben Paltiel	מגילת אחימעץ
76	R' Avraham HaNassi	מגילת המגלה
101	R' Shmuel Motot	מגילת סתרים
111	R' Shimon Duran (Rashbatz)	מגן אבות
93	R' David HaNaggid	מדרש דוד
99	R' David al-Adeni	מדרש הגדול
186	R' Tovyah ben Eliezer	מדרש לקח וטב
161	R' Moshe HaDarshan	מדרש רבתי
186	R' Menachem ben Shlomo	מדרש שכל טוב
165	R' Moshe Kimchi	מהלך שבילי הדעת
152	R' Yisrael Brunna	שו"ת מהר"י ברונא
151	R' Yaakov Weil (Mahariv)	שו"ת מהרי"ו
149	R' Yaakov Moelin (Maharil)	מהרי"ל
190	R' Yosef Colon (Maharik)	מהרי"ק
153	R' Moshe Mintz	שו"ת מהר"ם מינץ
140	R' Meir of Rothenburg (Maharam)	מהר"ם מרוטנבורג
89	R' Yosef ibn Aknin	המוסר
137	R' Elazar Rokeach of Worms	מורה חטאים
93	R' Shem Tov ibn Palquera	מורה המורה
82	R' Moshe Ben Maimon (Rambam)	מורה נבוכים
51	R' Menachem ben Saruk	מחברת
78	R' Shlomo Ibn Parchon	מחברת הערוך
124	R' Simchah of Vitry	מחזור ויטרי
103	R' Yerucham	מישרים
175	R' David ben Levi	המכתם

Page	Name of Author	Name of Work
187	R' Yeshayah of Trani I Hazaken (Rid)	רי"ד
99	R' Yom Tov ibn Asevilli	ריטב"א
70	R' Yosef ibn Migash	ר"י מגאש
65	R' Yitzchak al-Fasi	רי"ף
189	R' Menachem Recanati	ריקנטי
179	R' Levi ben Gershon (Ralbag)	רלב"ג
79	R' Moshe Ben Maimon (Rambam)	רמב"ם
90	R' Moshe Ben Nachman (Ramban)	רמב"ן
98	R' Moshe de Leon	הרמון
104	R' Nissim (Ran)	ר"ן
89	R' Yosef ibn Aknin	רפואת הנפשות
56	R' Yehudah ibn Chayug	הרקחה
64	R' Yonah ibn Janach	הרקמה
96	R' Shlomo ibn Aderes (Rashba)	רשב"א
126	R' Shmuel ben Meir (Rashbam)	רשב"ם
122	R' Shlomo Yitzchaki (Rashi)	רש"י
		ש
188	R' Tzidkiyah HaRofei	שבולי הלקט
100	R' Meir Aldabi	שבילי אמונה
95	R' Avraham Abulafia	שבע נתיבות התורה
102	R' Bachya (Bechaye) ben Asher	שובע שמחות
77	R' Yehudah of Barcelona	השטרות
102	R' Chaim of Tudela	שיטה לבעל הצרורות
71	R' Moshe ibn Ezra	שירת ישראל
102	R' Bachya (Bechaye) ben Asher	שלחן של ארבע
98	R' Moshe de Leon	השם
103	R' Yitzchak HaYisraeli II	שער המלואים
97	R' Todros Abulafia	שער הרזים
83	R' Yaakov Ben Sheshes	שער השמים
93	R' Yitzchak ibn Latif	שער השמים
99	R' Yosef Gikatilla	שער השמים
103	R' Yitzchak HaYisraeli II	שער השמים
172	R' Nassan ben Meir of Trinquetaille	שער התפיסה
98	R' Yosef Gikatilla	שערי אורה
141	R' Yitzchak of Duren	שערי דורא
88	R' Yonah of Gerona (Gerondi)	שערי העבודה

ᴇ§ Hebrew-English Geographical Names

The following table, given in Hebrew alphabetical order, gives the medieval Hebrew names of many of the geographical locations mentioned in this work along with their English equivalents. It should be understood that no formal orthographic system existed during this period and many of the names may be found with variant spellings.

Those locations that appear on a map in this book have the page number indicated.

א

33	Avignon	אויגנון, אויניון
33	Orleans	אורלייניש
45	Otranto	אטרנטה
33	Evreux	איברא
45	Italy	איטליה
19	Estella	איסטילה
28	Algiers	אלגזייאר, אלגזייר
28	Alexandria	אלכסנדריא
19	Andalusia	אנדלוסיה
45	Ancona	אנקונה
19	Aragon	ארגון
33	Arles	ארלש
31	Aleppo	ארם צובה
33	England	ארץ האי
37	Germany	אשכנז

ב

33	Bagnols	באויולש
45	Bari	בארי
31	Baghdad	בגדד
33	Beziers	בדריש, בדרש
37	Bonn	בונא
37	Bamberg	בונבערק, בונברק
33	Bagnols	בוניולש
19	Burgos	בורגוש
37	Bohemia	ביהם
33	Blois	בלויש
19	Valencia	בלנסיה
37	Brunn(Brno)	ברונא
37	Bern	ברן
19	Barcelona	ברצלונה

ג

19	Gerona	גירונה
37	Worms	גרמייזא ,גרמישא

ד

37	Duren	דורא
31	Damascus	דמשק
19	Denia	דניה
—	Dampierre, France	דנפיר

ה

33	Montpellier	ההר

ו

37	Vienna	וינא
37	Worms	וורמייזא ,וורמיישא
37	Wurtzburg	ווירצבורג
33	Vitry	ויטרי
45	Verona	וירונה
19	Valencia	ולנסיה

ז

37	Saxony	זכסן

ח

31	Tigris River	חדקל
31	Haifa	חיפה
31	Aleppo	חלב

ט

31	Tiberias	טבריה
19	Tudela	טודילה
—	Touques, France	טוך
19	Tolosa	טולושא
19	Toledo	טוליטולה
19	Tortosa	טורטושא
—	Tirnau, Bohemia	טירנא
45	Trani	טראני
33	Troyes	טרויש
33	Trinquetaille	טרנקאטאלייש
33	Trinquetaille	טרנקטיליש

׳

33 Joigny .... יואני
28 Greece.................... יון
33 Joigny .... יוני
— York, England .... יורק
31 Jerusalem................. ירושלים

ל

— London, England .... לונדריש
33 Lunel..................... לוניל
19 Lucena .... לוסינה
45 Lucca .... לוקה
33 Alsace-Lorraine .... לותר
19 Leon...................... ליאון
33 Limoges................... לימורגש
37 Landau.................... לנדא

מ

37 Mainz .... מגנצא
28 Maghreb [Morocco and Algiers]................... מגרב
33 Montpellier..... מונטפשליר, מונפשליר
31 Mosul..................... מוצול
19 Majorca................... מיורקה
37 Magdeburg................. מיידבורג
— Mainz, Germany .... מיינצא
33 Metz .... מיץ
37 Merseburg................. מירזבורג
19 Malaga.................... מלגה
33 Melun..................... מלון
19 Malaga.................... מלקה
45 Mantua .... מנטובא
37 Moravia................... מעהרן
28 Morocco and Algiers ...... מערב
28 Egypt .... מצרים
— Marvege, France........... מרויש
19 Merida.................... מרידה
33 Marseilles .... מרשייליש

נ

19 Navarre .... נבארא ,נבארה
37 Wiener-Neustadt........... נוישטאט
37 Nuremberg................. נירנבורג
33 Narbonne.................. נרבונא

ס

— Siponto, Italy ... סימפונטו, סיפונטו
45 Sicily.................... סיקיליא
19 Spain .... ספרד
19 Saragossa .... סרגוסה, סרקוסא

ע

31 Acre .... עכו
37 Erfurt .... ערפורט

פ

28 Fez .... פאס
45 Padua .... פדואה
37 Fulda .... פולדא
33 Pontoise .... פונטייזא
28 Fostat (Old Cairo) .... פוסטט
— Posquieres, Provence....... פושקיירש
37 Bohemia .... פיהם
45 Pesaro .... פיזרו
19 Penafiel .... פיניפיל
33 Perpignon .... פירפיניאן
45 Ferrara .... פיררא
33 Falaise................... פלייזא
19 Palma..................... פלמה
33 Pontoise .... פנטוישא
19 Penafiel .... פנפיאל
19 Pamplona .... פנפלונה
37 Prague .... פראג
33 Provence .... פרובינציה
33 Paris .... פריש
37 Frankfurt................. פרנקפורט
33 Perpignon .... פרפיגנן
31 Euphrates River .... פרת

צ

37 Zurich .... צוריך
31 Safed .... צפת
33 France.................... צרפת

ק

37 Cologne .... קולוניא
— Coucy, France............. קוצי
— Corbeil, France .... קורבייל
19 Cordova .... קורדובה
19 Catalonia .... קטלוניה
— Kiev, Russia .... קיוב
28 Kairouan .... קיירואן
33 Chinon .... קינון
— Kila Chamad, Algeria .... קלעה חמד
— Catalayud .... קלעת איוב
28 Crete (Candia) .... קנדיא
28 Kastoria .... קסטוריה
45 Capua .... קפואה
— Carthage, Tunisia .... קרטגינא
— Krems, Austria .... קרימז

33 Carpentras	קרפינטרץ	19 Granada	רמון ספרד

ש

33 Carcassone	קרקשונה	37 Styria	שטיירמרק
19 (Old) Castille	קשטיליה	19 Seville	שיביל
		— Salamanca	שלמאנקה , שלמנקה

ר

37 Regensburg	רגנשבורג
37 Rothenburg	רוטנבורג
45 Rome	רומא
37 Rhine River	רינוס
45 Recanati	ריקנטי

33 Sens	שנץ
37 Speyer	שפירא

ת

28 Tlemcen	תלמסאן, תלמסן

Index